Understanding and Using

Microsoft®

Windows™ 95

Ronald W. Maestas
Professor of Management Information Systems
New Mexico Highlands University

Steven C. Ross
Associate Professor of Management Information Systems
Western Washington University

WEST PUBLISHING COMPANY
Minneapolis/St. Paul • New York
Los Angeles • San Francisco

WEST'S COMMITMENT TO THE ENVIRONMENT

In 1906, West Publishing Company began recycling materials left over from the production of books. This began a tradition of efficient and responsible use of resources. Today, 100% of our legal bound volumes are printed on acid-free, recycled paper consisting of 50% new paper pulp and 50% paper that has undergone a de-inking process. We also use vegetable-based inks to print all of our books. West recycles nearly 27,700,000 pounds of scrap paper annually— the equivalent of 229,300 trees. Since the 1960s, West has devised ways to capture and recycle waste inks, solvents, oils, and vapors created in the printing process. We also recycle plastics of all kinds, wood, glass, corrugated cardboard, and batteries, and have eliminated the use of polystyrene book packaging. We at West are proud of the longevity and the scope of our commitment to the environment.

West pocket parts and advance sheets are printed on recyclable paper and can be collected and recycled with newspapers. Staples do not have to be removed. Bound volumes can be recycled after removing the cover.

Production, Prepress, Printing and Binding by West Publishing Company
Project Management by Labrecque Publishing Services

Microsoft® is a registered trademark and Windows™ is a trademark of Microsoft Corporation.

Screen shots reprinted with permission from Microsoft Corporation

 Text is Printed on 10% Post Consumer Recycled Paper

Library of Congress Cataloging-in-Publication Data

Ross, Steven C.
    Understanding and using Microsoft Windows 95 / Steven C. Ross, Ronald W. Maestas.
        p.   cm. — (The Microcomputing series)
    Includes index.
    ISBN 0-314-07240-3 (soft : alk. paper)
    1. Microsoft Windows 95.   2. Operating systems (Computers)
I. Maestas, Ronald W.   II. Title.   III. Series.
QA76.76.063R6917   1996
005.4 '469 — dc20
                                                                95-45674
                                                                    CIP

British Library Cataloguing-in-Publication Data. A catalogue record for this book is available from the British Library.

Contents

Windows Applications   111

... never cease to wonder when men say that only the wise are beautiful, with what physical senses they have seen that particular beauty, and with what eyes they have beheld the form of the flesh and the loveliness of wisdom.

St. Augustine

Understanding and Using Microsoft Windows 95 is about operating system software that can be used to replace the "usual" MS-DOS/PC-DOS environment—specifically, with the use of the popular program Microsoft Windows 95. Windows 95 is an attempt to make the computer more "user-friendly."

Drop-down menus, dialog boxes, and graphic symbols called icons provide an extremely efficient manner to execute commands. As technology changes, hardware and software provide faster and more intuitive methods of working with a personal computer. Operating systems are the foundation for the business student and professional alike to become skillful computer users.

Why This Book?

There are many books available that discuss Microsoft Windows 95. Why, then, would anyone write another book? We decided to do so because both our students and our colleagues at several universities desired a book tailored to the way personal computing is taught at the college and professional level. We saw that there was no book designed for use in academic or workshop settings. We saw a need for a book that would present concepts and skills as well as provide activities, applications, and questions for practice and teaching purposes. *Understanding and Using Microsoft Windows 95* is such a book.

Our goal was to support the efforts of the instructor by providing the essential facets of the software, together with activities and exercises, to reinforce and evaluate the student's learning experience. Examples are drawn from the fields of business administration and economics to illustrate how the software can be used in other course work as well as in the daily tasks performed by business professionals. The *Instructor's Manual* provides supplementary materials and suggestions for integrating this book with other course materials.

This book serves a different role than the reference manuals furnished with the Microsoft Windows 95 software. Those manuals are quite comprehensive, but often are difficult to read and fail to provide adequate examples. Accordingly, we sought to provide instruction in fundamental, intermediate, and advanced operations, supporting it with substantial reference material. When more detailed information is required, the user will have a significant foundation for finding and using it.

Finally, *Understanding and Using Microsoft Windows 95* serves as a member of THE MICROCOMPUTING SERIES published by West Publishing Company. It can be used alone, or in combination with other books in the series (listed in the Publisher's Note on pages xvii–xxiii), or as a supplement for any other book in a course where a knowledge of Microsoft Windows 95 is required.

How to Use This Book

You should complete the first six units in the order presented. With that background, the material in the remainder of the book can be covered in the order that suits you best—although several units do assume that you have completed earlier units and build on that knowledge base. The more work you do on the computer, the better you will learn the topics. As a minimum, you should complete the Guided Activities with each unit. Each activity is designed to illustrate points made in the previous units, and many contain additional material that is best presented during a computer session.

Each unit includes the following features:

LEARNING OBJECTIVES   the knowledge and skills addressed in the unit.

COMPUTER SCREENS   figures depicting the steps and results of most commands.

GUIDED ACTIVITIES   step-by-step, hands-on illustrations of operations discussed in the unit.

REVIEW QUESTIONS   questions designed to test your understanding of the material presented. The answers to selected Review Questions are contained in Appendix C.

KEY TERMS   a list of the important terms and concepts discussed in the unit. This list is designed for review and self-test.

Additional features of this book are as follows:

WINDOWS SETUP   Appendix A presents a short discussion of setting up Microsoft Windows 95.

KEYBOARD COMMANDS   Appendix B contains a list and short discussion of Microsoft Windows 95 keyboard commands.

INDEX   covers commands, functions, symbols, and other topics. It is designed to allow you to locate the relevant information quickly.

A Note of Thanks

From Steve Ross

- to Ron Maestas—getting a friend to write a book with you is tough, but finding one who will stay a friend throughout the process is even more difficult;

- to Greg Foy, Floyd Lewis, and T. J. Olney, my colleagues at Western Washington with whom I have discovered the joys of Windows;

- to Meredith, Kelly, and Shannon, still in love and having fun after all these years.

From Ron Maestas

- to Steven C. Ross, whose friendship, collegiality, and guidance helped me maintain my sanity;

- to Max Baca, Field Services/LAN Manager at New Mexico Highlands University, for getting me out of trouble; he has one of the brightest minds I know;

- to Luis Ortiz, a graduate student in Business Administration at New Mexico Highlands University, who assisted me in the preparation of the manuscript;

- to Georgia K. Ulibarri-Ortiz, an Elementary Education-Spanish major at New Mexico Highlands University, who assisted me in editing the manuscript;

- to Lori Vasquez, B.B.A. major at New Mexico Highlands University, who gave the manuscript a final polish;

- to Raymond B. Maestas, a B.B.A. and J.D. graduate from the University of New Mexico, who first encouraged me to write a book and who put his heart and soul into the manuscript; he gave the book a student's perspective in the Guided Activities and Review Questions;

- to C3C Dominic Maestas, United States Air Force Academy, whose intelligence, enthusiasm, and curiosity for computers are contagious;

- to Lisa Maestas, CPA, whose dedication, determination, and organization have taught me how to persevere;

- to my beautiful wife, Monica, whose love and support has *always* been with me in all of my endeavors starting in Alamosa, Colorado, to Tempe, Arizona; Minneapolis, Minnesota; Bloomington, Indiana; Seoul, South Korea; and finally to Las Vegas, New Mexico; I love you very much!

- to Lisa, Raymond, and Dominic Ron Maestas; I hope that I have made you as proud of me as I am of you; each of you has been an inspiration to me.

From Both of Us…

- to the many students and teachers who adopted the first edition of *Understanding and Using Windows 3.x*;

- to the reviewers of the previous version of this manuscript—John Nicholson of Johnson County Community College, Michelle Lenox of Nashville State Technical College, Joseph Franklin of Asheville–Buncombe Technical Community College, and Cliff Layton of Rogers State College—whose comments and careful reading of the manuscript helped us immensely as we labored to write about this exciting technology;

- to Rick Leyh and Sara Schroeder of West Publishing, for pushing this project through to completion…with a gentle touch; and, to Lisa Auer, Mark Woodworth, Jeanette Brinker, Carol Golden, and Mark Rhynsburger of Labrecque Publishing Services for producing this book.

R.W.M. & S.C.R.
Las Vegas, New Mexico, and Bellingham, Washington
August 1995

This book is part of THE MICROCOMPUTING SERIES. This popular series provides the most comprehensive list of books dealing with microcomputer applications software. We have expanded the number of software topics and provided a flexible set of instructional materials for all courses. This unique series includes five different types of books.

1. *West's Microcomputing Custom Editions* give instructors the power to create a spiral-bound microcomputer applications book especially for their course. Instructors can select the applications they want to teach and the amount of material they want to cover for each application—essentials or intermediate length. The following titles are a sample of what is available for the 1996 Microcomputing Series custom editions program:

Understanding Information Systems	*PageMaker 4.0*
Management, Information, and Systems: An Introduction to Information Systems	*PageMaker 5.0*
Understanding Networks	*Lotus 1-2-3 for Windows Release 4*
NetWare 3.x	*Lotus 1-2-3 for Windows Release 5*
DOS (3.x) and System	*Microsoft Excel 4*
DOS 5 and System	*Microsoft Excel 5*
DOS 6 and System	*Microsoft Excel for Windows 95*
Microsoft Windows 3.1	*Quattro Pro 5.0 for Windows*
Microsoft Windows 95	*Quattro Pro 6.0 for Windows*
WordPerfect 6.0	*dBASE IV Version 1.0/1.1/1.5*
WordPerfect 6.0 for Windows	*dBASE IV Version 2.0*
WordPerfect 6.1 for Windows	*Paradox 3.5*
Microsoft PowerPoint 4.0	*Paradox 4.5 for Windows*
Microsoft PowerPoint for Windows 95	*Microsoft Access 2.0*
Microsoft Word for Windows 6.0	*Microsoft Access for Windows 95*
Microsoft Word for Windows 95	*QBasic*
	Microsoft Visual Basic

   For more information about *West's Microcomputing Custom Editions*, please contact your local West Representative, or call West Publishing Company at (512) 327-3175.

2. General concepts books for teaching basic hardware and software philosophy and applications are available separately or in combination with hands-on applications. These books provide students with a general overview of computer fundamentals including history, social issues, and a synopsis of software and

hardware applications. These books include *Understanding Information Systems*, by Steven C. Ross; *Management, Information, and Systems: An Introduction to Information Systems*, by William Davis; and *Understanding and Using Information Technology*, by Judith C. Simon.

3. A series of hands-on laboratory tutorials (*Understanding and Using*) is software specific and covers a wide range of individual packages. These tutorials, written at an introductory level, combine tutorials with complete reference guides. A complete list of series titles can be found on the following pages.

4. Several larger volumes combining DOS with three application software packages are available in different combinations. These texts are titled *Understanding and Using Application Software*. They condense components of the individual lab manuals and add conceptual coverage for courses that require both software tutorials and microcomputer concepts in a single volume.

5. A series of advanced-level, hands-on lab manuals provides students with a strong project/systems orientation. These include *Understanding and Using Lotus 1-2-3: Advanced Techniques Releases 2.2 and 2.3*, by Judith C. Simon.

THE MICROCOMPUTING SERIES has been successful in providing you with a full range of applications books to suit your individual needs. We remain committed to excellence in offering the widest variety of current software packages. In addition, we are committed to producing microcomputing texts that provide you both the coverage you desire and also the level and format most appropriate for your students. The Executive Editor of the series is Rick Leyh of West Educational Publishing; the Developmental Editor is Sara Schroeder; the Consulting Editor is Steven Ross of Western Washington University. We are always planning for the future in this series. Please send us your comments and suggestions:

Rick Leyh
Executive Editor
West Educational Publishing
1515 Capital of Texas Highway South, Suite 402
Austin, TX 78746-6544
Internet: rleyh@research.westlaw.com

Sara Schroeder
Developmental Editor
West Educational Publishing
1515 Capital of Texas Highway South, Suite 402
Austin, TX 78746-6544
Internet: sschroed@research.westlaw.com

Steven Ross
Associate Professor/MIS
College of Business and Economics
Western Washington University
Bellingham, Washington 98225-9077
Internet: steveross@wwu.edu

We now offer these books in THE MICROCOMPUTING SERIES:

General Concepts

Understanding Information Systems
Steven C. Ross

Understanding Computer Information Systems
Paul W. Ross, H. Paul Haiduk, H. Willis Means, and Robert B. Sloger

Understanding and Using the Macintosh
Barbara Zukin Heiman and Nancy E. McGauley

Operating Systems/Environments

Understanding and Using the Internet
Bruce J. McLaren

Understanding and Using Microsoft Windows 95
Ronald W. Maestas and Steven C. Ross

Understanding and Using Microsoft Windows 3.1
Steven C. Ross and Ronald W. Maestas

Understanding and Using Microsoft Windows 3.0
Steven C. Ross and Ronald W. Maestas

Understanding and Using MS-DOS 6.0
Jonathan P. Bacon

Understanding and Using MS-DOS/PC DOS 5.0
Jonathan P. Bacon

Understanding and Using MS-DOS/PC DOS 4.0
Jonathan P. Bacon

Networks

Understanding Networks
E. Joseph Guay

Understanding and Using NetWare 3.x
Larry D. Smith

Programming

Understanding and Using Microsoft Visual Basic
Jonathan C. Barron

West's Essentials of Microsoft Visual Basic
Jonathan C. Barron

Understanding and Using QBasic
Jonathan C. Barron

Word Processors

Understanding and Using WordPerfect 6.1 for Windows
Jonathan P. Bacon

Understanding and Using WordPerfect 6.0 for Windows
Jonathan P. Bacon

Understanding and Using WordPerfect for Windows
Jonathan P. Bacon

Understanding and Using Microsoft Word for Windows 95
Emily M. Ketcham

Understanding and Using Microsoft Word for Windows 6.0
Emily M. Ketcham

Understanding and Using Microsoft Word for Windows 2.0
Larry Lozuk and Emily M. Ketcham

Understanding and Using Microsoft Word for Windows (1.1)
Larry Lozuk

Understanding and Using WordPerfect 6.0
Jonathan P. Bacon and Robert G. Sindt

Understanding and Using WordPerfect 5.1
Jonathan P. Bacon and Cody T. Copeland

Understanding and Using WordPerfect 5.0
Patsy H. Lund

Desktop Publishing

Understanding and Using PageMaker 5.0
John R. Nicholson

Understanding and Using PageMaker 4.0
John R. Nicholson

Spreadsheets

Understanding and Using Microsoft Excel for Windows 95
Steven C. Ross and Stephen V. Hutson

Understanding and Using Microsoft Excel 5
Steven C. Ross and Stephen V. Hutson

Understanding and Using Microsoft Excel 4
Steven C. Ross and Stephen V. Hutson

Understanding and Using Microsoft Excel 3
Steven C. Ross and Stephen V. Hutson

Understanding and Using Quattro Pro 6.0 for Windows
Lisa L. Friedrichsen

Understanding and Using Quattro Pro 5.0 for Windows
Larry D. Smith

Understanding and Using Quattro Pro 4
Steven C. Ross and Stephen V. Hutson

Understanding and Using Lotus 1-2-3 for Windows Release 5
Dolores Pusins and Steven C. Ross

Understanding and Using Lotus 1-2-3 for Windows Release 4
Steven C. Ross and Dolores Pusins

Understanding and Using Lotus 1-2-3 Release 3
Steven C. Ross

Understanding and Using Lotus 1-2-3 Release 2.3 and Release 2.4
Steven C. Ross

*Understanding and Using Lotus 1-2-3: Advanced Techniques
Releases 2.2 and 2.3*
Judith C. Simon

Understanding and Using Lotus 1-2-3 Release 2.2
Steven C. Ross

Understanding and Using Lotus 1-2-3 Release 2.01
Steven C. Ross

Database Management

Understanding and Using Microsoft Access for Windows 95
Bruce J. McLaren

Understanding and Using Microsoft Access 2.0
Bruce J. McLaren

Understanding and Using Microsoft Access 1.1
Bruce J. McLaren

Understanding and Using Paradox 4.5 for Windows
Larry D. Smith

Understanding and Using Paradox 3.5
Larry D. Smith

Understanding and Using dBASE IV Version 2.0
Steven C. Ross

Understanding and Using dBASE IV
Steven C. Ross

Understanding and Using dBASE III Plus, 2nd Edition
Steven C. Ross

Integrated Software

Understanding and Using Microsoft Office for Windows 95
Emily M. Ketcham

Understanding and Using Microsoft Works for Windows 3.0
Gary Bitter

Understanding and Using Microsoft Works 3.0 for the PC
Gary Bitter

Understanding and Using Microsoft Works 3.0 for the Macintosh
Gary Bitter

Understanding and Using Microsoft Works 2.0 on the Macintosh
Gary Bitter

Understanding and Using Microsoft Works 2.0 on the IBM PC
Gary Bitter

Understanding and Using ClarisWorks
Gary Bitter

Presentation Software

Understanding and Using Microsoft PowerPoint for Windows 95
Lisa L. Friedrichsen

Understanding and Using Microsoft PowerPoint 4.0
Edna Dixon

Combined Books

Understanding and Using Microsoft Office for Windows 95
Emily M. Ketcham

Essentials of Application Software, Volume 1: DOS, WordPerfect 5.0/5.1, Lotus 1-2-3 Release 2.2, dBASE III Plus
Steven C. Ross, Jonathan P. Bacon, and Cody T. Copeland

Understanding and Using Application Software, Volume 4: DOS, WordPerfect 5.0, Lotus 1-2-3 Release 2, dBASE IV
Patsy H. Lund, Jonathan P. Bacon, and Steven C. Ross

Understanding and Using Application Software, Volume 5: DOS, WordPerfect 5.0/5.1, Lotus 1-2-3 Release 2.2, dBASE III Plus
Steven C. Ross, Jonathan P. Bacon, and Cody T. Copeland

Advanced Books

Understanding and Using Lotus 1-2-3: Advanced Techniques Releases 2.2 and 2.3
Judith C. Simon

Steven C. Ross holds a B.S. degree in History from Oregon State University and M.S. and Ph.D. degrees in Business Administration from the University of Utah. He is an Associate Professor of Management Information Systems at Western Washington University, Bellingham. His previous positions were as Associate Professor of Information Systems at Montana State University, Bozeman, and Assistant Professor of Management at Marquette University in Milwaukee. His responsibilities include the introduction of microcomputers into the primary computer courses and the integration of computer applications throughout the curriculum.

Dr. Ross is the Consulting Editor for THE MICROCOMPUTING SERIES. In this capacity he advises both West Publishing and the authors on pedagogical, creative, editorial, design, and marketing issues. He is the author or coauthor of a dozen articles dealing with information management and education, and this is one of 25 books on microcomputing that he has written or edited. Two of his books in this series have been translated into French. He also consults with businesses of all sizes to integrate microcomputers into their managerial operations. His teaching and consulting experiences have provided ample material for this book.

Ronald W. Maestas holds B.A. and M.A. degrees in Business Education from Adams State College and an Ed.D. degree in Business Education from Arizona State University. He successfully completed the AACSB Information Systems Faculty Development Institute at the University of Minnesota and the Advanced Institute at Indiana University. He is a Full Professor of Management Information Systems at New Mexico Highlands University, Las Vegas, New Mexico. His current assignments include Director of the School of Business. He previously was Cross Country Coach at New Mexico Highlands University. His 1987 team was the NAIA runner-up champions. He served as the national distance coach for the Swaziland Olympic team at the 1988 Summer Olympics in Seoul, South Korea. His current responsibilities include the introduction of microcomputers into the business curriculum and the integration of computer applications throughout the business school.

Dr. Maestas is the coauthor with Steve Ross of *Understanding and Using Microsoft Windows 3.0 and 3.1.* He has received a National Science Foundation grant to integrate computers in the Information Analysis class. He has served as a reviewer for several books on microcomputers and has been a beta tester for Ashton–Tate's Digital VAX/VMS version of dBASE IV. He has made several presentations at regional and national conferences. His 20 years of teaching have provided him with a good foundation for this book.

Fundamental Windows Operations

■ **PART ONE** In this part we introduce Microsoft Windows 95. Unit 1, "The Windows Environment," illustrates concepts and features of the program, describes launching Windows, and provides an overview of other Windows products. Unit 2, "Basic Skills," contains a series of discussions and activities that provide practice in dealing with the different types of windows, using both the mouse and the keyboard for input.

Unit 3, "The Windows 95 User Interface," deals with the fundamental aspects of Windows. Here we discuss how to move among program groups and how to start application programs. Unit 4, "Windows Explorer," presents the numerous techniques available in that program for administering storage of data and programs in files, in folders, and on disks.

Unit 5 presents the "Control Panel," a program that allows you to change the visual and mechanical aspects of the Windows interface. You can, for instance, change both the colors of window borders and the background of your windows screen. Finally, Unit 6 discusses "Printing," the program that manages the printing of the output of most Windows programs.

Windows Operating System Product Line

Microsoft's operating system product line provides users with a rich set of services that take full advantage of the broad range of hardware platforms available today, from small portable systems to multiprocessor servers. The members of the Windows operating system family all share a consistent user interface programming environment, making the entire product line easier to learn and use for both end users and developers.

Currently the Windows operating system product line includes Microsoft Windows 95, Windows 3.1, and Microsoft Windows for Workgroups 3.11, which are designed to run personal and business productivity applications on mainstream personal computer platforms. Except for Windows 95 itself, the most recent additions to the product line are Microsoft Windows NT Workstation and Windows NT Server operating systems, which are designed to run the most demanding applications on high-end workstation and server platforms.

The major differences among versions of Windows have been behind-the-scenes performance improvements (for example, programs run faster and are less susceptible to certain types of errors), rather than differences in the manner in which the program is operated. Some visual differences are found in the Explorer program, and new menu items have been added to many of the Windows applications. This book should serve you well in understanding Windows 95.

Welcome to Windows 95

As the successor to Microsoft MS-DOS, Windows 3.1, and Windows for Workgroups 3.11, Windows 95 is the next major release of the standard operating system for the desktop and portable personal computer (PC). It has something for everyone, whether it's a more intuitive way to work, new capabilities like "surfing the information highway," or better support for managing a 1,000-PC installation site.

Windows 3.1 moved the PC platform forward by making PCs easier to use. Yet the problems encountered by PC users today only highlight the need to significantly further the ease, power, and overall usefulness of the PC. Windows 95 goes beyond simple ease of use. It not only empowers a new range of people to become proficient PC users by making their computers dramatically easier to use, but also enables a wide range of uses for the PC among existing users as follows:

- *Windows 95 makes PCs even easier to use.* Windows 3.1 put a friendly interface on top of MS-DOS to make common PC tasks far easier. In Windows 95, the goal is to make those tasks more intuitive or, where possible, automatic. The addition and configuration of new hardware devices on the PC is one example. Windows 95 automatically loads the appropriate driver sets and IRQs (interrupts), and notifies applications of the new capabilities of the hardware device without any action by the user. A redesigned user interface, highlighted by the Windows taskbar, makes computing more automatic for novices. Windows 95 usability tests show a tenfold improvement over Windows 3.1 in the time required to complete certain common tasks such as starting an application. The program also makes the power of the PC more readily discoverable, and even more enjoyable to use, for intermediate and advanced users.

■   *Windows 95 is altogether a faster and more powerful operating system.* Ease on the surface requires power and speed at the core, and Windows 95's modern, 32-bit architecture meets these requirements. Freed from the limitations of MS-DOS, Windows 95 preemptively multitasks for better PC responsiveness. Users will no longer have to wait while the system copies files, for example, and in addition they will notice that it delivers increased robustness and protection for applications.

■   *Windows 95 also provides the foundation for a new generation of easier, more powerful multithreaded 32-bit applications.* Multithreaded processing means that each window opened by the shell runs as a separately scheduled thread. You will see this innovation in action if you move the hourglass mouse cursor outside a window boundary. The cursor will change back to the normal arrow pointer and you can continue moving to another task. Another example of thread support involves a single application doing two things at once—perhaps writing a backup copy of the current document to disk while still allowing the user to edit the on-screen text. An application's ability under Win32 (in Windows 32-bit) to utilize multiple threads of execution provides a structured way to perform multitasking. Most important, Windows 95 delivers this power and robustness on today's average PC platform while taking advantage of additional memory and CPU cycles. Windows 95 integrates network connectivity and manageability. Windows 3.1 gave end users the power to better use their PCs, but it did not make the same strides for management information system (MIS) organizations. Windows 95 addresses this deficiency by providing a system architecture that makes basic network connectivity easy, by integrating high-performance, 32-bit client support into the operating system (including a 32-bit client for Novell NetWare) and going beyond simple connectivity (by enabling central management and control of the PC). Windows 95's user profiles, policies, and ability to pass through server-based security makes it much easier for MIS organizations to administer and support large numbers of PCs within the corporation.

■   *Windows 95 is more than the next generation of Windows.* It is a catalyst that will move the PC industry to a higher level of usefulness for end users. We can reasonably expect that the release of Windows 95 will spawn not only a new generation of PCs and peripherals that support Plug and Play, but a new generation of powerful, 32-bit Windows applications as well.

The Windows Environment

For you to appreciate Microsoft Windows 95, you need to become acquainted with some basic concepts that are unique to the program. Since Windows has become extremely popular, with more than 100 million copies in use (even before the summer 1995 release of Windows 95), you should learn, understand, and utilize its features to better prepare yourself for using personal computers in your career.

Learning Objectives

At the completion of this unit you should know

1. the concepts and features of Microsoft Windows 95,

2. what a user interface (UI) is,

3. some applications available with Windows 95,

4. how to start Windows 95,

5. how to exit Windows 95,

6. how to describe the Startup menu,

7. how to describe Windows and non-Windows applications.

Windows 95 Concepts

Windows is a *user interface*[1] (abbreviated as **UI**, pronounced *oo-ee*) that provides its users with more intuitive methods for working on personal computers and more visual cues than those offered by traditional *character-based user interfaces (CUI)*. An UI such as Windows permits a wide range of operations using a mouse or other pointing device. Those who are not good typists appreciate being relieved of the necessity of entering commands by typing—since a simple point, drag, or click of the mouse can perform sophisticated operations that require several keystrokes in a CUI environment.

The goal for the user interface of Windows 95 is to make computers easy for users at all levels to operate. Both novice and experienced users will find that the changes made to the user interface in Windows 95 make it even easier to learn and use than earlier versions of Windows. The system taskbar will make accessible all the functions most users need with a single click of a button. The taskbar will show all open windows and make it much easier to switch between windows by just clicking on a button representing that window. Instead of mastering different kinds of tools (Program Manager, File Manager, Print Manager, and Control Panel) to work with different resources on their computers, users of Windows 95 can browse for and access all resources in a consistent fashion with a single tool. All resources in the system will have property "sheets" that present tabbed-notebook-style interface settings that can be directly changed and customized. And a new integrated Help system makes it easy and fast to get context-sensitive help at all times.

Windows 95 will enable individuals who want to move gradually to the new user interface to continue running Program Manager and File Manager while they become familiar with the new user-interface features.

In Windows, the computer screen is referred to as a *desktop*. The Windows desktop is similar to the surface of the desk you use at work or at home. The desktop displays information in rectangular areas, or frames, called *windows*. You work with applications and documents within these windows. Figure 1.1 illustrates a desktop with various key terms noted.

Across the top of the window is the *window title*, which tells you what the window contains. The thin frame around the window is called the *window border*. Windows usually contain *applications*, computer programs used for a particular kind of work, such as word processing. Some applications programs allow you to have more than one *document* active at a time; for instance, you could be working on a term paper in one document window and a letter to a friend in the other. Windows can be arranged on the desktop, just as you can move work items around on an actual desk. For example, to review a spreadsheet and a report from two separate applications, you can change the size of the windows so that you view each side of the desktop simultaneously. Figure 1.1 shows two windows, one in the background containing

---

1 In this section, we introduce a number of terms, typeset in **boldface italics,** that deal with the operation of Windows. Some are defined here, while others are defined elsewhere in the book. As you read the text and work on your computer, develop your own definitions for these terms and concepts. The Key Terms section near the end of each unit lists the terms introduced in that unit.

FIGURE 1.1
Windows desktop

Window title

Control menu box

Application running in a window

Window border

Program icon

Close

Maximize

Minimize

Menu bar

Scroll bars

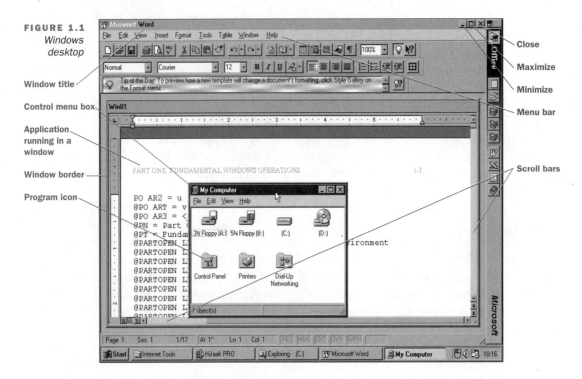

the program Word for Windows (a word processor) and one in the foreground containing My Computer, the usual starting place for Windows operations.

In most cases, the window containing an application or document is not large enough to display the entire document. *Scroll bars* (resembling vertical and horizontal elevator shafts) are used to move parts of a document into view when the entire document will not fit in a window. The *menu bar* at the top of each window contains many commands that are standard across Windows applications, as well as commands that are specific to the application contained in the window. (These commands will be printed in initial capitals in this text.)

Icons are small pictographs (symbols) that appear on some screens. Icons are used to represent running applications, documents, and program groups in My Computer. For example, a graphic illustration of a clock represents the Clock application. If you should choose to leave an application for a while, you can *minimize* (reduce) the window to an *application icon*. The application will continue to run even though it does not appear in a window. After you minimize an application, Windows will place its application icon at the lower edge of the *taskbar* until you *restore* it to window size again. In Figure 1.1, you see My Computer in the foreground, with a document window (a Word document) in the background. If you wish, you can *maximize* (expand) a window so that it occupies the entire screen. Maximized windows allow as much information as possible from a single application to be displayed on the screen.

With Windows, you can run several applications at once and switch quickly among them. For example, you can switch from a database application to a spreadsheet and then to a word processor with a few simple commands—and without having to wait while you quit one application and start another.

FIGURE 1.2
Windows Accessories

When you work with two or more applications, whether they are designed specifically for Windows or not, you can transfer information from one to the other. You select the information you want from one application, *cut* or *copy* it to the Clipboard, and *paste* it into another application. By moving information in this manner, you can combine into one single document the work you have done in a number of different applications.

Windows comes with a collection of useful accessory programs to help you manage the various tasks that are part of your daily work. These programs are contained in the Accessories program group, illustrated in Figure 1.2. These accessories include games, multimedia, a notepad, a card file, a calculator, and a character map. Windows also includes three full-featured applications: WordPad, Paint, and HyperTerminal Connection. These applications are useful when preparing and editing documents, creating illustrations, and connecting to computers and information services.

As you work with an application, you can pause at any time to take care of other tasks. For example, you might need to make some additions to the card files, or pull together some quick totals with Windows' electronic calculator.

Windows 95's Top Features

In many ways, Windows 95's development has been guided by the primary principle of making all its great technological improvements translate to practical benefits for users, while making these benefits easily and inexpensively available to everyone. This means several things:

- *Compatibility with existing MS-DOS and Windows-based applications.* Windows 95 is designed to add significant value to any PC without requiring additional software or hardware. It also ensures compatibility with existing Windows applications, yet goes a step beyond by fixing key compatibility deficiencies of Windows 3.1. It provides, for example, much better support for demanding MS-DOS and Windows applications. With Windows 95, you can run your cool games right from Windows.

- *Compatibility with existing hardware.* The wide range of available hardware for Windows 95, from scanners to plotters to fax modems to video capture boards, is enormously valuable to users. While providing support for new, easier-to-use peripherals through Plug and Play, Windows 95 also preserves the huge investment both users and manufacturers have made, by maintaining compatibility with existing peripherals and their associated device drivers.

■ *Windows 95 provides equal or better performance than Windows 3.1.* In keeping with the goal of adding value to existing PCs without requiring extra hardware and software, Windows 95 matches or exceeds the performance of Windows 3.1 on today's average PC (386DX with 4MB of RAM). As more memory is added to the PC, performance scales are faster than in Windows 3.1. For users this means that access to all of Windows 95's new features should not cost them any performance penalty.

Windows 95 makes the upgrade process as easy as possible with a Setup program that upgrades cleanly over Windows 3.*x*.

For end users and MIS organizations alike, improving ease of use goes beyond fixing problems with Windows itself; the improvements in Windows 95 encompass hardware, connectivity, and applications as well. Less-experienced users find the plethora of overlapping Windows, to say nothing of minimizing and maximizing, too complex to master easily. Yet more experienced users crave greater efficiency and more "toys". Windows 95 offers these solutions:

■ *New user interface.* A blizzard of improvements greatly enhance learnability, usability, and efficiency for users at all levels of expertise. New users can get started more quickly, while experienced users can unlock even more of the full power of their PCs.

■ *Plug and Play.* The goal of Plug and Play is simple: when a user installs a new hardware device, it just works.

■ *Long file names.* Long file names have put an end to the limitation of eight-characters-plus-a-three-character-extension file names. This alone is an important example of Windows 95's usability improvements.

MIS organizations increasingly find their job more difficult as the number of PCs in a given corporation increases more rapidly than their support staff. In addition, the introduction of Windows 3.1 led to a series of security, reliability, and management issues because of its lack of integrated connectivity and lack of infrastructure for being managed. Some features of Windows 95 that attack these problems are:

■ *Built-in networking.* Whether you're running NetWare or Microsoft Networks; IPX/SPX, TCP/IP, or NetBEUI; NDIS or ODI, Windows 95 has native, integrated support for your network. Additional LANs are easily supported.

■ *The Registry.* This holds all pertinent information about the system—installed hardware, installed software, and user preferences.

■ *User profiles.* Windows 95 enables multiple users to personalize and/or customize settings. A network administrator could, for example, prevent an employee from deleting program items no matter what PC he or she logs in on, or could securely enforce a policy that everyone in a particular group have passwords of at least six characters.

- *Pass-through user-level security.* A Windows 95 PC can require that a remote user and their password be passed through to and validated by a NetWare server or Windows NT Advanced Server before allowing the user to do something—for example, change the PC's Registry or access its files and printers either over the network or from a remote location.

- *Network backup agents.* Windows 95 includes agents that support industry-leading server backup products.

Microsoft Windows 95 is the most popular graphical user interface program to exploit the advanced features of computers introduced since the original IBM PC. With it, users of DOS computers have an operating system that is flexible and powerful enough to support applications of every kind, at every level of complexity and ambition. With more than 80 million new users since its initial release in May 1990, Microsoft Windows has become the new standard for personal computing. Customers are choosing Windows because it is easy to use and because the most powerful new applications designed for it are the focus of development activity and innovation at every major independent software vendor. There are several reasons for Windows' success.

First, an enormous range of Windows applications is available now. Windows users do not have to wait years for the kinds of applications promised, but not yet delivered, for other advanced operating systems.

Second, unlike some other systems, with relatively small numbers of computers sold and expensive hardware, Windows runs on millions of DOS-based machines. In fact, Windows can run on virtually any DOS-based machine with a suitable graphics adapter and monitor. True, good performance requires extra memory and a speedy microprocessor, but Windows 95 makes its appearance at an ideal historical moment, since RAM is inexpensive and 386SX, 486DX, and Pentium-based machines are less expensive than ever.

Third, Windows 95 is able to push any PC to its limit in ways that few other programs can. It exploits the power of a 486 or Pentium computer (with at least 4MB of RAM, since Windows 95 runs better with at least 16MB of RAM) by letting you multitask (operate more than one DOS session) while you run multiple Window applications. Windows 95 lets you multitask Windows applications and access up to 16MB of RAM.

Windows 95 allows your computer to operate with greater efficiency, unhampered by memory restrictions of previous operating environments.

Windows 95 makes efficient use of all the memory installed in your computer, enabling you to execute several programs simultaneously. Windows 95 also allows for the easy transfer of information from one program to another.

Windows 95 is in effect the computer cockpit that allows you to control all of your computer's capabilities with the click of a button. Like the pilot of a modern, sophisticated aircraft, you are guided quickly through Windows' numerous functions by graphic symbols. You use Windows applications in the same intuitive way that you use Windows itself. With little effort, you can master high-powered, Windows-based programs for desktop publishing, spreadsheets, word processing, database management, and graphics, such as PageMaker, Excel, Word, Access, and Paint.

Some of the other features found in Windows 95 include the following:

Explorer, which allows a full range of mouse operations to copy and move both files and folders by dragging their icons with your mouse.

The Control Panel, which lets you connect to network printers, set up additional ports, set multitasking options, and customize the appearance of your desktop.

DOS Prompt, which allows you to use many of the commands familiar to users of MS-DOS.

Clipboard Viewer, which is the temporary storage place for information being transferred from one application to another.

Read Me, a document that contains late-breaking information not available in online help screens or printed manuals.

A Quick Introduction to Working with the Mouse

If at all possible, use Windows 95 with a mouse or other pointing device. In this book we will tell you how to use some of the commands with the keyboard, although many operations are far easier using the mouse. The following terms are used to describe mouse operations. When we refer to the "mouse button" or the "active mouse button" we mean the left button on those mouse devices that have more than one button. If you are left-handed, you can change a multibutton mouse so that the right button is the active mouse button. Instructions for doing this are in Unit 2.

POINT   means to move the mouse pointer—often an arrow but sometimes another symbol—to an object. You will be instructed to point to an icon, a window title, the border of a window, a menu item, or various objects in a window, such as a spreadsheet cell.

CLICK   (also *choose* or *select*) means to press and then quickly release the active mouse button after you have pointed to the object to be selected. With most mouse devices, this produces a "click" sound. Clicking is used to instruct Windows to activate a window, open a menu, execute a command, or pick an item from a list.

DRAG   means to point to an object, then press the active mouse button and hold it down while you move the mouse on a flat surface. Dragging is used to move objects such as windows and icons as well as to change window size. Dragging is also used in applications programs to *mark* or *highlight* a range of objects (such as words or spreadsheet cells) before executing certain commands. For instance, you can highlight a group of words, and then use a command to italicize them.

DOUBLE-CLICK   means to press the mouse button twice, rapidly, after you have pointed to an object. Double-clicking is a shortcut method for selecting and executing some commands. Throughout this book, we will tell you where to use double-clicking.

Starting Windows 95

You have now been introduced to the basic concepts and terminology of Windows 95. This section shows you how to start and end a Windows session. The manner in which you load Windows will depend on your system configuration.

The procedure for starting Windows varies from place to place and perhaps even from computer to computer. In this section we discuss a typical procedure for hard disk systems. If necessary, your instructor or system manager can assist you with any differences within your school or organization. To use Windows, you need a computer that has Windows installed on the hard disk or network as well as a formatted disk to save the files you create. If Windows has not been installed on your system, consult Appendix A for installation procedures.

Once Windows 95 has been installed on your system, you may begin. The following Guided Activity assumes that your system *does not* have a "shell" or "menu" program that is executed when the computer is started. If this assumption is incorrect, your instructor or system manager will have to give you additional instructions in starting Windows.

GUIDED ACTIVITY 1.1

Starting Windows

1. Turn on your PC and monitor. Your computer will begin to load the various programs, drivers, and so on. After a couple of minutes, Windows 95 will automatically load up.

2. The monitor will display the Windows 95 copyright screen.

3. You will see a dialog box requesting your username and password. If this is the first time that you have used Windows 95, press the [Enter] key.

4. After a short pause, the Windows desktop appears. This might be a solid color, a design, or a picture, depending on your computer and your organization's preferences. On the desktop, you will see the My Computer icon, representing one program. We can't predict how your organization has set up Windows, so our instructions at this point are a bit equivocal.

Windows begins with the My Computer window open.[2]

---

2 If you have sufficient disk space, some schools and organizations may have loaded Windows 95 on top of a previous version of Windows (3.x). If so, you may switch versions by pressing the [F4] key prior to the Windows program's starting. Your instructor or lab manager should tell you if this is the case and should inform you how your local program differs.

GUIDED ACTIVITY 1.2

Opening the My Computer

1. Locate the My Computer icon, which looks like the icon in the margin.

2. If you are using a mouse, point to the My Computer icon. Double-click on the icon—that is, press the left button twice quickly.

GUIDED ACTIVITY 1.3

Exiting Windows

1. Close any active windows before leaving Windows. You will learn how to close active windows in later units as we discuss the Windows software.

2. Click on the Start button, and then click on Shutdown.

3. Respond to the dialog box to confirm your wish to shut down Windows. With a mouse, you can click once on the Yes button. With the keyboard, use the arrow keys to highlight the button (notice that the edges of the highlighted button are darker and wider), and then press ⏎Enter.

Additional Microsoft Software

Microsoft Windows 95 is capable of running many other programs, including drawing packages, smart utilities, and project and data managers. Some programs, written especially for Windows, are called *Windows applications*. These include software published by Microsoft as well as software from other publishers. At the time this book was written, Microsoft had published five Windows 95 applications: Project, PowerPoint, Word for Windows, Excel, and Access. Following is a brief description of each. See Unit 11 for examples of how these products are used and more complete discussions of their features.

Project takes full advantage of the graphical capabilities of the Windows environment, making project management easier, more powerful, and far more flexible to use than earlier programs of its kind. Project management is an inherently graphical application. Microsoft has used the Windows environment to create entirely new techniques for handling task relationships, resource management, reports, and data entry. Project goes beyond the arbitrary structures of conventional text-based project managers such as Time Line and Harvard Project Manager.

Microsoft PowerPoint is another program designed for Windows. It is a fast, easy way for you to create and manage your own high-quality overhead and 35mm-slide presentations. The uniqueness of PowerPoint software lies in its approach, for it addresses the needs of the businessperson, not the trained graphic designer. Microsoft PowerPoint is also unique with respect to its guiding principle: "A better process yields better results."

Capitalizing on the Microsoft Windows graphical environment, PowerPoint software makes the process of creating presentations simple, beginning with *WYSIWYG* (pronounced *wiz-ee-wig*, for "what you see is what you get") technology. WYSIWYG lets you create slides or overheads directly on screen. Add to that the ability to store all your presentation visuals in a single file, special presentation-management features that make organizing your presentation easy, plus a complete set of tools. In essence, PowerPoint gives you all you need to produce a professional-looking presentation yourself. It lets you remain in control of your presentation from start to finish.

Word for Windows is the word processing package developed by Microsoft for the Windows environment. It is a sophisticated program that includes a spell checker, a thesaurus, mail merge, and other utilities. Word permits the importing of pictures, charts, and stylized text directly into a document. It provides a number of character styles, including bold and italic character sets, single and double underlining, strike-through, superscript, subscript, and hidden text.

Word contains a number of paragraph formats that are helpful as you set up your text. A document can contain multiple formats, permitting you to have a standard format for most text—say, double-spaced and justified—but also to reserve special formats for headings and important paragraphs. These special formats can have left, center, or right alignment; a unique typeface; extra spacing before, after, or in the middle of the paragraph; and numerous other characteristics. The possibilities for arranging text are as many and varied as your imagination permits, while the ***graphical user interface*** (***GUI***, pronounced *goo-ee*) makes it easy for you to see the effect immediately.

Excel is a state-of-the-art spreadsheet package from Microsoft and the first popular package to use the graphical user interface extensively. Excel provides a broad range of formatting options, allowing you to enhance the visual appeal of your product with multiple fonts, borders, shading, customized number formats, and color. Excel is designed to allow you to construct powerful models, displaying and linking multiple spreadsheets on your screen. You can check your figures as well with an array of advanced, built-in auditing tools. Excel has 131 built-in worksheet functions and 224 macro functions. For graphic display of numbers, a gallery of 44 built-in chart types plus customization is available in Excel.

Excel uses the standard GUI features of user-defined menus, dialog boxes, and online help to facilitate your work. You can record macros as you work, store them on separate sheets, and apply them to any worksheet. Excel is compatible with Lotus 1-2-3, dBASE III Plus, and Microsoft Multiplan, supplementing these data analysis packages with its own set of features.

Finally, Windows permits you to use ***non-Windows applications*** (those created in the "DOS Age" and later reprogrammed to run in Windows), such as Lotus 1-2-3, Quattro Pro, dBASE IV or V, WordPerfect, Norton Utilities, and so on, without exiting from Windows.

Database management systems have traditionally split into two camps: those that are so complex that only a professional programmer can make them work, and the so-called easy-to-use database management systems that are so underpowered that they sacrifice speed or skimp on critical features.

With Microsoft Access, you do not have to scrap your existing and valuable investment in data. Microsoft Access directly reads and writes in all of the popular file formats—even across a network, simultaneously with other users! You can easily share data back and forth with others in your workgroup who use Paradox, dBASE, or other database management systems. Access allows you to get your data quickly by using graphical *query by example (QBE)*. With a mouse, just drag and drop tables, join fields, and specify criteria. Forms are built in minutes by using *visual form-generation* tools. Access allows you to quickly access database tools with the *dynamic toolbar*, create reports and forms using *Report Wizard* and *Form Wizard*. Cue Cards provide a step-by-step help on-line screen alongside the database task that you are working on. Finally, Access macros allow you to easily automate routine database management tasks, such as printing out a series of monthly reports. They provide an easy, fill-in-the-blank programming model for those who do not want to immerse themselves in Access Basic code.

Overview of This Book

This book is designed to teach the basics of Windows applications. Basic skills will be practiced and fundamental concepts will be illustrated to help you master Windows. You will learn how to operate within the Windows environment. Windows includes all the programs you need to manage your software applications and files easily and efficiently. Furthermore, you will learn ways to increase your computing power and knowledge. With its emphasis on essentials and its practice-oriented instructions (Guided Activities, Review Questions, and Key Terms), this book will help you learn how to use Windows for your daily work.

Additional topics to be covered in this book include other Windows applications—such as Word, Excel, Project, and PowerPoint. This book deals with the programs included with Windows—WordPad, Paint, and HyperTerminal—as well as Windows accessories (Calculator, Cardfile, Notepad, and so on). You will soon be exploring the Wonderful World of Windows!

Review Questions

The answers to questions marked with an asterisk are contained in Appendix C.

1. There are many ways in which Windows 95 applications parallel items on your desk. Describe as many of these as you can.

*2. Discuss the factors leading to the recent success of Microsoft Windows 95.

*3. Briefly, state and describe the features and capabilities of Windows 95. (*Hint:* Review the icons in this unit.) Where applicable, state the advantages gained by using these features.

*4. List the steps for starting Windows 95.

Key Terms

The following terms are introduced in this unit. Be sure you know what each of them means.

Application	Form Wizard	Report Wizard
Application icon	Graphical user interface	Restore
Character-based user	(GUI)	Scroll bar
interface (CUI)	Highlight	Select
Choose	Icon	Taskbar
Click	Mark	User interface (UI)
Copy	Maximize	Visual form generation
Cut	Menu bar	Window
Desktop	Minimize	Window border
Document	Non-Windows application	Window title
Double-click	Paste	Windows application
Drag	Point	WYSIWYG
Dynamic toolbar	Query by example (QBE)	

Basic Skills

Mastering basic concepts and skills is extremely important in learning new software. This is particularly true of Windows 95, which is unique since it utilizes specialized terminology as well as different approaches to execute commands. This unit introduces you to the use of both mouse and keyboard for entering commands, and then discusses the advantages and disadvantages of each method. In addition, you will learn the types of windows (application and document) that are used with Windows 95.

Learning Objectives

At the completion of this unit you should know

1. the terminology of Windows,

2. advantages and disadvantages of using the mouse for input,

3. advantages and disadvantages of using the keyboard for input,

4. the difference between an application window and a document window,

5. how to use both mouse and keyboard to enter commands,

6. how to open and close drop-down menus,

7. how to open dialog boxes and make entries in them,

8. how to move windows, icons, and dialog boxes,

9. how to change the size of a window,

10. how to minimize, maximize, and restore a window,

11. how to close an application window,

12. how to switch among application windows,

13. how to access and use Help.

Two Types of Windows

Throughout this book we will refer to various types of windows. The two most important types are application windows and document windows. Other types of windows are variations on these. An *application window* contains a program, such as Excel or Word. A *document window* contains a specific spreadsheet or graph in Excel, a document file in Word, and so on. Many Windows applications allow you to work with more than one document (whether spreadsheet, graph, or document) at once. The program group windows (for example, My Computer) on the desktop are also classified as document windows.

Using a Mouse

Microsoft Windows 95 can best be operated by using a mouse (or trackball or other rolling device). The mouse offers an easy way to work with Windows because it enables you to quickly move the cursor on the screen. When the mouse is rolled over a flat surface, the cursor moves in the same relative direction on the screen. You give instructions to Windows by using the mouse control functions introduced in Unit 1: pointing, clicking, choosing, selecting, dragging, marking, and double-clicking.

Normally, the left mouse button is the active button, which is convenient for right-handed users. The mouse can be configured for left-handed users, making the right mouse button the active button. To do so, double-click on the Control Panel (in the Start button on the taskbar under Settings), and then double-click the mouse icon. The mouse dialog box will appear. Choose the button configuration (Right-handed or Left-handed) by clicking inside the *option button* (the circle), and then click on the OK button to exit.

Using a Keyboard

This unit and all subsequent units contain activities that require you to enter information from the keyboard. Your input must be accurate or the results will vary from what is described in the text. We have established a number of typographical conventions that will make it easier for you to know exactly which keys to press.

The word *Press* is used whenever you are instructed to push a single keystroke. For instance, after highlighting a command option, you will be instructed to

Press [Enter].
or
Press the [Enter] key.

This means you press the Enter or Return ([Return]) key on your keyboard once. On older PC keyboards, the [Enter] key is unlabeled except for a broken (bent) arrow. In this text, that key is always referred to with the symbol [Enter].

Other keys that you press are listed below, with their symbols shown in the first column.

[Alt]	Alt or Alternate key
[Backspace]	Backspace key
[CapsLock]	Caps Lock or Capitals Lock key
[Ctrl]	Ctrl or Control key
[Del]	Del or Delete key
[↓]	Down arrow key
[End]	End key on numeric or cursor movement pad
[Esc]	Esc or Escape key
[F1]	Function key labeled F1
[F2]	Function key labeled F2
[F3]	Function key labeled F3
[F4]	Function key labeled F4
[F5]	Function key labeled F5
[F6]	Function key labeled F6
[F7]	Function key labeled F7
[F8]	Function key labeled F8
[F9]	Function key labeled F9
[F10]	Function key labeled F10
[F11]	Function key labeled F11
[F12]	Function key labeled F12
[Home]	Home key on numeric or cursor movement pad
[Ins]	Ins or Insert key
[←]	Left arrow key

`Num Lock`	Num Lock or Numeric Lock key
`PgDn`	PgDn or Page Down key
`PgUp`	PgUp or Page Up key
`PrtSc`	PrtSc or Print Screen key
`→`	Right arrow key
`Shift`	Shift key
`Spacebar`	Spacebar key
`Tab`	Tab key
`↑`	Up arrow key

Three of these keys (`Alt`, `Ctrl`, and `Shift`) are used in combination with a second key. For example, if instructed to press `Alt` `Tab`, you would hold down `Alt`, press the `Tab` key once, and then release `Alt`.

When keys are pressed one right after another, as opposed to the first key being held and the next pressed, the key notations are separated by commas. For example, press `Alt` `H`, `I`. In this case, you would press `Alt` then `H`, release both, and then press `I` once.

The words *Type* or *Enter* are used to indicate that multiple keystrokes must be entered on the keyboard. The specific keys to be typed are shown in the following monofont typeface:

Type `Good Morning, Good People.`

In this example, you would type "Good Morning, Good People." (without the quotation marks but including the period).

Keyboard operations (commands) are generally the same from one Windows application to another. Sometimes the keyboard allows you to use a single-key short-cut, which replaces any mouse movements.

If you are using Microsoft Word (word processor) and you wish to access the menus listed in the menu bar, press the `Alt` key or the `F10` function key. Each menu or command name contains an underlined letter and is chosen by next pressing that letter on the keyboard. In rare cases, the underlined letter is duplicated and you can select the second instance only by using the arrow keys to highlight that command and then pressing `Enter`.

There are times when using the mouse will not be efficient or even possible. In some instances, you might find it easier to use a combination of keyboard commands and mouse functions, or just the keyboard commands alone (keeping both hands on the keyboard). In any case, becoming familiar with both the mouse and keyboard will enhance your ability to use Windows 95.

≋ **NOTE** *A list of keyboard commands for all applications included with Windows 95 is contained in Appendix B to this book.*

Opening and Exiting Programs

To open a program, point and click on the Start button on the lower left of the desktop. Figure 2.1 shows the Help menu after it has been opened.

FIGURE 2.1
*Windows Help
menu*

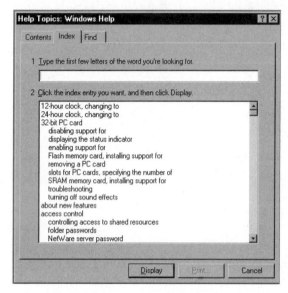

Selecting Menu Commands

Items listed on menus are often commands that represent choices. You select one of these to carry out a desired task. In addition, items listed on menus can be format-ting effects for text (such as bold or centered), a list of open windows or files, or the names of *cascading menus*, which are menus that list more commands.

To choose an item from a selected menu, click on the item name. For example, if you wish to open a file using Microsoft Word for Windows, click on the *File* menu, and then select the *Open* command. If you are using the keyboard for command selection, press [Alt], then arrow to File, press [Enter], then arrow down to Open, and once again press [Enter]. (See Figure 2.2.)

When choosing menu commands you will notice that some menu items appear dimmed (gray instead of black), some have check marks next to them, several have ellipses (...), and others have key combinations listed across from them. (We will not print the ellipses in this text.) Windows applications all follow certain conventions when listing items on a menu. These conventions signal extra information about the menu commands that follow.

Menu Convention	*What It Means*
Command name dimmed	The command is not available at the moment. You might have to select something (such as a paragraph or a spread-sheet cell) before you can use the command, or it may just be that the command cannot be used with your particular application.

FIGURE 2.2
File Open

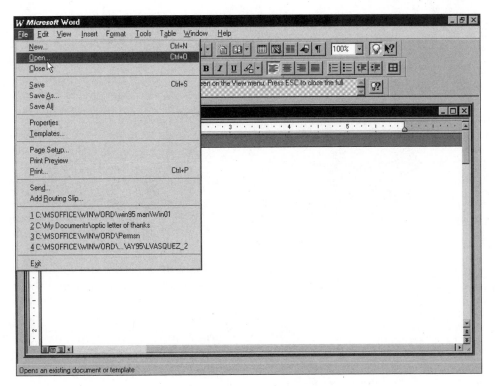

Menu Convention	What It Means
An ellipsis (…) after the name	A dialog box will appear when the command is chosen, asking for information that the application needs to carry out the command.
A check mark next to the name	The command is active. This convention is used for commands that *toggle* (switch) between one state and another.
An X next to the name	The command is active. Marks a command that can be used along with other X'd commands in the same section of a dialog box.
A key combination after the name	The key combination is a shortcut for this command. Use this key combination to choose the menu command without first opening the menu.
An arrowhead at the right side of a menu command	The command leads to a cascading menu, which lists additional commands that are available.

Dialog Boxes

Windows uses *dialog boxes* to request information from you as well as provide information to you. Whenever you see an ellipsis (…) after a menu command, a dialog box follows. For example, when you select Font from the Word for Windows 7.0 Format command, the program displays a dialog box asking for details on how you

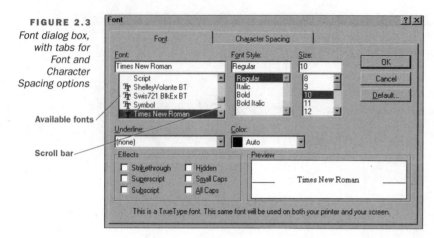

FIGURE 2.3
*Font dialog box,
with tabs for
Font and
Character
Spacing options*

Available fonts

Scroll bar

want the character(s) to appear. You may change the font or character spacing from this dialog box. You complete the dialog (or interchange with the computer) by providing the requested information. The Font dialog box illustrated in Figure 2.3 appears after you request a font format in Word for Windows.

FIGURE 2.4
*Drop-down
list box*

Drop-down
list box

If you are using a mouse, you can click the various features you desire. The fonts are contained in a *drop-down list box*. To choose a font, click on the arrow next to the font box (illustrated in Figure 2.4). To see additional fonts, click on the vertical scroll bar. Select the font you want. You can format text as bold, italic, or bold italic. In addition you can select character Size (10 or 12, depending on the font you choose). You may Underline the text with single, double, or dotted lines. Color can be changed to emphasize certain parts of the text. Finally, you can add special Effects to include strikethrough, superscript, subscript, small caps, or all caps. *Command buttons*, such as *OK* and *Cancel*, are self-explanatory and usually exit the menu or call additional menus.

Working with Windows

When you work with an application or create a document, you will most likely have several different windows open on your desktop. Windows can be moved, changed, shrunk, enlarged, restored, and ultimately closed. Using and understanding the elements of windows will help you arrange and control your workspace. For example, the Calculator window can be enlarged, compressed, or moved, depending on your wishes. You can accomplish these tasks with the mouse or by using the arrow keys.

Calculator Maximized:

Calculator Minimized:

A window is a rectangular area where applications are run, documents are created, and other activities take place. A window is composed of a frame, the Control menu box, title bar, menu bar, maximize-minimize box, the actual workspace, and the mouse pointer. The Control menu box is located in the upper-left corner of the screen and appears as a small icon of the application being used. Most of these terms have been introduced earlier in this book. Locate each element and familiarize yourself with each of them. Learning to navigate through the window is important! The next several Guided Activities illustrate the use of these Windows control features.

Switching Among Application and Document Windows

At times when you have more than one application window open on your desktop, you may want to switch to a window other than the *active window*. The active window is distinguished from the inactive window(s) by a title bar of a different color or intensity. In Figure 2.5, Calculator is the active application window and NotePad is the active document window. An active window will be placed in the foreground (in front of the other windows that are open), covering all or portions of any *inactive windows*. Part of the application window can be moved beyond the borders of the desktop, placing some of the window's contents outside your view. To switch to an application window, simply click any area within the window with your mouse, or press [Alt][Tab] on the keyboard repeatedly until the icon you want is active. To switch to a document window, click any area within the window with your mouse.

FIGURE 2.5
Calculator

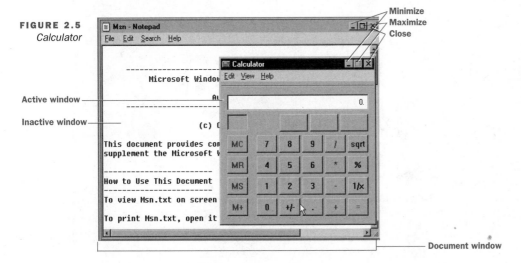

Taskbar

Another method of switching instantly to an application window is to use the *taskbar*. To use the taskbar to switch application windows:

1. Press the Start button.

2. Select Program and then choose the program from the list that appears. The dialog box illustrated in Figure 2.6 will open, but your list of tasks will probably be different than that illustrated here.

3. Click on the application to which you wish to switch.

FIGURE 2.6
Taskbar

Window List

When you are working in an application that allows multiple document windows, the Window menu usually allows you to switch between the documents. Click on Window, or press [Alt] [Tab], and a list of available windows will be displayed (Figure 2.7). Click on the title bar of the desired window, or use the arrow keys to highlight it and press [Enter].

FIGURE 2.7
List of open windows

Notice that the taskbar has doubled in size to accommodate the open programs

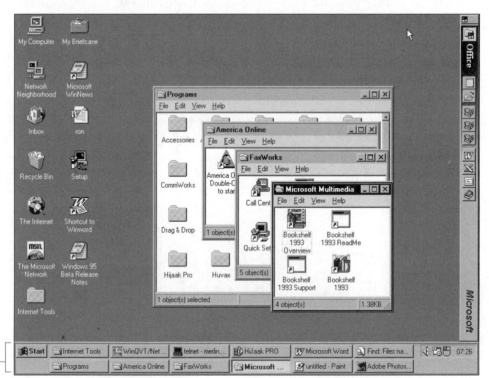

GUIDED ACTIVITY 2.1

Switching Applications

1. Press [Ctrl] and [Esc] to bring up the Start button. Select Taskbar.

2. Choose Calculator by pressing [←] or [→] to select the application in the list box.

3. Press [Enter].

Moving Windows and Icons

As your work with Windows becomes more complex, you will feel the need to rearrange the windows and icons on the desktop so that you can see more at one time. The following Guided Activity gives simple instructions for moving objects on the desktop.

GUIDED ACTIVITY 2.2

Moving a Window or Icon

1. Point either to the title bar of the window or dialog box, or to the center of the icon you wish to move. Choose the Calculator window for this activity.

2. Press and hold the mouse button to drag the title bar (or icon) to a new location. As you move a window or dialog box, an outline of the window or dialog box moves with it. As you move an icon, the mouse pointer changes to a black-and-white outline of the icon, which moves as you slide the mouse.

3. When the window, icon, or dialog box is in the desired location, release the mouse button. You can press [Esc] anytime before you release the mouse button to cancel the move.

Changing the Size of a Window

There will be times when you want to change the size and shape of the windows that are opened on your desktop. You can make a window occupy the entire screen, have it take up only a portion of the screen, or even reduce it to the taskbar.

GUIDED ACTIVITY 2.3

Sizing a Window

1. Select the window you want to change. For this activity, open *WordPad*, the word processing application that comes with Windows 95.

2. Point to a border or corner that you want to move. (The pointer changes to a two-headed arrow.)

3. Press and hold the mouse button to drag the corner or border until the window is the size you want.

4. Release the mouse button.

Windows can be changed both horizontally and vertically by choosing the Size command, by pressing two arrow keys alternately (for example, ⬆ and then ➡), and finally by pressing Enter to complete the action. You may cancel the resizing when using the mouse or keyboard by pressing Esc before you either release the mouse button or press Enter.

Minimizing a Window to an Icon

Windows on your desktop may become crowded because as you progress through various windows, your workspace becomes limited. To make room for other applications, you can shrink a window to the taskbar without actually closing the application. To shrink a window, use the minimize button located in the top-right corner of the window (see Figure 2.5). Placing the pointer on the minimize button and using a single click will reduce the window to the taskbar. When you shrink an application window to a taskbar, the application still runs in memory, but its window is not taking up space on your desktop. Application windows reduced to the taskbar can be restored instantly for use at a later time.

GUIDED ACTIVITY 2.4

Minimizing a Window

1. Select the WordPad window.

2. Minimize the window to an icon:

   Move the mouse pointer to the minimize button in the upper-right corner of the WordPad window and click.

   To restore a minimized window, click on the application's taskbar at the bottom of the screen.

Maximizing a Window

A window can be expanded to fill the entire desktop. For example, if you are working with *Paint* (Windows 95's drawing program), you will want as much work-space as possible. To enlarge the window, place the pointer in the maximize button located in the upper-right corner of the window (see Figure 2.5) and click the mouse button to complete the action. The window enlarges to its maximum size and the maximize button is replaced by the restore button. When one window is maximized, you cannot see the other windows and icons, although they are still available through the taskbar or using the ⌧Alt⌧⌧Tab⌧ shortcut method.

GUIDED ACTIVITY 2.5

Maximizing a Window

1. Select the Paint window.

2. Maximize the window to full-screen size:

   Move the mouse pointer to the maximize box in the upper-right corner of the Paint window and click.

GUIDED ACTIVITY 2.6

Restoring a Window from Maximum Size

  A window or an icon that has been maximized can be restored to its previous size (less than full-screen) by simply clicking the Restore button in the upper-right corner of the window. You usually restore a window to its previous size so that you can view and access other windows. Note that this does not reverse the effect of a window-sizing operation; it merely changes from full-screen to whatever size the window was before maximizing.

1. Using the mouse, click on the Restore button to reduce the Paint application to its normal size.

Closing an Application

  When you are finished with a particular application window, it should be closed. Open applications, even those that have been reduced to the taskbar, take up computer memory and processing time, making other operations less efficient (especially on older computers with less memory).

There are several ways to close a window. One method is to exit from the application by double-clicking on the document icon at the upper-left corner of the window, or alternatively, you can open the Control menu with a single click (or ⌧Alt⌧⌧Shift⌧), and then choose *Close.*

Most application programs that deal with separate files (for example, spreadsheets, word processors) will know whether you have saved your work since the last changes were made and will ask if you want to save before exiting. Often a simple mouse click or press of the ⌧Enter⌧ key is all that is necessary to answer "Yes" and save before exiting.

The document window Control menu, summoned by ⌧Alt⌧⌧-⌧ (hyphen), contains a Close command that is used to close document windows, such as the program groups in Explorer or documents in Word, but this does not close the application, only the document within the application.

GUIDED ACTIVITY 2.7

Closing an Application

1. Make Paint the active window by clicking on it or pressing [Alt] [Tab] as needed.

2. Close the window:

   Double-click on the Paint icon in the upper-left corner of the screen. If your clicks aren't quick enough, choose Close from the Control menu.

   Press [Alt] [Spacebar], and then choose Close.

3. The Paint application should disappear from the screen. If you want it back, you must restart the program as discussed earlier in this unit.

Getting Help

Windows 95 provides excellent on-line *help*. For example, if you are in Desktop and have a question, help is readily available through the pop-up menu shown in Figure 2.8.

FIGURE 2.8
Windows Help

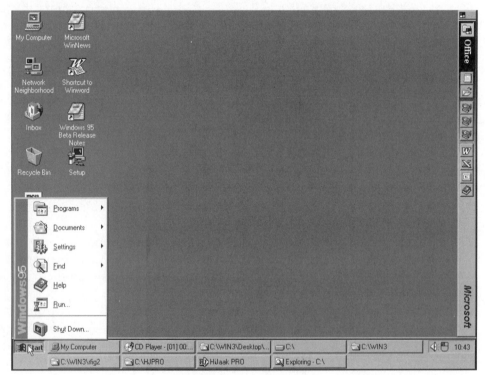

Using Help

Help answers questions about the keyboard, basic skills, commands, and procedures, and it also provides a glossary. Windows 95 has approximately 318 topics that you can get information on.

GUIDED ACTIVITY 2.8

Starting Help

1. Click on the Start button.

2. Place the mouse pointer on Help and click.

GUIDED ACTIVITY 2.9

Using the Help Index

1. Select *Index* using the mouse. This will produce a dialog box where you can either type the word(s) you want to find or select some matching words to narrow your search. When you find the topic, click on *Display*.

2. Place the mouse pointer on the box that asks you to type the word(s) you want and type Taskbar. Then click Display.

GUIDED ACTIVITY 2.10

Using the Back Button

1. Place the mouse pointer on the *Back* button and click to go to the previous topic, the portion of the index from which you selected Taskbar.

2. Choose Back once again to arrive back at the original Index window.

GUIDED ACTIVITY 2.11

Using the Option Button

1. Choose the *Option* button from Help with the mouse.

2. The available options include Annotate, Copy, Print Topic, Font, Keep Help on Top, and Use System Colors. Print this topic (Taskbar) on your printer.

Review Questions

The answers to questions marked with an asterisk are contained in Appendix C.

1. Can Windows 95 help you customize the mouse for a right- vs. a left-handed operator?

*2. What is a principal advantage in using the keyboard for input as opposed to using the mouse? Discuss the purpose of the [Alt] key or the [F10] (function key) in keyboard commands.

3. Which mouse command(s) would be used to open a file? Which keyboard command(s) would be used?

*4. When a menu command has an ellipsis (…) after the name, what does this indicate? A command in gray (dimmed)? A check mark? A key combination?

*5. What is a dialog box, and when does it appear?

Key Terms

The following terms are introduced in this unit. Be sure you know what each of them means.

Active window	Display	Open
Application window	Document window	Option
Back	Drop-down list box	Option button
Cancel	File	Paint
Cascading menus	Help	Taskbar
Close	Index	Toggle
Command button	Inactive window	WordPad
Dialog box	OK	

The Windows 95 User Interface

The Windows 95 user interface replaces the Windows 3.1 manager programs such as Program Manager, File Manager, Task Manager, and Print Manager. The Windows 95 shell consolidates the manager functions into a single program that is always accessible and will be the means by which most users will view and use a Windows 95 system.

Windows 95 looks as dramatically different from Windows 3.0 (and 3.1) as Windows 3.0 did from its predecessors. From the moment you start Windows 95, you can see that the appearance of Windows has been completely altered.

Learning Objectives

At the completion of this unit you should know

1. the elements of the Windows 95 shell,

2. the procedures for starting applications,

3. how to start applications from Windows 95,

4. how to use program groups in Windows 95,

5. how to shut down Windows 95.

Windows 95 User Interface

FIGURE 3.1
Office Manager

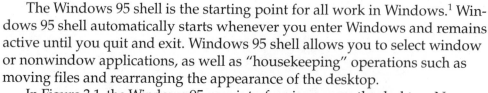

The Windows 95 shell is the starting point for all work in Windows.[1] Windows 95 shell automatically starts whenever you enter Windows and remains active until you quit and exit. Windows 95 shell allows you to select window or nonwindow applications, as well as "housekeeping" operations such as moving files and rearranging the appearance of the desktop.

In Figure 3.1, the Windows 95 user interface is open on the desktop. Non-Windows applications installed on your hard disk will also be represented by icons in this set of Office Manager icons. For example, if you have Lotus 1-2-3 SmartSuite or Microsoft Office Suite on your hard disk, your system manager places their icons on top of your screen (Figure 3.1).

Folders and Shortcuts

The Windows 95 user interface implements two new concepts that need immediate discussion: *folders* and *shortcuts*. Folders are the foundation of the shell design, and as you use Windows 95, you will quickly see that shortcuts are very useful.

Folders

A folder is a logical container that allows you to group any collection of items you choose. Folders can contain documents created with your word processor. The items a folder can contain include individual files, other folders, or shortcuts. Figure 3.2 illustrates some folders and their names.

The shell provides a view of both the local and network system that is an exact replica of the file system—that is, an object shown in one of the shell's windows is actually a file or a directory on the disk. Folders are directories and even shortcuts, stored as files.

Shortcuts

You will find **shortcuts** to be an abstract but extremely powerful tool for increasing efficiency. They are especially useful in a networked environment. A user can create a shortcut to any object (such as a file, program, network folder, Control Panel tool, or disk drive) in the UI (user interface) in Windows 95 and can then place it anywhere else in the UI or in an application. Making a shortcut allows you to create a reference to an object without having to make a copy of the object. For example, you might create a folder containing several word processing documents together with a shortcut to the printer. The icon in the margin illustrates how this shortcut would appear. To print the document, you would open the folder, click on the document

---

1 Some replacement shell products, such as Symantec's Norton Desktop for Windows, have been successful.

FIGURE 3.2
Windows folders

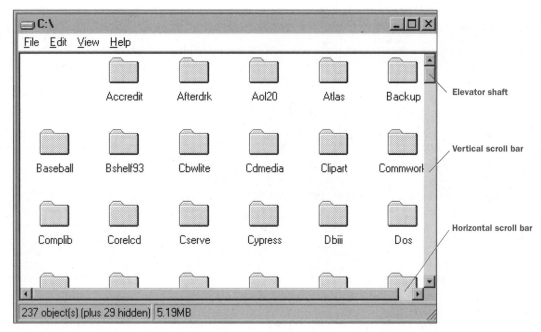

icon, drag the icon to the printer icon, and drop it. The document would begin printing. The shell takes care of loading the appropriate application and starting the printing.

Windows 95 uses shortcuts extensively. Windows 95 also uses a hierarchical (ranked order) file system. Therefore, using the shortcut mechanism makes it possible for you to organize your files or documents the way you want them. If you keep several folders of documents that need the use of a calculator, you can create and store a shortcut to a calculator in each folder.

GUIDED ACTIVITY 3.1

Using the Start Menu

1. Select Settings, Taskbar from the Start button.

2. The *Start Menu* folder will open up (it is a subfolder of the *Windows* folder). The *Programs* folder contains the items that appear under the Programs item on the Start button.

3. Note that all of the shortcuts and folders are exactly those that appear in the Programs menu off the Start button. You can add or delete shortcuts and folders. This will change the items that appear in the Programs menu.

GUIDED ACTIVITY 3.2

Customizing a Shortcut Icon

1. Choose Start, Settings, Taskbar.

2. Open the *Programs* folder.

3. Right-click on any shortcut. Choose Properties.

4. Select the Shortcut tab.

5. Click on the Change Icon button.

6. Select a new icon for the shortcut and choose OK.

7. Select Refresh from the View menu on the *C:\Windows\Start Menu\Programs* dialog box.

The Initial Desktop

After you start the computer, you are presented with the new desktop in Windows 95. The initial desktop appears as Figure 3.3. It is neat and clean with only a few graphical objects on the screen. It is like moving into a new office before you have the chance to really get messy. The simplicity of the desktop appeals to experienced users' sense of organization, but also serves to focus beginning users on the essentials of the following.

FIGURE 3.3
Windows 95 desktop

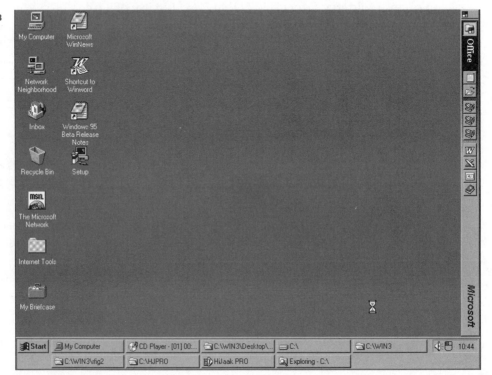

- *Taskbar*. Allows you to quickly start a program or open a document from the Start button. In addition, you can easily switch between tasks.

- *My Computer*. Makes browsing around for files and programs in your personal computer extremely logical and easy.

- *Network Neighborhood*. In a world of mapped drives and complex interfaces, few users are able to browse freeely in their own network. The Network Neighborhood makes browsing networks possible and easy, independent of the network provider (such as Windows NT Server, a NetWare server, or Windows 95 itself).

- *Recycle Bin*. The recycle bin allows the user to recover deleted files. Files that have been deleted can be easily returned to their original location on the user's local system.

The Taskbar

More than any other feature, the taskbar exemplifies the order-of-magnitude improvement in the ease of use and learnability of the user interface provided by Windows 95. It is the anchor of the UI. Its purpose is to make 95 percent of what a typical user wants to do with the operating system easily accessible at all times. The taskbar, shown in Figure 3.4, is designed for the novice user as a program launcher; however, its simplicity and power have been effectively used by more experienced Windows users. Windows 95 uses the taskbar—a user interface that serves as a common storage point for several different types of objects. The taskbar is always visible. A maximized window occupies the entire display except for the area at the bottom used by the taskbar. If you turn off the Always on Top property for the taskbar, a maximized window can obscure the taskbar.

FIGURE 3.4
Taskbar

If you select the Auto Hide option, the taskbar will appear only when you move the mouse cursor to the edge of the screen at the point where the taskbar would normally be placed. The taskbar disappears when the cursor moves away from the edge of the screen.

In the taskbar, you will see the following: (1) the Start button, the single button that provides immediate access to some common system function: help or shutdown, and (2) a resting place for all active windows. The system will put a button representing each active window into the taskbar.

The major function of the taskbar is to provide a consistent "home position," or anchor point, for the user. If you accept the taskbar's default behavior, the taskbar is always visible. If you get confused or the desktop gets messed up, the taskbar is always there as a place to return to for help or other systems functions.

The two key features of the taskbar are the Start button and push-button task switching.

Task Switching

The objective of the taskbar is to make switching among multiple applications as simple as changing channels on a television set. Every new window that is opened automatically gets a button on the taskbar—this greatly improves a user's ability to visualize which windows or applications are presently open. To change tasks, all the user must do is go to the taskbar and select the desired "channel," or application. No more minimized program icons, no more disappearing windows. No matter where the user is, he or she can see all of his or her active tasks simply by looking at the taskbar, in effect the Windows *TV Guide*.

Task buttons resize automatically depending on the number of active tasks. Should the buttons get too small (because you minimized several applications), you can configure the taskbar to two lines or more. Finally, you will notice animation when a task is minimized into the taskbar or maximized from the taskbar. The animated effect helps the user to understand "where" a program goes when it is minimized.

Start Button

Windows 95 begins with the Start button on the lower-left corner of the screen. The area at the bottom of the screen is called the *system taskbar*. Clicking on the Start button will call up a screen similar to Figure 3.5. You can select to open a Program, open a Document, change Settings, Find, ask for Help, Run, or Shut Down. Figures 3.6 and 3.7 illustrate the continuation of menus from the Start button.

FIGURE 3.5
Start menu

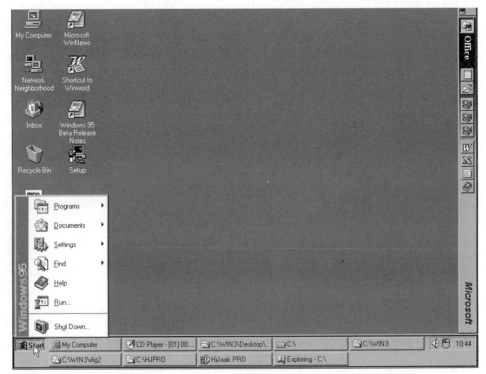

FIGURE 3.6
*Applications
available from
the Programs
button*

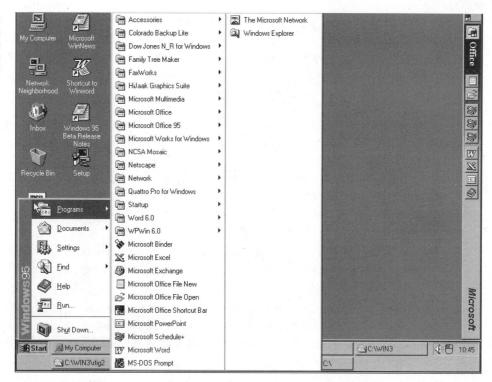

A user can Start a program by moving the mouse to and clicking on one of the items listed in Figure 3.7. One more click, and you are running the application or loading a document associated with it. For example, after clicking on the Start button,

FIGURE 3.7
*Documents
menu*

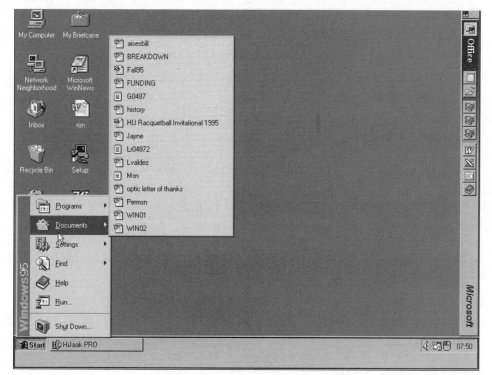

the user can move the mouse to Programs, and then to Accessories; and an additional menu of accessories appears. You might select Games to practice starting an application. Windows 95 comes with four games: FreeCell, Hearts, Minesweeper, and Solitaire. You may select the game you wish to play.

The ability to get an application running with two clicks is what makes Windows 95 easier to learn.

Other methods by which you can start the initial desktop are through My Computer (which you can rename) and through *Network Neighborhood* (if a network connection is recognized).

The Start button is designed to get you up and running in a matter of seconds. A beginning user of Windows 95 can quickly launch a program and get it to work. However, the Start button is much more than a super-efficient program launcher. It provides fast access to the following:

PROGRAMS The *Programs* item on the Start button provides quick access to launching programs. This menu item is equivalent to Program Manager under Windows 3.1.

DOCUMENTS The *Documents* menu of the Start button contains a list of the last 15 documents the user opened. It provides virtually instantaneous access to information most recently worked with. This helps prevent time-consuming and frustrating browsing and helps the user to begin to think of their work in terms of documents rather than applications.

SETTINGS Gives quick access to the changing or viewing *settings* and options of the PC, including the Control Panel (for computer settings), the taskbar, and the *Printers* folder. You can customize the taskbar to suit your personal work preferences.

FIND *Find* is a new feature of Windows 95 that goes far beyond File Manager's File Search feature in Windows 3.1. Searches do not need to conform to the *.* wildcard searching syntax, and criteria such as last modification date, size of file, and actual text within a document can now be used to find information.

HELP *Help* is provided for easy access from the Start menu.

RUN *Run* permits you to install new software and provides enhanced command line functionality.

SHUT DOWN Allows the user to *Shut Down* the computer easily and safely, as well as to restart or log off.

GUIDED ACTIVITY 3.3

Customizing the Start Button

1. Select Start, Settings, Taskbar.

2. From the Start Menu Programs property sheet, choose which programs you would like to appear either at the first level of the Start button or inside the program group.

3. Close and check your new configuration by pushing the Start button. (*Power user hint:* You can also put a program on the Start button by dragging and dropping a shortcut to the program directly on the button.)

GUIDED ACTIVITY 3.4

Bringing up the Start Button

   1.   Press [Ctrl][Esc] and the Start menu will pop up.

The Desktop

The Windows 95 Desktop provides a new look over Windows 3.1. This new look and feel is consistent across all objects. Drag-and-drop operations are available everywhere. You can move folders by dragging and dropping them to their new location. You can print documents by dragging them to the printer.

As you gain experience with Windows 95, you can customize your desktop to include the folders or shortcuts that you prefer.

On-Screen Appearance

From the moment you start Windows 95 you will probably notice many of the changes in its on-screen appearance. Some changes, such as the introduction of the taskbar, are obvious, but there are many other subtle changes as well. The minimize and maximize icons on the application title bar have changed. Notice too that the application buttons are changed slightly; in the taskbar, some of the black outline disappears, and the shading details change. Figure 3.8 illustrates the new Windows 95 design.

Another example of the new Windows 95 design is the use of visual cues. Figure 3.9 illustrates the screen properties for drive C:, the hard disk. The type of drive (the hard disk graphic) and the space used in comparison to the available free space (the pie graph) are shown. In addition to the General properties, you will notice tabs for Tools and Sharing.

Properties

Property sheets like that shown in Figure 3.9 are an all-inclusive feature of Windows 95. All objects in the user interface contain properties boxes that can be accessed and customized by selecting File Properties or by pointing to the object and right-clicking.

GUIDED ACTIVITY 3.5

Renaming a Hard Drive in Disk Properties

   1.   From the Windows Explorer (on the Programs submenu) or My Computer, select your hard disk and right-click. From My Computer, you must select your hard disk, right-click, and then choose Properties.

2. Choose Properties.

3. Type a new name in the Label box. Choose OK.

4. Choose View Refresh.

FIGURE 3.8
Windows 95 appearance

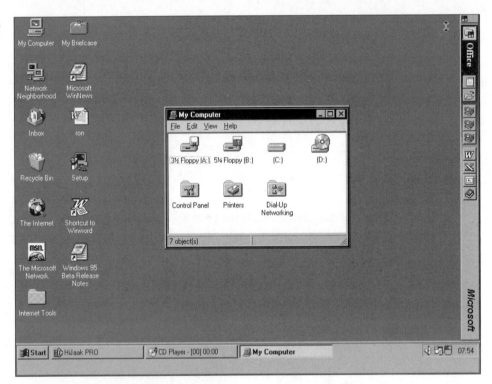

FIGURE 3.9
Screen properties

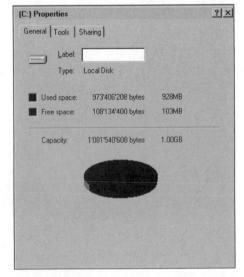

GUIDED ACTIVITY 3.6

Sharing a Folder (for Network Users)

1. From the Windows Explorer, right-click a folder that you wish to make available on your network. Right-clicking selects it. Choose Properties.

2. Select the Sharing tab.

3. Select Shared, and then complete the other fields in this dialog box.

Right-Clicking

Like properties, **right-clicking** is another all-inclusive feature of Windows 95. (*Right-clicking* refers to clicking the secondary mouse button—the right mouse button for right-handed people.) Right-clicking can be used as a shortcut for most common menu commands.

GUIDED ACTIVITY 3.7

Customizing the Desktop

1. Right-click any unused space on the desktop.

2. Choose Properties.

3. Click on the Background Tab and select Bricks as a pattern.

4. Click on the OK button to finish the selection.

GUIDED ACTIVITY 3.8

Creating a Shortcut

1. Right-click any unused space on the desktop.

2. Click on New.

3. Select Shortcut.

4. From the Create Shortcut, click on Browse.

5. Select a file from your C: drive to create the shortcut.

GUIDED ACTIVITY 3.9

Changing the Screensaver

1. Right-click an unused area of the desktop and choose Properties.

2. Select Screensaver.

3. Click on Color and Curves.

Light Source

FIGURE 3.10
*Windows 95
light source*

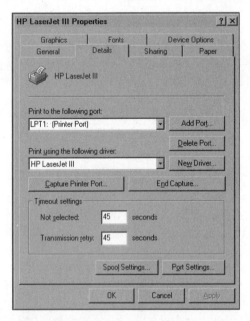

Another aspect of the Windows 95 design is the use of a consistent light source. The imaginary source "shines" from high and wide over your left shoulder as you look at the screen. All the shading for the three-dimensional effects uses the same light source. Figure 3.10 illustrates this consistency. The sunken field containing the LPT1: string, for example, is shaded on the left and upper edges, and the raised New Driver button is darker on the bottom and right edges. Although this graphics change is minor, it is intended to make the appearance more polished and pleasing to the eye.

GUIDED ACTIVITY 3.10
_____

Minimizing and Maximizing Windows

1. Open Explorer from the Start menu (Programs submenu).

2. Click on the minimize ("–") button.

3. To restore the window to its original position, click on the Exploring button on the toolbar.

4. Click on the Maximize button.

5. To restore the window to its original position, click on the Restore button (second button in the upper-right corner). Then close the Explorer window.

MS-DOS Prompt

One of the applications available is called "MS-DOS." This aids users who are familiar with DOS and want to execute a DOS procedure (such as checking the directories of several floppy disks or formatting a floppy disk) without using the appropriate Windows programs. *It is not a good idea to use the MS-DOS to execute a non-Windows program such as Lotus 1-2-3; in fact, memory restrictions often prevent your doing so.* Do not use the CHKDSK command from within Windows' MS-DOS—for it will report errors that do not exist, because Windows stores temporary data on the disk in such a way that CHKDSK will interpret it to be in error. Once the DOS procedure is accomplished, type exit and press Enter to return to Windows.

GUIDED ACTIVITY 3.11

Executing the MS-DOS Prompt Application

1. Press the Start button and select Programs.

2. Select the DOS Prompt application.

3. Put a floppy disk in drive A, type the command `dir a:`, and press ⏎. Perform other DOS commands if you wish.

4. Return to Windows by typing `exit` and pressing ⏎ at the DOS prompt.

GUIDED ACTIVITY 3.12

Opening Other Programs in Explorer

1. Activate the following program group windows (if they are not already active). On your system some of these might not be present, or the names might vary slightly:

- Accessories

- Windows Applications

- Games

- Non-Windows Applications

Typical Windows Program Groups

One of the selling points of Windows 95 is the ease with which a system manager can configure it to meet the needs of a particular organization. We cannot in this short book begin to cover all the possible arrangements of program groups and programs within Windows, although in this section we review some fairly typical groups. As you read this section, compare what we describe with what is available on your system. You might have more, or fewer, or different programs.

FIGURE 3.11
My Computer

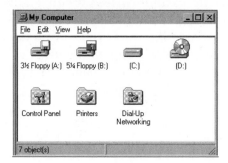

My Computer (see Figure 3.11) displays icons for 3½ Floppy drive (A:), 5¼ Floppy drive (B:), hard disk drive (C:), *Control Panel* folder, and *Printers* folder.

FIGURE 3.12
Accessories

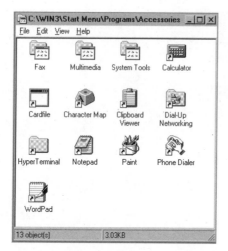

Accessories group (some of which are shown in Figure 3.12) includes Fax, Games, Multimedia, System Tools, Calculator, Cardfile, Character Map, Clipboard Viewer, HyperTerminal Connection, WordPad, Paint, and Phone Dialer.

FIGURE 3.13
Windows applications

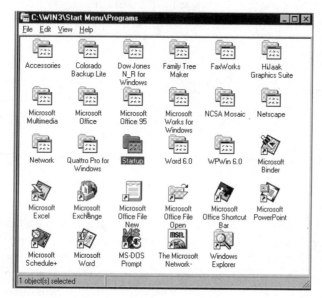

Windows applications group (programs group) (Figure 3.13) contains programs such as Microsoft Word (word processing) and Microsoft Excel (spreadsheet). The programs in this group vary from one organization or system to another, depending on what has been purchased. These programs are not included in the basic Windows package.

FIGURE 3.14
Non-Windows applications

Non-Windows applications group (Figure 3.14) contains programs such as WordPerfect, Quattro Pro, dBASE IV, Lotus 1-2-3, and Norton Utilities. Your laboratory configuration may vary depending on the specific non-Windows applications that your system manager has decided to install.

FIGURE 3.15
*Windows 95
Games*

Games group (Figure 3.15) displays four games, FreeCell, Hearts, Solitaire, and Minesweeper. Your organization might have added additional games— or might have removed this group entirely so that you won't be distracted!

Exiting Windows 95

To end your Windows 95 session, you simply click on the Start button and select Shut Down. An information window appears, to let you know that you are about to terminate your Windows session, as shown in Figure 3.16. The dialog box will ask you if you want to (1) shut down; (2) restart Windows; (3) Restart in MS-DOS mode; or (4) close all programs and log in as a different user. In many lab situations, your lab supervisor would prefer that you *do not* save changes, so that the Windows environment for the next user will be the organization's standard.

FIGURE 3.16
*Exiting
Windows 95*

GUIDED ACTIVITY 3.13

Exiting Windows

1. Click on the Start button.

2. Select Shut Down, and then select your choice from the dialog box.

Review Questions

1. Can you recover lost items, and how?

*2. Why is the taskbar thought of as a kind of *TV Guide*?

*3. Shortcuts can help you print. How?

*4. Program group windows can be arranged in two ways. What are they, and how are they different?

*5. Name the five typical program groups, and briefly describe the contents of each.

Key Terms

Accessories group	Network Neighborhood	Shortcut
Documents	Non-Windows	Shutdown
Find	Applications group	Windows Applications
Games group	Programs	group
Help (on Start)	Right-click	
My Computer	Settings	

Windows Explorer

Explorer is the Windows 95 shell program. The name embodies an important feature of the shell's function. The Windows 95 shell is intended to be the program you will use to explore the system—not just your own desktop system, but also the network system you are connected to. The Windows 95 shell replaces the Windows 3.1 manager programs such as Program Manager, File Manager, Task Manager, and Print Manager. The Windows 95 shell combines all manager-type functions into a single program that is always accessible and, at least by intent, will be the means by which most users will view and use a Windows 95 system.

Learning Objectives

At the completion of this unit you should know

1. the purpose of Explorer,

2. the features of Explorer,

3. how to start and quit Explorer,

4. how to work with the folder tree,

5. how to create folders,

6. how to search files and folders,

7. how to move and copy files,

8. how to delete files and folders,

9. how to rename files,

10. how to use a folder window,

11. how to format and copy disks.

Introduction to Explorer

Explorer displays a two-pane window. Moving through the hierarchy (or ranked series) causes the contents of the right-hand pane to be replaced with the contents of the next folder window that you open.

Explorer provides the user with the ability to browse files, folders, and other resources.

Explorer is a powerful tool that helps you to organize your files and folders. A *folder* is a collection of files stored under the same folder name (equivalent to a subdirectory in earlier versions of Windows and DOS). You use Explorer to view your files and then build a structure for those files and folders in a fashion that makes sense to you. Folders allow for the overall organization of files, similar to a file cabinet in your office where you dedicate a drawer for certain subjects and then further divide the drawer into logical sections.

Explorer is a Windows *shell program*. A shell program is defined as an alternate interface intended to facilitate your use of the computer. The shell program in Windows is used as a starting point for all Windows applications. If you designate Explorer as the *default shell*, Windows sessions will start and end with Explorer.

Explorer is much more than a program starter, however. It is designed to help you organize the files on your hard disk, network, or floppy disks. If you work with many applications and store a large number of files, you will find it easier to keep track of these files if you maintain a logical and orderly filing system.

By organizing related files in their own folders, you develop your own filing system. For example, you may organize memos and letters in one folder and spreadsheets in another. Most of your application programs will be set up within their own individual folders (for example, Microsoft Word, WordPerfect, Lotus 1-2-3). Folders will enable you to operate more efficiently by identifying where related files and programs are located.

GUIDED ACTIVITY 4.1

Viewing the Hierarchy of Folders on a Disk Drive

1. Click the Start button.

2. Point to Programs, and then click Windows Explorer.

3. Click a folder on the left side of the window to display its contents on the right. Click the plus sign (+) to display more folders.

You can change the size of either side of the window by dragging the bar that separates the two sides. To quickly open a folder and display its subfolders, double-click the folder on the left side of the window.

Starting Explorer

Explorer is started from the Start button. Point to Programs, and then click on Windows Explorer. The icon for Explorer appears in the list as illustrated in Figure 4.1.

Click on the Windows Explorer icon. Click on a folder on the left side of the window to display its contents on the right side (Figure 4.2). If a folder has a plus (+) sign, then subfolders are contained. Click on the plus (+) sign to display these subfolders.

FIGURE 4.1
Explorer icon

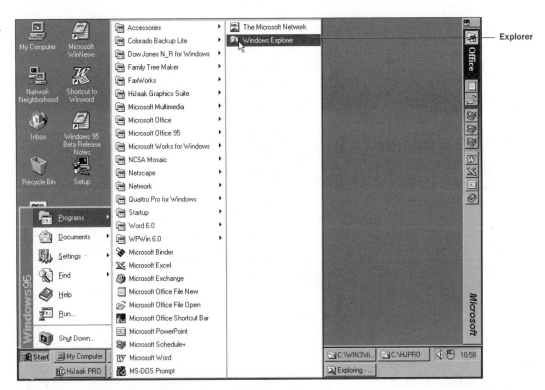

FIGURE 4.2
Folder contents

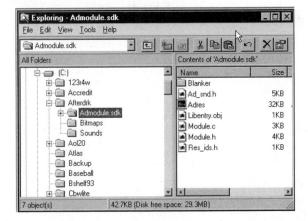

To change the size of either pane of the window, drag the bar that separates the two panes. To quickly open a folder and display its subfolders, double-click the folder of the left pane of the window.

Starting a Program Automatically When Windows Starts

To start a program each time Windows 95 starts, click on the Start button, and then point to Settings. Click on Taskbar; the Taskbar Properties dialog box (Figure 4.3) will appear. Next click on the Start Menu Programs tab (Figure 4.4). Click on Add (Figure 4.5), and then click Browse (Figure 4.6). Locate the program you want to start (Figure 4.7), and then double-click it. For example, assume you wish to start Windows with Microsoft Word (a word processing program). Click Next, and then double-click the *StartUp* folder. Type the name that you want to see on the *StartUp* folder, and then click on Finish. If Windows prompts you to choose an icon, click one (like that shown in the margin), and then click Finish.

FIGURE 4.3
*Taskbar
Properties
dialog box*

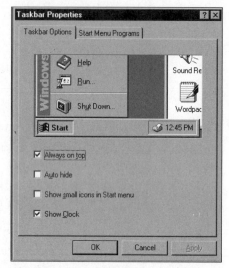

FIGURE 4.4
*Start Menu
Programs tab*

Add button ——————

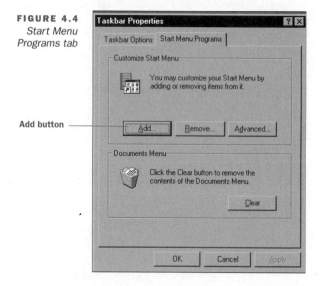

FIGURE 4.5
Add button

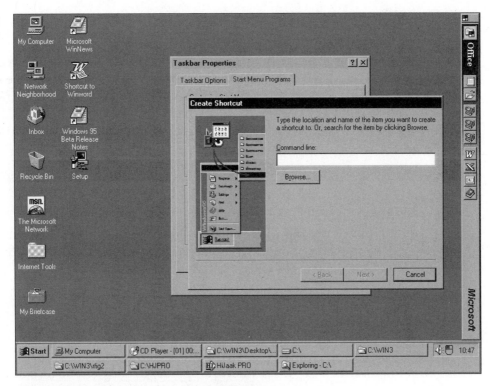

FIGURE 4.6
Browse

FIGURE 4.7
List of programs

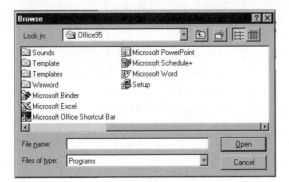

Selecting the Disk Drive

Explorer usually starts with drive C: as its default, as illustrated in Figure 4.2. Often, you will want to deal with your data disk, which will (usually) be in drive A:. To change disk drives with a mouse, click on the drive folder, down arrow, and then click on the drive A: icon. After you have changed drives, the folder tree for the new drive will appear. A *tree* is the hierarchical representation of the folders on your disk or computer.

Quitting Explorer

To quit Explorer, double-click on the exploring icon on the upper left of the screen. Another method of quitting Explorer is to click on the Close button at the upper right of the screen. The Close button is represented by an X.

Preparation of Disks

With Explorer you can format new floppy disks, copy all the files or one disk to another, and label a disk. You will *not* be able to inadvertently format a hard disk, which can lead to a disastrous result—the loss of all data.

Purpose of Formatting Disks

The purpose of formatting a disk is to prepare it for storing data. If you format an old disk, any data or information contained on that disk will be erased.

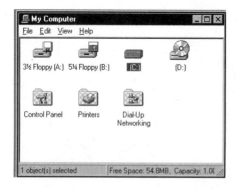

FIGURE 4.8
My Computer icon

To format a floppy disk, insert the disk you want to format in the floppy disk drive (drive A: or drive B:). Then, double-click the My Computer icon (Figure 4.8), and then click the disk you want to format (be sure not to double-click the disk icon, because you cannot format a disk if it is open in My Computer or Explorer). On the File menu, click Format (Figure 4.9). After this is done, a Format dialog box will appear (Figure 4.10). Formatting a disk removes all information from the disk (not after formatting, just after you click Format).

You will be prompted to select certain options. For example, if the disk that you want formatted is a high-capacity disk (1.44MB or 720KB), you will then see the choices for disk capacity (1.44MB or 720KB); click on the type of disk being formatted. Other options include the ability to use a Label for your disk. You could label your disk as "Homework" or any other name you choose.

FIGURE 4.9
Format command

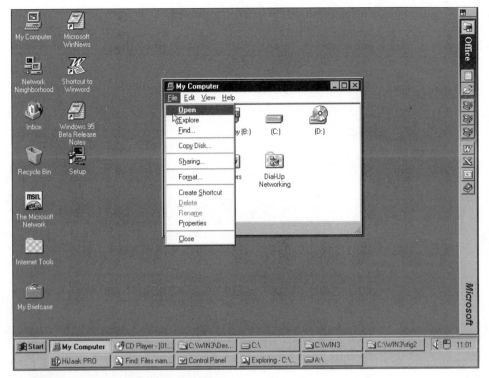

FIGURE 4.10
Format dialog box

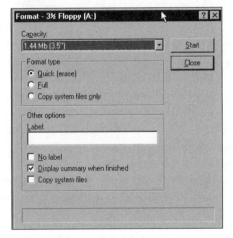

Finally, click on Start to begin the formatting process. A status message will appear to let you know that the formatting process has begun. A Format Results message box (Figure 4.11) will appear when the formatting has been completed. You can now select the Close button.

FIGURE 4.11
Format Results

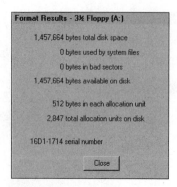

Format Results - 3½ Floppy (A:)

1,457,664 bytes total disk space

0 bytes used by system files

0 bytes in bad sectors

1,457,664 bytes available on disk

512 bytes in each allocation unit

2,847 total allocation units on disk

16D1-1714 serial number

Close

GUIDED ACTIVITY 4.2

Formatting a Disk

1. Insert the disk you want to format in the floppy disk drive.

2. Double-click the My Computer icon, and then click the disk you want to format.

3. On the File menu, click Format. When formatting is complete, click on Close on the Format Results dialog box.

Copying a Disk

The entire contents of one disk can be copied to another disk. You use this capability when you want to make an exact backup copy of a disk. Using this procedure, you can copy only disks that have the same disk capacity. For example, if the original disk (the disk you want to copy from) holds 720KB, the destination disk must also be a 720KB disk (in a disk drive that writes 720KB disks). You can copy from and to the same disk drive; you will be told when to insert the original and the destination disks. To make a copy of a disk, click on the My Computer icon, and select the 3½ floppy (A:) Programs. Select Edit from the menu and then choose Copy. Replace the source disk with a properly formatted disk. Select the 3½ floppy (A:) icon again. This time, select Paste from the Edit command. The new files should appear on this disk. Don't forget to remove your copy disk.

GUIDED ACTIVITY 4.3

Making a Copy of the Student Data Disk

A Student Data Disk has been furnished to your instructor with the *Instructor's Manual* for this book. This disk contains a few folders and files to allow you to try the features of Explorer. In this Guided Activity you make a copy of the Student Data Disk for your own experimentation. You can use the disk you make for other purposes after you finish this unit.

Before starting on this activity, you must have a floppy disk that is the proper size and format for your computer. Your instructor will tell you which of the following you should obtain: 5.25-inch double-sided, double- or high-density, or 3.5-inch double-sided, double- or high-density. These are often referred to by their formatted capacity: the 5.25-inch disks are 360KB or 1.2MB, while the 3.5-inch disks are 720KB or 1.44MB, respectively. You can work with a "used" disk from another class, but ensure that the disk does not contain any files you want to keep because they will be erased in the following activity.

In this activity, we assume that your system has only one disk drive—or, if it has two drives, that they are different sizes. Therefore, we give you the instructions for a single-drive copy. If you have two disk drives of the same size and capacity in your computer, your instructor will give you slightly modified instructions for the following.

1. Start Windows and enter the Explorer program.

2. Put *your* disk in the disk drive (normally drive A:, although your instructor might tell you otherwise).

3. Format your disk:

   a. Insert the disk you want to format in the floppy disk drive.

   b. Double-click the My Computer icon, and then click the disk you want to format.

   c. On the File menu, click Format.

4. Copy the Student Data Disk:

   a. Put the original Student Data Disk in the disk drive (normally drive A:, although your instructor might tell you otherwise).

   b. Click on the My Computer icon and then click on the 3½ floppy (A:) icon.

   c. Select Copy from the Edit command.

   d. Remove the original Student Data Disk and insert the copy disk.

   e. Click on the 3½ floppy (A:) icon and select Paste from the Edit command.

5. Remove your disk and label it with your name and "Copy of Student Data Disk for Windows." Return the original Student Data Disk to your instructor or lab supervisor.

Folders

Folders list the structure of your files. The term directory was used in Windows 3.1 and 3.0, while subfolder was used in Windows 3.11. In Windows 95, folders are now referred to as such. In DOS, almost all folders are actually subordinate to another folder and the terms are interchangeable. The folder tree shows all the folders present on the disk drive. This structure resembles the branches of a tree. The tree begins with the *root folder*, which is the first or top-level folder on the disk. The root folder is created when you format a disk. It is represented by the backslash (\). Your workstation will probably designate C:\ as its root folder.

NOTE *You may wish to consult with your instructor or system manager to learn about your specific system.*

From the folder tree, you can open folders to list files, as well as open any subfolders for your individual folders. You can also select different disk drives to view their folder structures. For example, you may want to list the files in a particular folder on drive A: or drive B:. To do so, click on the appropriate folder icon in My Computer.

While exploring a folder, you will notice the following parts (Figure 4.12):

1. The *Name of Folder* represents the current folder that you are viewing. The path of the current folder is listed on the fourth line of the title bar. For example, Figure 4.12 illustrates the folder entitled *Accredit*.

2. The *Go to a Different Folder* allows you to select a different folder.

3. The *Up One Level* is designed to back up a level in the event that you have subfolders.

4. The *Map Network Drive* represents a way in which you can work in the Network Neighborhood.

5. The *Disconnect Net Drive* allows you to disconnect from the Network Neighborhood.

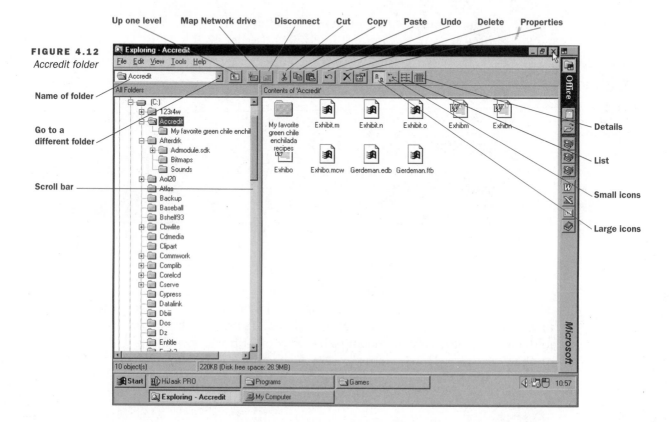

FIGURE 4.12
Accredit folder

6. *Cut, Copy, and Paste* icons are represented by scissors, a document with a turned-up corner, and a clipboard.

7. *Undo and Delete* are used to delete or restore folders.

8. *Properties* provide additional information about the folder.

9. *Large and Small Icons* provide a graphical user interface for individual folders (Figures 4.13 and 4.14).

FIGURE 4.13
Large icons

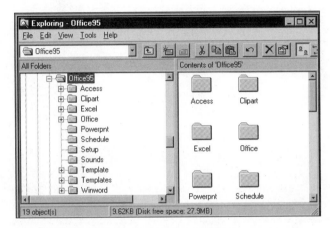

FIGURE 4.14
Small icons

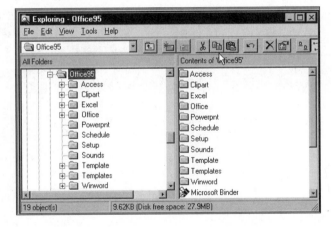

10. *List and Details* provide a comprehensive listing of the individual folders. List includes the individual folders/subfolders, while Details lists attributes of the folders to include Folder Name, Size, Type, and Modified (Figures 4.15 and 4.16).

11. *Minimize, Restore, Close* icons are used to temporarily set aside a folder/subfolder to the taskbar, restore the folder/subfolder to the desktop, or close the folder/subfolder.

12. A *scroll bar* appears if there are more folders and subfolders than will fit in the window.

FIGURE 4.15
*Folder Name,
Size, Type*

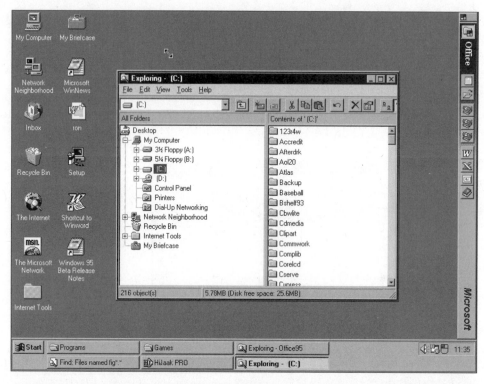

FIGURE 4.16
Folder modified

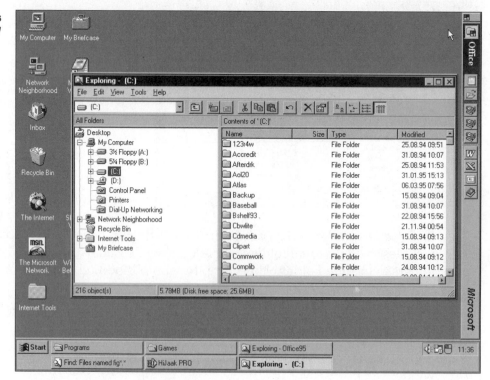

Subfolders

The folder tree in Explorer will also display any subfolders. The left side of the window contains a folder tree, but there might not be a plus or minus sign indicating expanded or collapsed folders. The default configuration of Explorer does not indicate expandable folders (Figure 4.17). The current folder is indicated by an open file folder icon, and the subfolders to the current folder are listed on the right side of the screen in conjunction with files in the current folder. You may notice that the folder in Figure 4.18 contains a plus sign (+) in the icon for *Afterdrk*. The plus sign means that one or more subfolders exist beneath that folder.

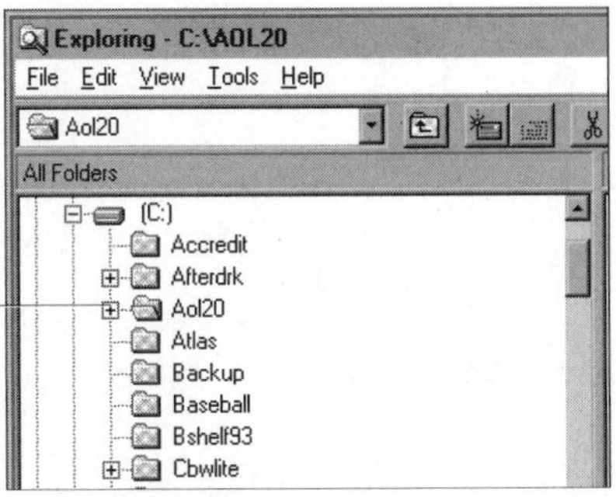

You can click on any folder icon with a plus sign to reveal the subfolders associated with its parent folder. This is called *expanding* the folder. The folder icon for an expanded folder contains a minus sign (–) as shown in the folder *Afterdrk* in Figure 4.19.

To select a new current folder, click once on its file folder icon. If there are subfolders to the current folder, they will be listed on the right pane of the window. To display the subfolders of a folder on the left pane of the window, double-click on its icon. To remove the display of subfolders on the left side, double-click on the icon a second time. Figure 4.20 shows the structure of the Student Data Disk, with all folders expanded. The right pane of the window shows the contents of the *Exploring \Cabin* folder.

FIGURE 4.17
Subfolders

Plus (+) sign indicates additional files

FIGURE 4.18
Afterdrk folder with + sign

FIGURE 4.19
Afterdrk folder with – sign

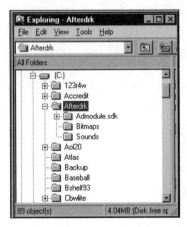

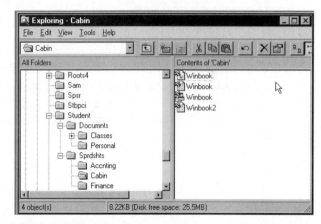

GUIDED ACTIVITY 4.4

Expanding a Folder

1. Click the plus sign (+) in the folder icon next to the name of the folder you want to expand.

Changing Folders

The highlighted folder is the *active* (current) *folder*. If you want to change to another folder, simply position the selection cursor (mouse pointer) on the folder desired. Click on the folder name that you want to select.

Use the following keys to select a folder:

To Move To	Press
A folder in the list above or below the root folder	⬆️⬇️
The root folder, which is always the first folder in the list	Home
The last folder in the list	End
The first subfolder of an expanded folder	➡️
The folder level above the current folder	⬅️
The folder one window up from the current folder	PgUp

To Move To	Press
The folder one window down from the current folder	`PgDn`
A specific folder	The first letter of the folder name, then ⏎ if necessary

Folder Windows

The folder tree shows the overall structure of your folders. To list the individual files, you must open a *folder window*. With such a window, you can list the files of other folders, change the information you see, or rearrange the listed files (Figure 4.21).

FIGURE 4.21
Folder window

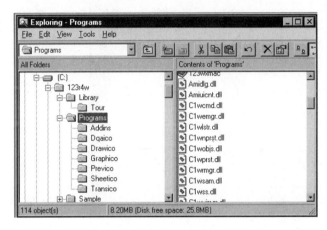

The icon to the left of the file name shows whether the file is a folder, a program file, a document file, or another type of file. The interpretation of these icons is as follows:

Kind of Icon	Kind of File
Folder icons	Folders are listed first, in alphabetical order
Program file icons	Program files and batch files, with extensions .exe, .com, .pif, and .bat; these are executable files used to start applications
Document item icons	Document files, created by specific applications and recognized as such by Windows
Open file folder icons	Indicates the current open folder
Data file icons	Other files

Changing Information Displayed in Folder Windows

File names in a folder window are usually listed alphabetically, but you can change the way that they are listed. The *View Option* menu in Explorer is used to rearrange files and to specify the information to be displayed.

From the View tab (Figure 4.22) of the Options menu you can select Hidden Files, All Files, or Hide Files by Types (that is, with extensions of .dll, .sys, .vxd, .386, or .drv). In addition, you can specify Display the Full MS-DOS Path in Title Bar, Hide MS-DOS File Extension for File Types that Are Registered, or Include Description Bar for Right and Left Panes. Finally, you can select the File Types tab (Figure 4.23). Some File Types include *Applications*, *AudioCD*, and *Configuration Settings*, among others.

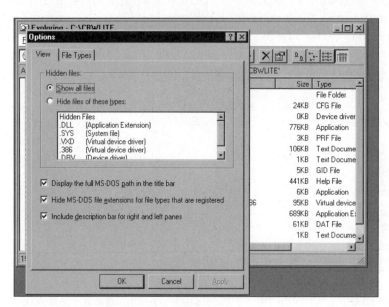

FIGURE 4.22
View Options

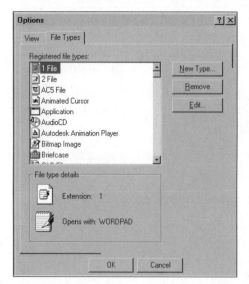

FIGURE 4.23
File Types

You can sort the files and folders by Name, Type, Size, or Date the file was last modified. The Sort commands do not affect the folder tree. If you select By Name, the current folder will be sorted (alphabetically) first by folders, then by files. To sort files and folders by type, select View, and then choose Arrange Icons By Type. Folders and then files will be listed alphabetically by extension in the active folder window. In addition, you can sort files by size. Select View, and then choose By Size. Files are listed by size, with the largest file listed first. Finally, you can sort by last modification date. From the View menu, choose Arrange Icons By Date. Folders are listed first, sorted by date, and then files are listed by date, with the most recently modified file listed first.

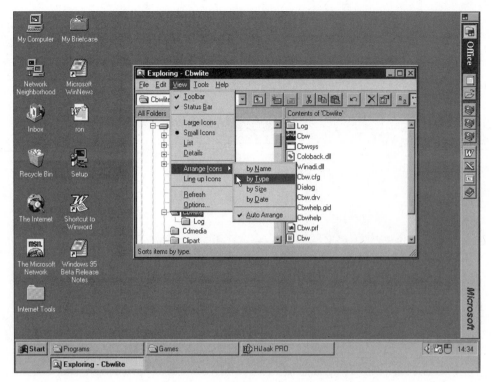

FIGURE 4.24
Files by Type

Finally, you can select the type of file to display. You may wish to have Explorer display certain types of files, or files with similar file names or extensions. Choose By Type from the View menu and Arrange Icons submenu; the results of this command are illustrated in Figure 4.24. Select the options that indicate the files you want to display (folders, programs, documents, other files, or hidden/system files).

Closing a Folder Window

To close an active folder window, double-click on the Folder icon, located in the upper-left corner of the window (Figure 4.25). If you are not using a mouse, press [Alt] [Spacebar] [-] (hyphen), and choose Close from the dialog box or press [Alt].

GUIDED ACTIVITY 4.5

Exploring the Folder Tree on Drive A:

1. Open Explorer from the Start button.

2. Make sure you have your copy of the Student Data Disk in drive A:. Click on Desktop from the folder tree.

3. Click on the 3½ Disk Drive icon from the left pane in Explorer.

4. Click on a folder icon. Note the tree structure of this disk.

5. When finished, close the folder tree window by double-clicking on the Explorer icon in the top-left corner of your desktop.

FIGURE 4.25
Creating folders

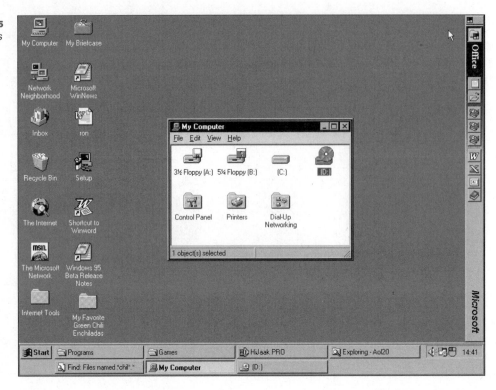

Files and Folders

Explorer allows you to perform such operations as naming, creating, searching for, copying, renaming, moving, and deleting both files and folders. Windows 95 supports long file names. The use of long file names in Windows 95 overcomes the sometimes cryptic MS-DOS file name conventions of eight-character names plus three-character extensions, to allow more "friendly" file names. MS-DOS 8.3 file names are still maintained and tracked by the system to support compatibility with existing Windows 16-bit and MS-DOS based applications that only manipulate 8.3 file names, but as users migrate to Win 32-based applications the use of 8.3 file name conventions is hidden from the user. Win 16 refers to 16-bit applications written for earlier Windows versions (Windows 3.*x*). Long file names can be up to 255 characters in length and can include spaces. For example, you can now name a file *My favorite green chili chicken enchiladas recipe*—and not have to use *Mfgccere.doc*, which only ensured that a month later you wouldn't have the vaguest idea what the file contains.

NOTE *You cannot use as file names the following reserved words, which address hardware devices: CON, AUX, COM1, COM2, COM3, COM4, COM5, LPT1, LPT2, LPT3, LPT4, NUL, or PRN.*

Creating Folders

Folders can be created on the hard disk as well as on a floppy disk.

To create a new folder, double-click on the My Computer icon or Windows Explorer, and then open the folder in which you want to create a new subfolder. On

FIGURE 4.26
New Folder

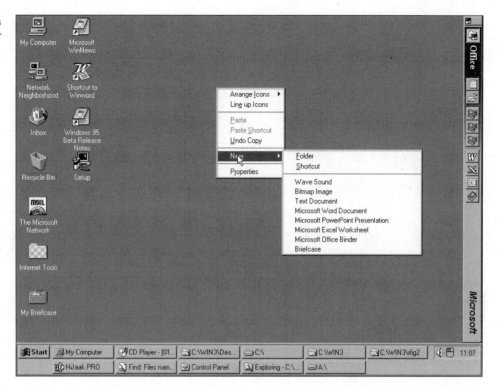

the File menu, point to New, and then click Folder. The new folder appears with a temporary name. Type a name for the new folder, and then press ⟦Enter⟧.

In addition, you can create a new folder by clicking the right mouse button. A dialog box will appear as illustrated in Figure 4.26. Point to New, and select folder. You will then be prompted to supply a file name for this folder. Remember, you are no longer restricted to the 8.3 file name convention. You will then see a new folder created on the desktop (Figure 4.27). It is also possible to create a subfolder using this same approach.

GUIDED ACTIVITY 4.6

Creating a Folder

1. To create a new folder, using My Computer or Windows Explorer, open the folder in which you want to create a new folder.

2. On the File menu, point to New, and then click Folder. The new folder appears with a temporary name.

3. Type the name Research Papers for the new folder, and then press ⟦Enter⟧.

FIGURE 4.27
*File name
convention*

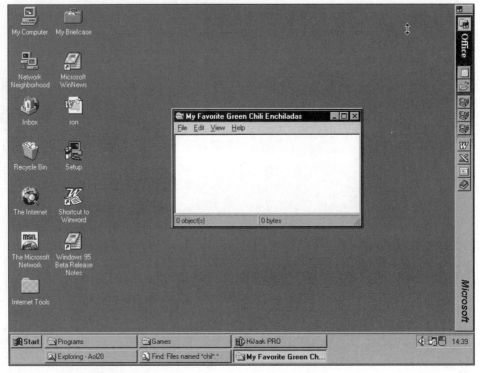

Searching for Files and Folders

As you spend time on your computer, you will most likely create many hundreds of files and dozens of folders. It may become difficult to remember where a particular file is located. You can use the Find command from the Start button to locate files

FIGURE 4.28
Find All Files

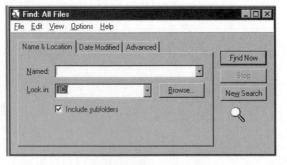

or folders. A Find All Files dialog box will appear (Figure 4.28). It contains a text entry box, which requests the name and location for the file or folder you are looking for. The dialog box also contains a drop-down list box that prompts you where to Look In. For example, you can look in C:, My Computer, 3½ Floppy (A:), 5¼ Floppy (B:), or D:, which usually is your CD-ROM drive (Figure 4.29).

Type the name of the file or folder in the Named text box. Use *wildcards* if you want to search for a group of files or folders with similar names or extensions. For example, if you want to search for all files with a *.doc* extension, you would type * . DOC (the * is a DOS wildcard). To complete the action, click or choose Find Now. Windows 95 will search for all such files on the entire disk and then provide the results in a Find window (Figure 4.30).

The Find window appears as a folder window, except that the full pathname (for example, *B:\Documnts\Classes\Managemt\ Quotes.doc*) is portrayed. The Find

FIGURE 4.29
CD-ROM drive

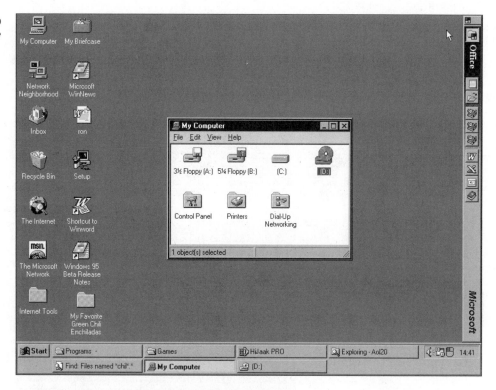

FIGURE 4.30
Find Now

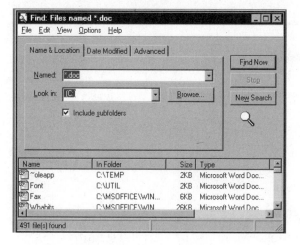

window lists the results by Name, In Folder, Size, and Type (Figure 4.31). You can use the scroll bar on the right border to move through the window if there are more "hits" than fit in the window. In addition, the Browse button provides a quick method to locate files. You will be able to copy or move files to other disks or folders using the techniques discussed later in this unit.

Finding Files or Folders by Date Modified

Files and folders can be found by date modified. Figure 4.32 illustrates the options available for this type of a find. You can find by selecting All Files, Find All

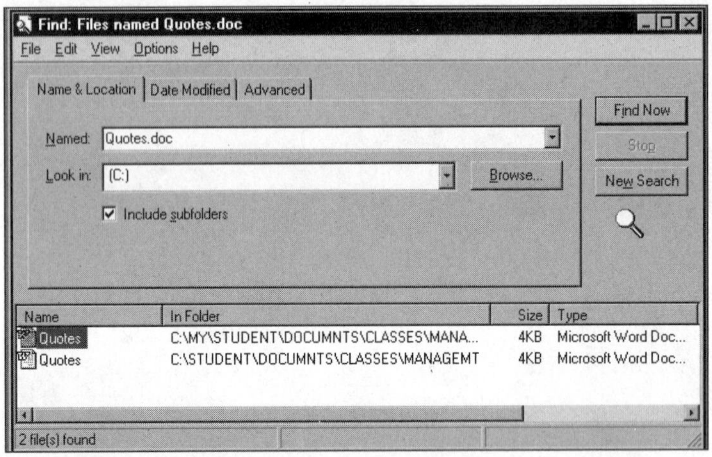

FIGURE 4.31
Find window list

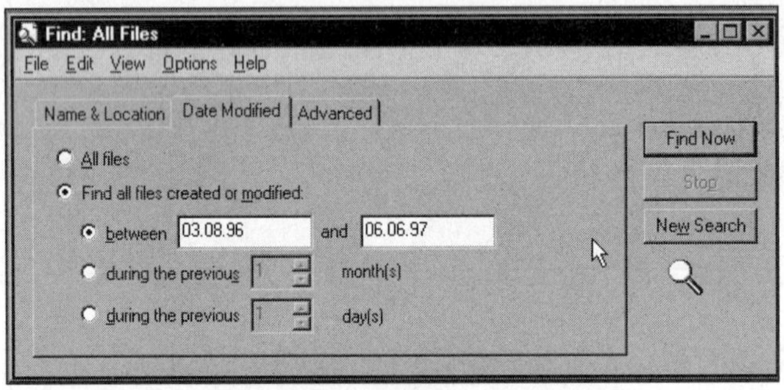

FIGURE 4.32
*Folders by Date
Modified*

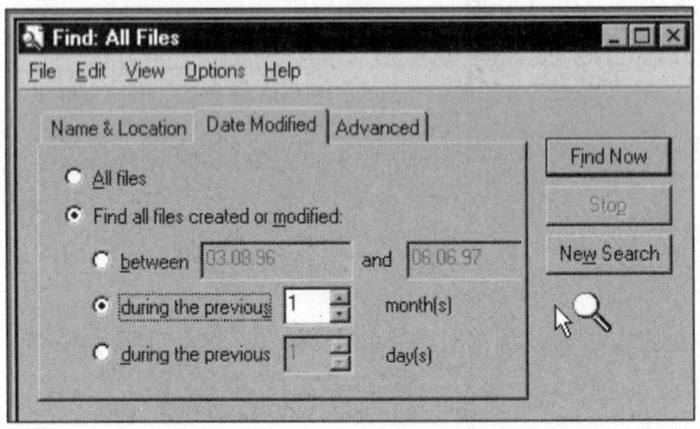

FIGURE 4.33
*Folders during
Previous Months*

Files Created or Modified Between 3/8/96 and 6/6/97, Find All Files Created or Modified During the Previous *x* Month(s) or *x* Day(s) (Figure 4.33).

There are some advanced commands that you may find very useful. Figure 4.34 presents those advanced find commands. They include Of Type, Containing Text (which you fill in), Size Is at least *x* KB or at most *x* KB.

The search can be saved with the Save Search command under the File command (Figure 4.35). Finally, you can select Options and then select *Case Sensitive* to enable you to enable/disable this particular feature. This command is especially useful whenever you do not remember the exact file name.

FIGURE 4.34
Advanced Find commands

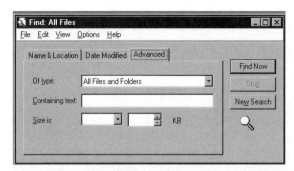

FIGURE 4.35
Save Search

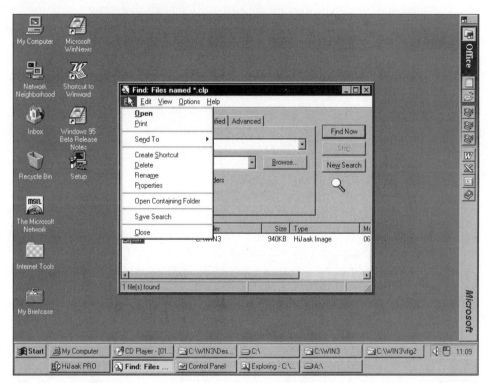

GUIDED ACTIVITY 4.7

Searching for a Specific Program File

1. Open Find Files or Folders from the Start button. Select drive C:.

2. Type the file name `write.exe`.

3. Ensure that the **Look In** box reads `C:\` and the Include Subfolders box is checked.

4. Click on Find Now to start the search.

5. The search will probably find one file named *Write.exe* in the *C:\Windows* folder, unless your system has been configured differently by the system manager.

> 6. Close the Search Results window by clicking on the Find icon in the upper-left corner of the desktop and selecting Close.

Copying and Moving Files and Folders

As you work with files, you will often want to have a second copy of a file, perhaps as a backup copy on a separate disk or as a record of the file at a point in time, prior to changing the file. To *copy* a file means to create a duplicate of the file. The duplicate can be on a different disk or folder with the same file name as the original file, or it can be on the same disk or folder with a different name than the original, or it can be on a disk/folder with a different name.

There are also occasions when you have a file on one disk or folder and you want it on another. To *move* a file means to copy it to another disk or folder and to erase it from its original disk or folder. Moving a file from one disk to another frees space on the original disk and occupies space on the destination disk. By contrast, copying a file from one disk to another has no effect on the space available on the original disk but occupies space on the destination disk.

Moving Files

Files or folders can be moved from one location (source) to another (destination) by dragging the source file or folder with the mouse or by using the Cut command from the Edit menu. If you are using the mouse, the file being moved and the destination (disk drive icon) must both be visible (Figure 4.36). You simply select the source (file or folder), hold down the key, and drag it to its destination (drive A:, drive B:, or another folder that you select). Make certain that there is a disk inserted in the disk drive you are designating, or you will receive an error message (Figure 4.37).

To move a file or folder, select the My Computer icon or Windows Explorer, and click the file or folder you want to move.

FIGURE 4.36
Moving files

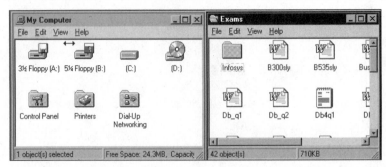

Click on Cut from the Edit menu. The file or folder is stored in a temporary location until you paste it where you want it. Open the folder where you want to put the file or folder. Finally click Paste from the Edit menu. To select more than one file or folder to move, hold down the Ctrl key, and then click the items you want.

FIGURE 4.37
Move dialog box

To move a file or folder to a disk in a different disk drive:

1. Using the techniques discussed earlier in this unit, open Explorer, or My Computer.

2. Click on the 3½ floppy (A:) icon. Select the file you want to move.

3. Choose Cut from the Edit command.

4. Remove the original disk and insert the destination disk. Select Paste from the Edit command.

Once you select the destination drive, you will see the copying dialog box on your screen.

GUIDED ACTIVITY 4.8

Moving a File to a Subfolder

1. Open Explorer. Make sure the Student Data Disk is in drive A:. Click on the drive A: icon.

2. Click (once) on each folder icon in turn to expand the *A:*, *Documnts*, and *Classes* folders. Double-click on *Managemt* to open a folder window.

3. Press and hold the Shift key, and then drag the icon for *Pbmacapp.doc* to the folder for *Wpdoc* in the folder tree window.

4. Open a folder window for *Wpdoc* to verify that the move has been successful.

Copying Files

The procedure for copying files is very similar to the move procedure. To copy a file or folder, open My Computer or Windows Explorer and click the file or folder you want to copy. Click Copy on the Edit menu (Figure 4.38). The file or folder is stored in a temporary location until you paste it where you want it. Open the folder or disk where you want to put the copy. Finally, click Paste on the Edit menu.

You can use drag-and-drop instead of menus to copy a file or folder. In My Computer or Windows Explorer, find the file or folder you want to work with. Make sure that the place you want to drag the file or folder to is visible. Drag the file or folder to

FIGURE 4.38
Copy command

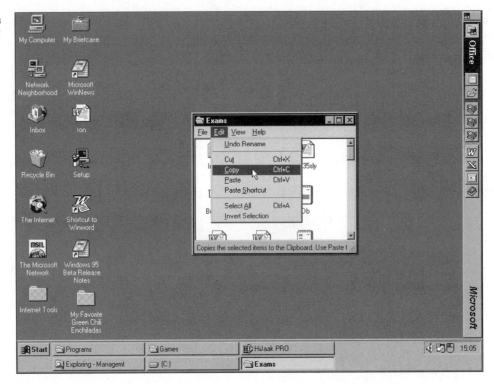

the destination. The result depends on the type of file you selected and the destination. For example, to print a file, drag it to the printer icon. If you use your right mouse button to drag, a menu will appear with the available options. If you drag a file to a folder on the same disk, it will be moved. If you drag it to a folder on another disk, it will be copied. You can hold down a key while dragging for the following:

- To move a file, use Shift.

- To copy a file, use Ctrl.

- To create a shortcut, use Ctrl Shift.

GUIDED ACTIVITY 4.9

Copying a File to a Folder

1. Open My Computer. Make sure the Student Data Disk is in drive A:. Click on the drive A: icon.

2. Click (once) on the folder icons to expand the *A:*, *Documnts*, and *Classes* folders. Double-click on *Wpdoc* to open a folder window. Click on Copy from the Edit menu.

3. Select the destination folder where you wish to copy the file. Finally, click on Paste from the Edit menu.

Deleting Files and Folders

Files and folders can be deleted from any disk drive. Before you can delete a file or folder, however, you must first select it from the folder tree or folder window. Explorer is much more efficient for deleting folders than is the command for deleting in DOS. If you delete a folder, all files and all subfolders within the folder will be deleted.

To delete files from the Recycle Bin, click the icon, then click on Empty Recycle Bin from the File menu. If you want to use different settings for different drives, click Configure Drives Independently, and then click the tab of the drive whose settings you want to change.

If you want to use the same settings for all drives, click Use One Setting for All Drives. Make sure the Do Not Move Files to the Recycle Bin box is checked. Note, however, that if this box is checked, you will be unable to recover any files you delete.

To retrieve a deleted file, folder, or shortcut, double-click the Recycle Bin icon. Click the file you want to retrieve. To retrieve several files, hold down the Ctrl key while clicking each one. On the File menu, click Restore.

To delete a file or folder, open My Computer or Windows Explorer and locate the file or folder you want to delete.

Click the file or folder. On the File menu (Figure 4.39), click Delete.

If you want to retrieve a file you have deleted, look in the Recycle Bin (Figure 4.40). Your deleted file will remain in the Recycle Bin until you empty it.

To retrieve a deleted file, click on the Recycle Bin icon and select the Undo command from the Edit menu.

You can also cancel the deletion if you happen to change your mind.

FIGURE 4.39
Delete files

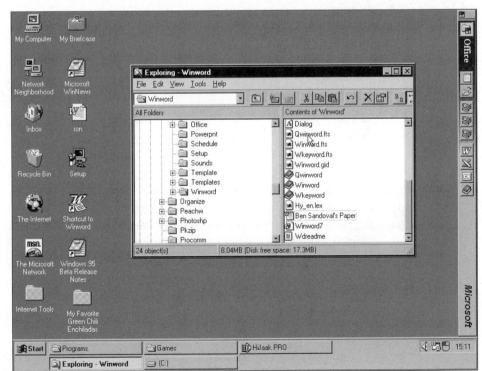

FIGURE 4.40
Recycle Bin

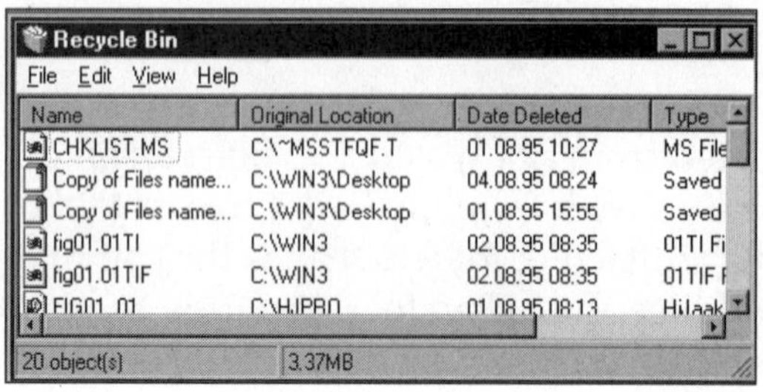

CAUTION *Delete Files from the Recycle Bin permanently removes the file or folder along with subfolders from the disk!*

GUIDED ACTIVITY 4.10

Deleting a File in a Subfolder

1. Open My Computer. Make sure the Student Data Disk is in drive A:. Click on the drive A: icon.

2. Select the file *Pbmacapp.doc* in the *Wpdoc* folder.

3. Click on File and then on Delete.

GUIDED ACTIVITY 4.11

Deleting a Subfolder

1. Open Explorer. Make sure the Student Data Disk is in drive A:. Click on the drive A: icon.

2. Click on the folder *Wpdoc*.

3. Click on Delete from the File menu.

Close Explorer by clicking on the Control menu box and then on Close.

Renaming Files and Folders

To change the name of a file or folder, open My Computer or Windows Explorer, and then click the file or folder you want to rename. You do not need to open it. On the File menu (Figure 4.41), click Rename. Type the new name, and then press ⏎Enter.

A file name can contain up to 255 characters, including spaces and underscore characters (_). But it cannot contain any of the following characters: \ ? : * " < > |

FIGURE 4.41
*Renaming files
or folders*

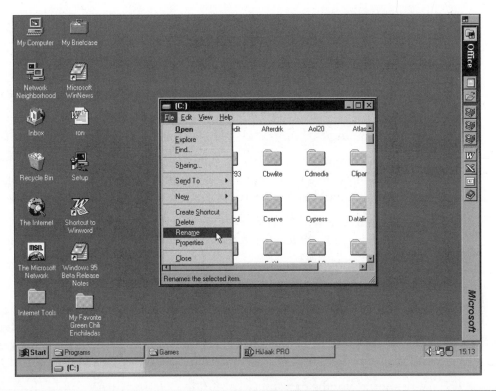

GUIDED ACTIVITY 4.12

Renaming a File

1. Open My Computer. Make sure the Student Data Disk is in drive A:. Click on the drive A: icon.

2. Open a folder window that contains the file *A:\Student\Documnts\Personal\Canada.doc* and highlight the file.

3. Click on File and then on Rename.

4. Type in a new name for the file: `Permissn.doc`. Close My Computer.

Review Questions

*1. What is the role of Explorer? How is it started?

2. Draw a folder tree with the following individual folders: *Var, Temp, Memo,* with the root folder being *A:*. The emphasis is on the structure and not on the quality or shape of the drawing. Include the following: disk drive representation, folder path, current folder, and folder representation.

*3. How are folders that have subfolders represented in the folder tree?

4. To change to the root folder, which key has to be pressed? (Review other situations involving changing folders.)

*5. If you wanted to list the individual files in a particular folder, what must you do?

*6. Briefly, list and describe the different icons used to represent files, folders, and programs.

7. Describe the process that involves displaying only certain files (for example, programs, documents, spreadsheets).

8. What are the mouse commands to close an active folder? Keyboard commands?

*9. What is the maximum number of characters that a file name may contain? What type(s) of characters may begin a file name? Identify at least three reserved words that cannot be used as file names. Explain why they cannot be used.

10. To create a folder within Windows 95, would you select File | New Folder *for* a menu or File | New Folder *from* the menu? (Select the correct sequence.)

11. Can files be copied from or moved to the Search Results window? What is the purpose of the Search command?

12. If you are using the mouse to move a file or a folder, is it possible to do so without using the keyboard (other than using the [Alt] or [Ctrl] keys)? What about if you want to copy them? (This may be a difficult question to answer. Review the steps and perform them on your computer to see if your answer is correct.)

*13. Why should you be extremely careful in deleting files?

14. Review the processes to rename files or folders, format and copy disks, and quit Explorer.

15. How many characters can you use to name a file? Give an example.

Key Terms

Active folder	Expanding a folder	Open file folder icon
Application file type	Folder	Program file icon
AudioCD	Folder icon	Properties
Case Sensitive	Folder window	Recycle Bin
Configuration Settings	Go to a Different Folder	Root folder
Copy	Large Icons	Shell program
Data file icon	List and Details	Small Icons
Default shell	Look In	Undo
Delete	Map Network Drives	Up One Level
Disconnect Network Drive	Move	Wildcard
Document item icon	Name of Folder	

Control Panel

Control Panel allows you to customize Windows automatic startup settings (the defaults) by changing color schemes, Mail and Fax, Microsoft Mail, modems, multimedia, networks, passwords, printer configuration, regional settings, sounds, mouse and keyboard speed, joysticks, fonts, and monitor type.

Learning Objectives

At the completion of this unit you should know

1. the features available with Control Panel for customizing Windows,

2. how to start and exit Control Panel,

3. how to change a color scheme,

4. how to change or remove fonts,

5. how to make desktop changes,

6. how to adjust keyboard speed,

7. how to change system date and time,

8. how to configure the printer.

Introduction to the Control Panel

This unit presents the basic *Control Panel* features that affect your hardware and connections. Control Panel consists of 22 icons, shown in Figure 5.1. Some of these allow you to change color, fonts, mouse, desktop, keyboard, joystick, date/time, printers, and so on. The remaining icons are for advanced operations, including adding new hardware, adding/removing programs, mailing and faxing documents, changing regional settings, choosing passwords, accessing a network, and using sound. You may need to consult the Microsoft Windows 95 *User's Guide* for detailed discussions of these advanced topics, and make liberal use of online Help.

FIGURE 5.1
Control Panel

To start Control Panel, you must first click the Start button. Point to the Control Panel icon under Settings. Windows 95 will then display the Control Panel window illustrated in Figure 5.1. The individual icons are the entry points for all operations. Each icon has its particular purpose and meaning:

Icon	Purpose
Add New Hardware	Provides a *wizard* that helps you install new hardware devices; Windows 95 uses Plug and Play technology to make this process easier, even for devices that do not support Plug and Play technology
Accessibility Options	Accessibility options for people with disabilities: "restricted movements, low vision, or hearing difficulty"
Add/Remove Programs	To install a Windows component after Windows 95 has been installed
Date/Time	To change the computer's date or time
Display	To change the way items on your desktop look

Icon	Purpose
Find Fast	Allows you to create an index for locating files
Fonts	To add or remove fonts for printer and monitor
Joystick	To calibrate your joystick, if your computer has this hardware
Keyboard	To adjust repeat speed of key
Mail and Fax	To connect to The Microsoft Network
Modems	To use telecommunications (connecting to a remote computer)
Mouse	To change the appearance or speed of the mouse pointer
Multimedia	To use the CD player to play compact discs; to play multi-media files; to use sound recorder to record, play, and edit sound files; volume control to vary sound; adjusting volume; assigning sounds; calibrating joystick; changing priority of audio compression drivers; changing the size of video clip windows; changing sound quality for recordings; moving a MIDI instrument to another sound card; setting up a MIDI instrument; and switching between CD players
Network	To use a cable to connect to a computer on the network; using dial-up networking to connect to a computer or network; using HyperTerminal to connect to a remote computer; changing dialing settings for dial-up connections, modem settings, settings for direct cable connections, your new password, a password for a NetWare connection, or Windows password; connecting to another computer on the network, the Internet, or The Microsoft Network; logging off the network, the domain for Client for Microsoft Networks, or the network; setting your computer to connect to the network; starting a program by using the Run command; troubleshooting dial-up connections, network problems, modem problems; and using a shared network printer

Icon	*Purpose*
Passwords	To assign or change computer password(s) for remote administration, dial-up connection, folder, printer, screen savers, windows, NetWare, network; enabling multiple users to personalize settings; and setting up access control for shared resources
Printers	To change printer settings; controlling access; default printers; finding a printer on a network; mapping drive letters; pausing or restarting printers; sending files to the printer; sharing printers; shortcuts for printing; troubleshooting; using disconnected printers; and using shared printers
Regional Settings	To change number, currency, time, date settings; change the way currency values appear and the way your computer displays numbers, date, and time; and using a different language or keyboard layout
Sounds	To access sound features; assigning program events; customizing the computer by using sound; editing sound, turning off PC card sound effects; playing and recording sounds; and adjusting sound
System	Provides general properties pertaining to the system being used, to whom registered, and computer type (for example, Pentium 16MB); device manager by type and connection; hardware profiles; performance of memory, system resources, file system, virtual memory, disk compression, PC cards; advanced settings to include hard disk and CD-ROM optimization; troubleshooting (CAUTION: *It is recommended that only advanced users and system administrators change these settings*); graphics hardware acceleration; and virtual memory —let Windows manage virtual memory (recommended) or let the user specify virtual memory

Accessibility Options

Windows 95 provides several accessibility features to make computers more accessible to people with disabilities. For example, if you have restricted movements, you can tell Windows to use the keyboard for the mouse pointer and you can also adjust your keyboard settings, as shown in Figure 5.2. For people with low vision, bigger fonts and high-color contrast schemes are readily available. Finally, for people who are deaf or with hearing impairment, Windows can visually indicate when your computer makes a sound. Accessibility Options in Control Panel are used to change Keyboard, Sound, Display, Mouse, or General settings.

FIGURE 5.2
Keyboard settings

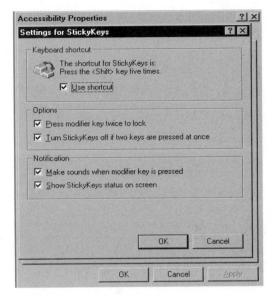

Add New Hardware

Windows 95 has a new feature to allow you to add new hardware to your computer. The Add New Hardware icon in Control Panel provides a wizard that helps

FIGURE 5.3
Add New Hardware

you install new hardware devices on your computer. If your hardware is already installed, you can have windows try to detect it. Otherwise, select the hardware from the list. To add new hardware, select Settings from the Start button and point to Control Panel. Double-click on the Add New Hardware icon; you will see the Add New Hardware Wizard dialog box, shown in Figure 5.3. Installing new hardware is very easy! You are prompted in each step by clicking on the Next button.

Add/Remove Programs

Adding or removing programs in Windows 95 has been greatly improved. Simply double-click on the *Add/Remove Programs* icon in Control Panel and you will automatically be taken into the Add/Remove Programs Properties dialog box, shown in Figure 5.4. The dialog box enables you to install/uninstall a program from a floppy disk, CD-ROM, or network, or to add or delete a program from a Windows component after Windows 95 itself has been installed. To add or remove a component, click the check box on the Windows Setup tab. A shaded box means that only part of the component will be installed. To see what is included in a component, click on Details.

FIGURE 5.4
*Add/Remove
Programs
Properties
dialog box*

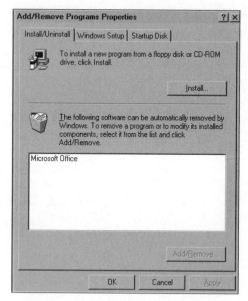

The Add/Remove Programs Properties dialog box is organized by tabs. At the top of the dialog box, you will notice the tabs for Install/Uninstall, Windows Setup, and Startup Disk. Each of the tabs is executed with the OK button. You can, of course, change your mind with the Cancel button.

Accessibility Properties

Windows 95 allows you to specify Accessibility Properties. Figure 5.5 illustrates the General Accessibility Properties where you can automatically reset the Accessibility feature after a specified number of minutes. In addition, you can give a warning message when turning a feature on. Finally, you can enable serial key devices which allow alternative access to keyboard and mouse features.

FIGURE 5.5
*Accessibility
Properties*

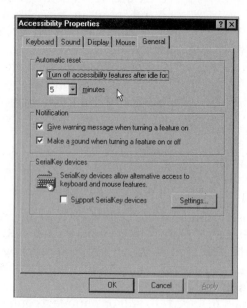

Changing the System Date and Time

You can alter the system date and time by double-clicking on or choosing the Date/Time icon in the Control Panel. The time and date are used in Clock and Calendar. Time and date are also used to time- and date-stamp files saved on your disk. If your computer system has a built-in clock, you may not have to worry about changing the date or time. (Over time, some PCs "lose" a little clock accuracy.) Check with your instructor or laboratory manager if you have any questions regarding system default dates and times.

When you select the Date/Time icon from the Control Panel, a Date/Time Properties dialog box will appear, as shown in Figure 5.6.

FIGURE 5.6
Date/Time Properties dialog box

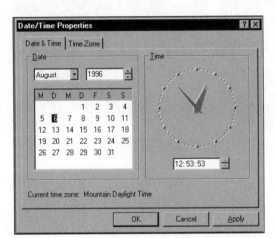

Select the part of the date (day, month, or year) that you want to change. To do this, place the cursor pointer on the button that you want to change. For example, you can click on the month and a listing will appear. You can select the new month. The year and the time can be increased/decreased in the same manner. Position the cursor on the time box, and click the part of the time (hour, minute, second, A.M. or P.M.) that you want changed. To complete the change, click or choose OK. Of course, you can cancel the command if you change your mind.

GUIDED ACTIVITY 5.1

Looking at Date/Time (change only if necessary)

1. Open Control Panel from Settings on the Start button.

2. Double-click on the Date/Time icon.

3. If the Date is not correct, click on and highlight the part of the date that is incorrect. You can make the appropriate change by clicking on the up or down arrow to the right of the Date.

4. Repeat step 3 to correct Time.

5. Click on OK to complete the change.

6. Close Control Panel.

FIGURE 5.7
*Properties
command*

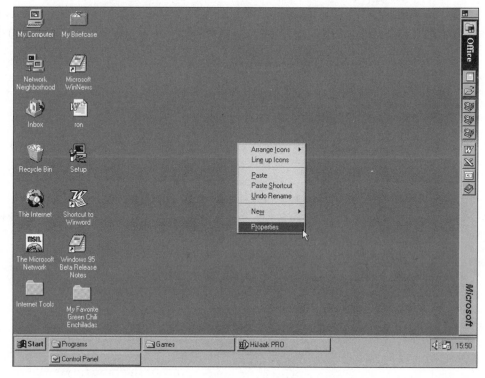

Display Properties

You can customize almost any screen element in Windows by using the right mouse button on the desktop and then clicking Properties (Figure 5.7). In the Display Properties dialog box (Figure 5.8), you can change the background color or add a bitmap to the desktop. You can change the font used for your menus, title bars, and other elements. You can choose different screen savers.

FIGURE 5.8
*Display
Properties
dialog box*

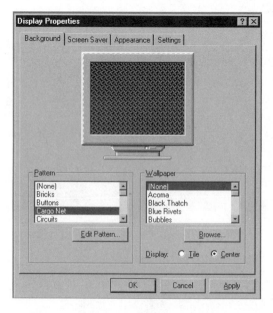

If you want to change the appearance of the desktop, choose the Display icon from the Control Panel. A Display Properties dialog box will appear (Figure 5.8), listing the parts of the four tabs entitled *Background*, *Screen Saver*, *Appearance*, and *Settings*. Select the Appearance tab to inspect the current (default) settings (Figure 5.9). You may notice the arrangement of the Display Properties dialog box, which includes Scheme, Item, and Font. The current *scheme* is probably Windows Standard. However, if you click on the Scheme button, you will see additional choices. Some Schemes that are available are Bricks, Desert, Eggplant, Flat, Flat Large, High Contrast Black, High Contrast

FIGURE 5.9
Display appearance tabs

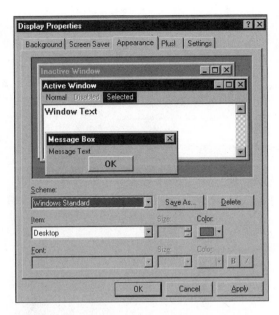

Black Large, Lilac, Plum, and Maple. You can scroll through the list and select a scheme that you like. Click or choose OK to complete the choice of scheme.

Changing an Existing Color Scheme

If you prefer another color scheme, you can change any of the default color schemes. The default color schemes are the predetermined colors provided by Microsoft. To change the scheme, select the Color Scheme you want from the Color list box. A small color list box will appear where a few basic colors are displayed. Click on Other to see the *color palette* where you can design your own color scheme.

Figure 5.10 shows a list of elements, a palette of basic colors, and, until you select additional colors, an empty color palette called Custom Colors. In the color sample

FIGURE 5.10
Color Schemes elements

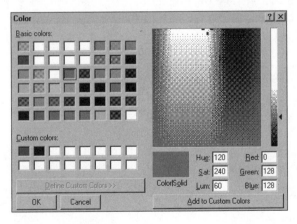

screen, click the element whose color you wish to change. The illustration in this text will not be the same as on your monitor. Remember that your monitor is probably a color monitor and accordingly should show the Basic Colors palette in color. When you are finished selecting the color of your choice, click or choose Save As, and type a name for the scheme. We developed the "West White 3a" scheme for this book to provide clearer black-and-white screen images.

FIGURE 5.11
Desktop Items

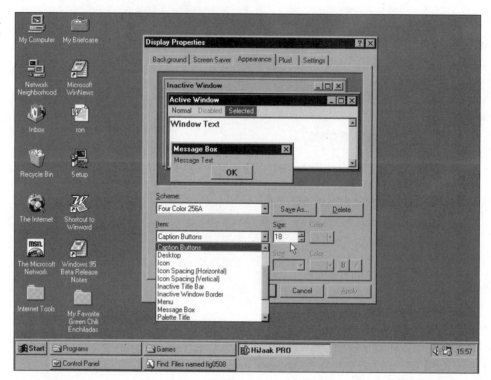

Changing Desktop Items

Desktop items can also be changed in the Display icon in the Control Panel. Double-click on the Display icon and click on the Appearance tab. Slightly below the Scheme list box, you will notice the Item list box (Figure 5.11). Click on the Item button to see the entire list. Some of the items include 3D Objects, Active/Inactive Title Bar, Active/Inactive Window Border, Caption Button, Desktop, Icon, Menu, Message Box, Palette Title, Scroll Bar, Selected Items, Tool Tip, Window, and so on. You may wish to experiment with different choices to see the effect of each. To accept the current Item selections, click on the OK button. You can, of course, change your mind with the Cancel button. You can also save the the settings by clicking on the Save As button.

GUIDED ACTIVITY 5.2

Changing the Color Scheme

1. Open the Control Panel window from Settings on the Start button. Remember, to open the window, you will have to point to the Control Panel icon.

2. Double-click on the Display icon.

3. Click on the Appearance tab.

4. Click on Color. This area is on the lower-right corner of the Display Properties dialog box. In the box, the name of the particular area that you clicked on will appear. If a color is changed, only the color in that particular area will change.

5. Look at the Colors palette on the right side of the screen.

6. Experiment with the other screen elements and with different color combinations.

7. If your instructor requests, save the color selections by clicking on Save As and giving it a file name. Click on OK to complete the process. If your instructor does not want you to alter the color scheme, click on Cancel.

Find Fast

You can use Find Fast to create indexes for various types of documents. Figure 5.12 reflects the dialog box for this.

FIGURE 5.12
Find Fast

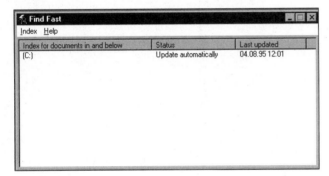

Using Fonts

The manner in which the characters appear on the screen will depend on the fonts that you choose. If you want to change the font, select (double-click) the Fonts icon in the Control Panel. A *font* is a graphic design that affects numerals, symbols, and characters. Different fonts are available for providing emphasis (bold, italics, or underline). They allow you to give your work a professional or casual appearance. Selecting the right font will take some practice, however.

 CAUTION *We strongly recommend that you do not change the system font.*

When you select the Fonts icon in the Control Panel, the Fonts dialog box in Figure 5.13 will appear. The fonts on your system may be different from those in the figure.

GUIDED ACTIVITY 5.3

Looking at Fonts

1. If Control Panel is still open, close it by double-clicking the Control menu box.

2. Open WordPad in the Accessories program group from the Start button.

3. Compose a couple of paragraphs of text—perhaps a short letter to Mom explaining why you need to buy a new racquet.

4. Close WordPad by pressing [Spacebar], and then selecting Close.

 NOTE *Font options are determined by the printer type. Therefore, your selection will depend on the type of printer you have available, and might not correspond with what is illustrated in this book.*

FIGURE 5.13
Fonts dialog box

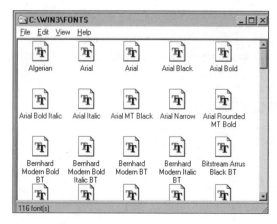

Removing a Font

Fonts that have been added to your system will use memory. If you are not planning to use one or more of the fonts that you added, it is best to remove them. You will soon appreciate the need for memory conservation for your other applications, since any wasted memory will result in storage problems later. To remove a font, click the Fonts icon in Control Panel; when the Fonts dialog box appears, select the font you wish to remove. Next, click or choose Delete from the File menu and another dialog box will appear, asking you to verify that you wish to remove the selected font to the Recycle Bin. To complete this process, click or choose Yes or No.

GUIDED ACTIVITY 5.4

Removing a Font (optional)

 CAUTION   *To be completed only if instructor approves!*

1. Open Control Panel from the Settings menu on the Start button.

2. Double-click on the Fonts icon.

3. Click on the scroll bar to view the Installed Fonts.

> *If your instructor approves removing the font:*
>
> 4. Click on the font you wish to remove.
>
> 5. Click on File Delete. Verify the removal by clicking on Yes.
>
> 6. Close Fonts by clicking on OK.
>
> 7. Close Control Panel by double-clicking on the Control menu box.

Calibrating the Joystick

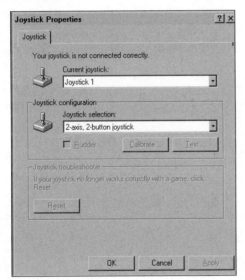

FIGURE 5.14
Joystick Properties dialog box

Joysticks are used to play your favorite games. Not every PC has one. To calibrate your joystick, click on the *Joystick* icon in the Control Panel. You can also use the Shortcut method from the Help menu on the Start button. The Joystick Properties dialog box will appear (Figure 5.14). In the Joystick Selection list, click the joystick you are using. If your joystick is not listed, click Custom. Click Calibrate, and then follow the instructions on your screen. If your joystick has external rudder controls, make sure the Rudder box is checked. If you have not yet installed your joystick, the Hardware Installation wizard will install it automatically. Simply click on its shortcut in the Help menu from the Start button.

Using Microsoft Exchange to Send and Receive Messages

With Microsoft Exchange, you can send and receive electronic mail or fax messages. You send messages from and store all messages in Microsoft Exchange, so there's one convenient place to look for all your messages. To open Microsoft Exchange to send or receive a message, double-click the Inbox icon on your desktop or the Mail and Fax icon on the Control Panel.

If Microsoft Exchange is not on your desktop, you can install it by double-clicking the Add/Remove Programs icon in Control Panel.

Microsoft Exchange gives you the ability to communicate with a number of electronic mail systems, including Microsoft Mail. You can use Microsoft Exchange to gain access to your mailbox if it is in a *post office* created by: Microsoft Mail for PC Networks version 3.0 or later; Microsoft Windows for Workgroups version 3.1 or later; Microsoft Windows NT version 1.1 or later.

When you start Microsoft Exchange for the first time, a wizard helps you create your profile. A *profile* contains default settings for how messages are delivered to and from your mailbox. If you have used Microsoft Mail before, you can also use the wizard to move the messages in your message file to your Microsoft Exchange mailbox. How you work with mail will determine whether you need more than one profile. If you use one computer, typically you have one profile that specifies a mailbox located on your computer or possibly on a network server. You may also want to store your mailbox on your computer if you have a dockable computer, if you frequently work in locations where the post office is unavailable, or if your message delivery is slow.

If you work on more than one computer and you use different information services on each, you need to create separate profiles listing the information services. If you share a computer with another person, each person must have his or her own profile.

Mail and Fax

You can inspect the Microsoft Exchange Profile by clicking on the Mail and Fax icon in Control Panel (shown in the margin). Then click on the *Properties* button where you will have the opportunity to Add/Remove Personal Address Book (Figure 5.15), Personal Folders (Figure 5.16), or Microsoft Network Online Services (Figure 5.17).

FIGURE 5.15
*Personal
Address Book*

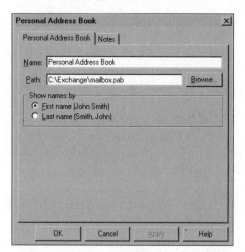

FIGURE 5.16
Personal Folders

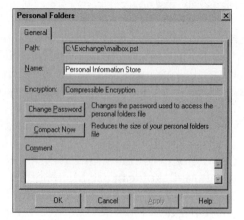

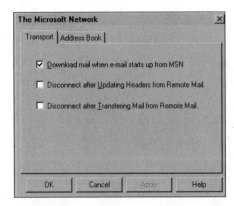

FIGURE 5.17
*Microsoft
Network Online
Services*

Installing Modems

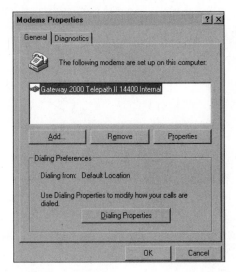

FIGURE 5.18
*Modem
Properties
dialog box*

Modems are very easy to install with the use of the modem wizard. You can select the Modems icon in Control Panel from the Settings menu on the Start button, or you can use the wizard from Help. Help, you will recall, is also in the Start button menu. Simply type in the word `modem` and the Help dialog box will take you directly into the Modem Properties dialog box (Figure 5.18). If you prefer to use the first method, double-click on the Modems icon in Control Panel.

Adjusting the Mouse

A mouse can be installed the same way that the modem is installed. (Your mouse has probably already been installed.) You can use the Mouse icon in Control Panel or you can use the wizard in Help. If you double-click on the Mouse icon, you will see the Mouse Properties dialog box (Figure 5.19). The Mouse Properties dialog box contains tabs for Buttons, Pointers, Motion, and General.

The Buttons tab (Figure 5.20) is used to adjust the mouse for right-handed or left-handed users. You can also set the Double-Click Speed and see the Test Area, which demonstrates the speed that you selected. To confirm the adjustments, select Apply. You may wish to experiment with this feature! However, be careful not to set the double-click speed to the highest speed possible, because you will be unable to click the mouse button fast enough. Normally, the speed should be somewhere in the middle.

FIGURE 5.19
*Mouse
Properties
dialog box*

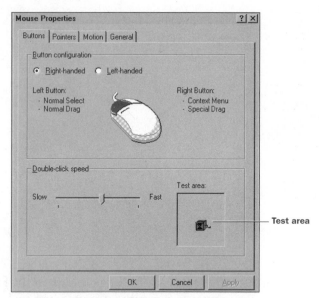

FIGURE 5.20
Mouse Buttons

FIGURE 5.21
Mouse Motion

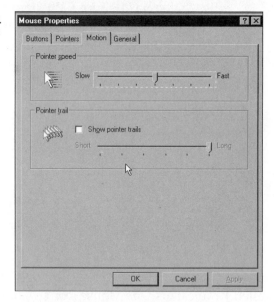

Pointers (Figure 5.21) allows you to select a Scheme and Save the scheme for later use. In addition, you can select Various Pointers from the list. Click on this button and you will see an extensive list of pointers.

Motion allows you to set the Pointer Speed and Pointer Trail.

From the General tab, you can activate the Mouse Manager (Figure 5.22) where you can experiment with the Options button. Options allow you to change the Orientation (Figure 5.23) where you can customize your mouse for either hand or in a variety of positions. You can also set the primary and secondary mouse buttons. Another option is to inspect the Sensitivity of the mouse.

FIGURE 5.22
Mouse Manager

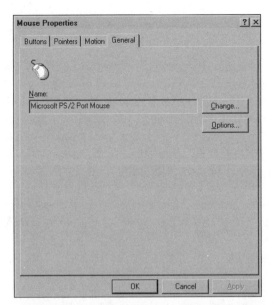

FIGURE 5.23
*Mouse
Orientation*

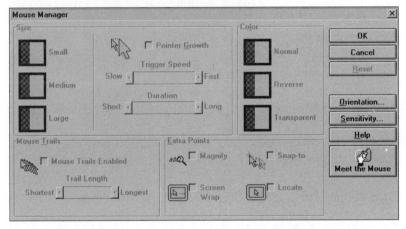

Installing Multimedia

To set up new multimedia hardware, click on Help from the Start menu where you will see a shortcut icon that activates the Add New Hardware wizard. Follow the instructions on your screen.

If you connected your hardware or installed its components in your computer before running the wizard, select the option to automatically detect your hardware. Multimedia devices that can be installed include CD Player, Sound Recorder, MIDI instruments, and so on. Once they are installed, use the Multimedia icon on the Control Panel to adjust the multimedia properties.

Connecting to the Network

With Dial-Up Networking, you can use shared information on another computer even when you are not on a network. If the computer you are dialing into is connected to a network, you may also be able to gain access to the network.

For example, if you have a computer at home, you can dial in and connect to your work computer and its network. Both your home computer and your work computer must have modems installed. To start the Dial-Up Networking setup wizard, double-click My Computer, and then double-click Dial-Up Networking. To connect to an online service such as a bulletin board, use HyperTerminal rather than Dial-Up Networking. If the Dial-Up Networking icon is not in My Computer, it is not installed. To install it, double-click the Add/ Remove Programs icon in Control Panel.

Connecting to the Internet

There are two ways you can connect to the Internet using Windows: (1) you can sign up for The Microsoft Network; (2) you can install the appropriate networking protocols and create a Dial-Up Networking connection to the Internet through an Internet access provider.

Signing Up for The Microsoft Network

Click the Start button, point to Programs, point to Accessories, and then click Dial-Up Networking.

If this option does not appear on the Accessories menu, then you did not install The Microsoft Network when you installed Windows.

Connecting to the Internet Using Dial-Up Networking

To connect using Dial-Up Networking, you will need the following components: communications hardware, software to connect to the Internet, and an account with an Internet access provider.

You need a modem (9600 bps or faster); or, if you have a direct network connection to the Internet, you can use a network adapter card instead of a modem.

Software Needed to Connect to the Internet

All of the following software is included with Windows (although it may not have been installed at the time you installed Windows): Dial-Up Networking, the Windows 95 TCP/IP protocol bound to the Dial-Up Adapter or to a network adapter, and software for browsing and downloading information from the Internet.

Windows includes a *File Transfer Program (FTP)* and Telnet for navigating the Internet. Other, more graphical tools, such as Mosaic or Gopher, are available from third parties at a cost, or you can find them on the Internet in the public domain.

Internet Account Information

When you call an Internet access provider to sign up for an Internet account, you need to get the following identification information: access provider's phone number, PPP account, Domain Name System (DNS) server host name and domain name, DNS search order (if required), IP address and subnet mask, and gateway address.

WHERE TO ENTER THIS INFORMATION

To enter address information, click Help from the Start button and type in the help topic `address information` to display network properties. Click TCP/IP/Dial-Up Adapter, and then click Properties. On the IP Address tab, type your IP address and subnet mask. On the DNS Configuration tab, type your host and domain names, and the DNS server search order, if applicable. On the Gateway tab, type your gateway address in the space provided.

If you are using a direct network connection to the Internet, click Obtain an IP Address from a DHCP Server on the IP address tab. Type your name and password in the Connect To dialog box in Dial-Up Networking, after you have defined a connection to the Internet.

To log on to the network, click the Start button, and then click Shut Down. Click Close All Programs and Log On as a Different User. Click Yes. In the Enter Network Password box, type your user name and password. If you want to log on to Windows and the network at the same time, you can do so by making your Windows and network passwords the same.

Using Networks from Explorer

To connect to a network from Explorer, click on the Start button and point to Programs. Select Explorer from the Programs dialog box. On the third line where the various icons are placed (Figure 5.24), click on the Map Network Drive icon (shown in the margin).

FIGURE 5.24
*Windows 95
Explorer*

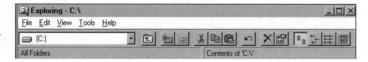

The Map Network Drive dialog box will appear (Figure 5.25). Click the mouse pointer in the Path box and type the access path to your mainframe computer. For example, I would type `\\Merlin\RonMaestas` to enter the computer at my institution. You will then see the listing on the first pane of Explorer. You might need to

FIGURE 5.25
*Map Network
Drive dialog box*

FIGURE 5.26
*Network Drive
list box*

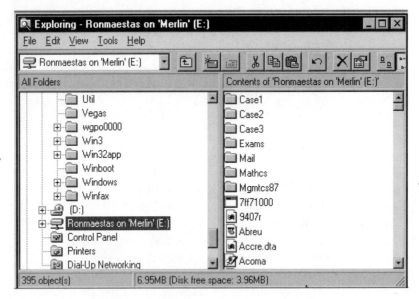

scroll down the list to find your connection (Figure 5.26). The icon will probably be listed as Drive E:\. Double-click on this icon and you will then see a complete listing of all files on your mainframe (Figure 5.27).

Network Neighborhood

If you are using a *network*, or group of computers and associated devices linked by communications facilities, the Network Neighborhood icon appears on your

FIGURE 5.27
Mainframe files

FIGURE 5.28
*Network
Neighborhood*

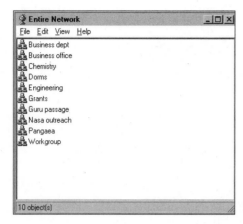

desktop. Double-click the icon to browse through the computers on your workgroup and the computers on your entire network. The Entire Network (see a sample in Figure 5.28) will consist of Microsoft Windows NT 3.5 and 3.51 (when released), plus Microsoft Windows for Workgroups 3.11. To connect to another computer on your network, click on that computer icon.

If you installed networking when you set up Windows 95, you can easily connect to other computers on your network (sometimes referred to as a local area network or LAN). Just double-click the Network Neighborhood icon on your desktop, and then double-click the computer you want. If you don't see the computer you want, double-click the Entire Network icon. If you don't have networking available (the Network Neighborhood window is empty or the icon is missing), you need to set up networking.

To Find a Computer on Your Network

Click the Start button, and then point to Find. Click on Computer. If you know only the name of the computer you are looking for, type it in the Named box—for example, marketing. If you know the path to the shared folder you are searching for, you can specify both the computer and folder name—for example, \\marketing\reports. Click Find Now.

You can also find a computer by double-clicking the Network Neighborhood icon on the desktop.

To see what network printers and folders are available to you, double-click the Network Neighborhood icon. To see additional printers and folders that are available, click Entire Network. Double-click the computer whose shared resources you want to view. If you can't see a resource you are looking for, you might not have access permission. Contact the person who shared the resource.

To see a hierarchical view of the network, click a computer (or Entire Network), click File, and then click Explore.

Setting Passwords

Passwords can be set or changed for various resources on your computer. These resources include remote administration, folders, NetWare server, printers, screen savers, or Windows itself. You can set passwords in the Control Panel or from the Help menu using the Shortcut. To enable others to see resource use on your computer, click on the Shortcut icon to display the Passwords Properties, shown in Figure 5.29. Then click the Remote Administration tab, and then mouse to Enable Remote Administration of This Server. If your computer is set up with user-level access control, click Add. Then, in the list on the left, click the person or group that you want to be able to view the resource use on your computer, and finally click Add. If your computer is set up

FIGURE 5.29
*Passwords
Properties*

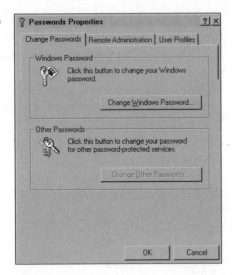

with share-level access control, type the password you want to assign to your computer in the Password box. Then type it again in the Confirm Password box.

To Change your Network Password

Click on the Shortcut icon on the Help menu for Password to display Passwords Properties (Figure 5.29). Click Change Other Passwords. Click the password you want to change, and then click Change.   Type your old password. Type your new password, and then type it again in the Confirm New Password box.

 NOTE *If you are using a NetWare server, click Related Topics for information about changing your password.*

To Change the Password for a Shared Resource

In My Computer, click the folder you want to share. On the File menu, click Properties. Mouse to the Sharing tab, and then change the password. To protect your files by assigning a screen-saver password, click the Shortcut icon in the Help menu to view Display Properties. In the list in the Screen Saver area, click the screen saver you want to use.

Make sure Password Protected is checked, and then click Change. Type your password, and then confirm the password by typing it again.

NOTE *If you assign a password to a screen saver, people who do not know the password cannot clear the screen saver, and therefore cannot easily gain access to your computer.*

To Change your Windows Password

Click on the Shortcut icon in the Help menu to display Passwords Properties. Click Change Windows Password. If you have other network passwords, these will be listed so that you can change them to match your new Windows password if you want to. Type your old password. Type your new password, and then type it again in the Confirm New Password box.

If you are using Windows with a network, you need to be logged on to the network to change your Windows password.

Accessing Printers

To control access to a folder or printer in My Computer, click the shared folder or printer you want to limit access to. On the File menu, click Properties. Click Sharing. If you are using user-level access control, click Add to specify the people you want to be able to use your resources.

If you are using share-level access control, type the password you want to use for the folder or printer.

You can control access to your folders or printers by using passwords or by listing names of people you want to have access to these resources.

To quickly send files to another place, use the right mouse button to click the file you want to send. Mouse to Send To, and then click the destination. You can add other destinations to the Send To command. In the Send To folder, located in your Windows folder, create shortcuts to the destinations you often send files to; for example, a printer, fax, or particular folder.

Changing Regional Settings

The Regional Settings icon in the Control Panel lets you change number, currency, time, and date settings. To change settings, click on the Shortcut icon in Help or click on the icon in Control Panel to display properties for regional settings (Figure 5.30). In the list, click the region whose date, time, number, and currency format you want to use.

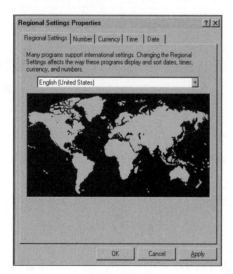

FIGURE 5.30
Regional Settings Properties

If you change the regional settings, you might also have to add a language or keyboard layout. To change the language or keyboard layout, you may wish to refer to the earlier discussion.

When Enable Indicator on Taskbar is checked, and you have two or more languages installed, an indicator representing the default language appears on the taskbar. To quickly switch between languages, click the indicator, and then click the language you want to use.

Checking the System

System properties can be viewed, changed, or removed. Simply click on the System icon in the Control Panel and the System Properties dialog box will appear (Figure 5.31). Tabs appear for General, Device Manager, Hardware Profiles, and Performance. You should be *extremely careful* not to change system properties. This discussion is merely to illustrate to you that system properties can be inspected. Your laboratory manager or your instructor should be consulted for any changes to be made to system properties.

FIGURE 5.31
System
Properties

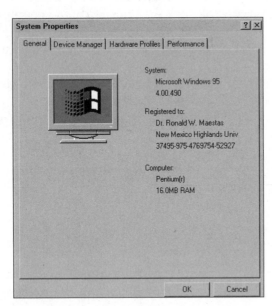

Review Questions

*1. How many icons are in Control Panel, and what do they allow you to do?

*2. What is a font? Why is it recommended that you remove any fonts that will not be used?

*3. What new feature allows you to send and receive electronic mail?

*4. What is the name of an empty color palette?

Key Terms

Add/Remove Programs
Appearance
Background
Color palette
Control Panel
Desktop
File transfer Program
  (FTP)

Font
Joystick
Local Area Network
  (LAN)
Modem
Network
Post Office
Profile

Properties
Scheme
Screen Saver
Settings
Wizard

Printing

Printing with Windows 95 sends information or data that you created through Windows application utilities (such as documents and pictures) to a printer. Printing allows you to send several documents to the printer at the same time.

This unit assumes that you have properly connected a local printer (or a network printer) to your computer and that the appropriate printer drivers have been installed. If you are running Windows in a network, you may need to consult with your system's laboratory supervisor for specific questions on printing.

Learning Objectives

At the completion of this unit, you should know

1. the purpose of printing,

2. the various commands and options available while printing,

3. how to make print settings,

4. how to see the status of the files you are printing,

5. how to pause and resume printing,

6. how to delete files waiting to be printed.

Printing a Document

To print a document (if the document is open), click the File menu, and then click Print. If the document is not open, drag the document from My Computer or Windows Explorer to your printer in the Printers folder. While a document is printing, a printer icon appears next to the clock on the taskbar. When this icon disappears, your document has finished printing. For easy access to your printer, you can create a shortcut to it on the desktop.

Printer Settings

Printing is done in the **background,** which means that once you send a document to the printer you can continue to work with another application in the **foreground**. You do not have to wait until the printing is completed to go on with your work.

If you have more than one printer connected to your system, Windows 95 will handle the assignment of a specific printer to a particular application. Windows manages a separate *queue* for each printer and sends the data to each printer as it is selected. A queue is a list of items to be printed. For example, you may want to print several documents on a laser printer and others on a shared network printer. If so, Windows serves as a "traffic controller," directing the printing in the manner that you select.

Windows is extremely efficient if you have large printing jobs from different applications. In practice, there may be times when you wish to print non-Windows applications directly, rather than using Windows. These applications are normally printed through DOS or through their own print facility. However, keep in mind that you may have to wait until the document is printed before any other work can be done on that document or application or before you can return to Windows.

Printers

To change printer settings, click Start, then click on Help and select Print Settings from the Help Topics. Change printer settings, then click on the Shortcut icon. The *Printers* folder (shown in the margin) will appear. Click the icon for the printer you are using. From the File menu, click Properties. The settings that you can change depend on the type of printer you have. Click the different tabs to see all of the options you can set. For Help on an item, click on the question mark at the top of the dialog box and then click the item. Changing the ***printer properties*** will change them for all the documents you print on this printer. To change these settings for one document, use the Page Setup or Print Setup command on the File menu in your program.

From the Printers dialog box, you will notice the command menu. The command menu includes File, Edit, View, and Help. If you click on File, you will be able to Open, Pause printing, Purge a print job, Share a printer, Create a shortcut, Delete, Rename, Close, and inspect Properties.

Printer Properties

You can set Printer Properties from the Printers dialog box. From the File command, mouse to Properties (Figure 6.1). There are individual tabs for General, Details, Sharing (if you are connected to a network), Paper, Graphics, Fonts, and Device Options. For example, you can inspect or change the Printers Properties Details tab. The dialog box for Details (Figure 6.2) lists those printer attributes that can be changed. They include Print to the Following **Port**, Print Using the Following **Driver**, Add/Delete a port, New Driver, Timeout Settings, as well as **Spool** and Port

FIGURE 6.1
*Printer
Properties*

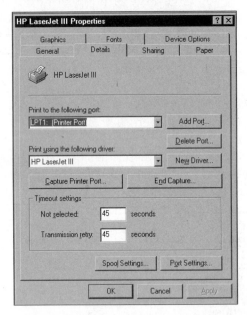

FIGURE 6.2
*Printer
Properties
detail box*

Settings. We recommend that you only inspect these settings and *not* change them unless your instructor directs you to do so.

Fonts can also be changed from the Printer Properties dialog box. Select the Fonts tab (Figure 6.3). The Fonts tab includes Cartridges and TrueType fonts. You can install printer fonts as well as restore defaults. Once again, we strongly recommend that you only inspect these settings and *not* change them unless directed to do so.

FIGURE 6.3
Fonts tab

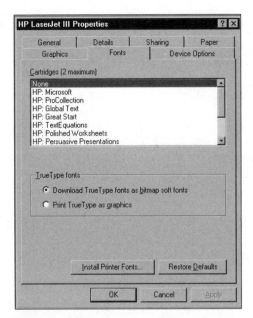

GUIDED ACTIVITY 6.1

Printing a File

1. Open WordPad from the Accessories program group by double-clicking on its icon.

2. Click on File from the menu bar and then on Open.

3. From the File Open dialog box, double-click on the file *Readme*. The file will appear in the WordPad window.

4. Print the file by clicking on File and then on Print. (Make sure the printer is on and print only the first page).

5. Close WordPad by clicking on the WordPad icon and then on Close.

The print queue is where Windows maintains the status for any pending print jobs. The dialog box that appears when Printers is activated will list those files that are currently being printed, as well as those files waiting to be printed, as shown in Figure 6.4. A file's status can be changed anytime prior to the time that the Print command is executed. For example, you can Pause the printing, Resume printing after it has been paused, or Delete a job from the print queue.

Windows has two types of print queues: local and network. The *local print queue* means that a printer is connected by a cable directly to your computer. The *network queue* refers to the print queue on the network server. It is managed by a completely separate network print manager, which is different from the one found in Windows 95. Your instructor or laboratory system supervisor should be consulted if you have any questions about using a network.

FIGURE 6.4
Print queue

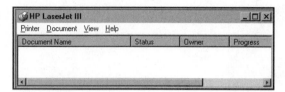

Quick Printing

Windows 95 offers a new "drag-and-drop" printing feature that prints a file if you drag the icon of the file from Explorer to the Printers icon. To use this feature, do the following:

1. Open My Computer by double-clicking on its icon, and then resize the dialog box to a smaller size.

2. Open Explorer and locate the file to be printed.

3. Drag the file icon from Explorer to your printer icon. Using the general Printers icon does not work if you have more than one printer attached (for example, a fax printer).

The application that created the file will be opened if it is not already open. This feature allows you to obtain a quick printout of a file without going through the steps of opening its original application.

INSPECTING THE PRINT QUEUE

When you select a file to be printed in an application such as WordPad, printing is started automatically. Its icon will appear on the taskbar. If you maximize (enlarge) the icon to a window, you will see the print queue for any active printer installed on your computer. If you have more than one printer connected to your computer, you will see multiple printer queue information lines, as well as a print queue for each printer.

GUIDED ACTIVITY 6.2
_____

Inspecting the Print Queue

1. If the *Readme* file is still printing from Guided Activity 6.1, go to step 2. If the file is not printing, open WordPad, open the file, and print it again. Then, immediately proceed with step 2.

2. Double-click on the Printers icon. The ***printer properties*** dialog box (Figure 6.5) will tell you (a) the name of the document, (b) the status of the job, (c) the owner (which computer sent the job to the queue), (d) the progress of the job, and (e) the time printing started. For example, if you wanted to inspect the printer for a file being printed, you would click on the Printers icon on the taskbar on the bottom of the desktop (Figure 6.6). The printer dialog box would appear.

FIGURE 6.5
Printer
Properties
dialog box

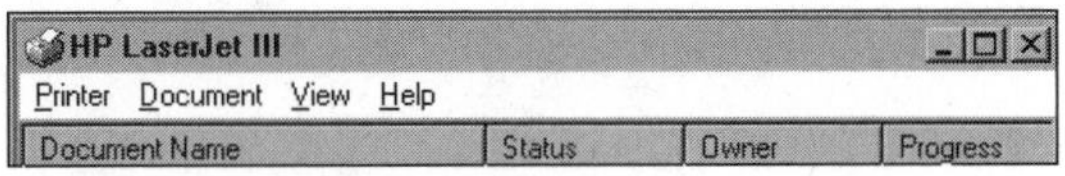

FIGURE 6.6
Printer
dialog box

Viewing Documents Waiting to Be Printed

Click the Start button, point to Settings, and then click Printers. Double-click the icon for the printer you want to look at. The print queue with all of the print jobs listed appears.

In the printer window, you can find information such as the status of print jobs and the owner of a document. If you want to cancel or pause the printing of any of the documents you have sent, click the document and then use the commands on the Document menu.

Using a Printer That Is Not Currently Connected [1]

Click the *Printers* folder in My Computer or use the shortcut method in Help. Click the icon for the printer that you want to print to. On the File menu, mouse over to Work Offline. When you send a document to this printer, it will be stored until you turn the printer online by clicking the Work Offline command again. The Work Offline command is available only for portable computers or for computers using a network printer. For local printers, use the Pause Printing command.

If you have a laptop computer with a docking station and you start Windows while the computer is undocked, your print jobs are automatically saved. Then, when you start Windows with your computer docked, the documents are sent to the printer. If you have turned off spooling in your printer properties, you cannot print offline.

Changing the Order of the Queue

To change the order of documents in a print queue, click on Help from the Start button or select the *Printers* folder from My Computer. Double-click the icon for the printer you are using.

Click the document you want to move, and then drag it to its new position in the queue.

✎ **NOTE** *You cannot move a document that is in the process of printing.*

---

1 Adapted from the online help for the Windows programs. Portions of the following are copyright © 1990–1995 by Microsoft Corporation.

Pausing and Resuming Printing

To pause or restart your printer, click Help from the Start button or the *Printers* folder from My Computer. Double-click the icon for the printer you want to pause or restart (Figure 6.7). On the Printer menu, click Pause Printing. If there is a check mark next to the command, the printer is paused. To restart the printer, click this command again. You can pause a printer only if it is attached to the computer you are using. For example, you cannot pause a network printer from your own computer.

FIGURE 6.7
Selecting a printer

Double-click to
pause or resume
printing

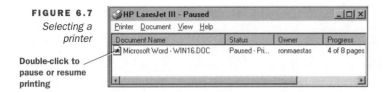

The Pause Printing command is unavailable if you have turned off spooling in your printer properties.

GUIDED ACTIVITY 6.3

Working with the Print Queue Using the Mouse

1. Open WordPad and click on File. Then click on Open. Double-click on a listed file, for instance *Readme*.

2. Click on File and then Print to print the file.

3. To inspect the queue, immediately click on the Printers icon, which appears on the taskbar on the lower-right of your screen.

4. To interrupt printing, click on the document name and then click on the Document command. The information line will indicate that printing has paused, but the printer might not stop immediately if special hardware or software, called a *buffer*, has been installed. To continue printing after the pause, click on the information line for the printer queue. Then, click on the Document command, and select Pause Printing. A check mark will be removed from this command, thereby allowing you to resume printing. The selected information line changes to indicate that printing has resumed. Your network printer driver may not permit you to pause during printing.

GUIDED ACTIVITY 6.4

Working with the Print Queue Using the Keyboard

1. Open WordPad and press [Alt][F]. Select File, Open. Press [Enter], [Tab], then highlight a listed file, for instance *Readme*, and press [Enter].

2. Press [Alt][F] for the File menu. Select Print to print the file.

3. To inspect the queue, immediately press [Alt][Tab] until the Printers icon is high-lighted, then release [Alt] (only if the Printer dialog box is already open).

4. To interrupt printing, press [Alt][P] on the Document command and then arrow to Pause Printing. The information line will indicate that printing has paused, but the printer might not stop immediately if special hardware or software, called a *buffer*, has been installed. To continue printing after the pause, highlight the information line for the printer queue. Then, press [Alt][D] on the Document com-mand and arrow to Pause Printing. The selected information line changes to indicate that printing has resumed. Your network printer driver may not permit you to pause during printing.

Print Troubleshooting [2]

Troubleshooter (located in Help) helps you identify and solve printer problems. Some problems encountered in printing include:

- My document didn't print at all.

- My document printed, but it doesn't look right, or it printed only partially.

- Printing is unusually slow.

- Only a partial page printed.

Your instructor or laboratory system supervisor may be able to help you if you encounter these or other printing problems.

NOTE *Keep in mind that procedures for printing on a network will differ from those for printing on a local printer. If you are using a **Novell network**, you may need to refer to the Novell user's manual for help with any problems you encounter during printing.*

Review Questions

*1. What is meant by printing in the background?

*2. Briefly identify and describe the types of print queues in Windows.

3. List the steps required to change the order of print jobs in a queue.

4. How is the printing of a document temporarily interrupted? How is a file deleted from a print queue?

*5. State at least four problems that may occur while printing.

---

2 Adapted from the online help for the Windows Programs. Portions of the following are copyright © 1990–1995 by Microsoft Corporation.

Key Terms

Background	Local print queue	Printer properties
Buffer	Network queue	Queue
Driver	Novell network	Spool
Foreground	Port	

Windows Applications

■ **PART TWO** introduces various Windows 95 applications. Unit 7 illustrates Windows' built-in word processing capabilities, contained in the program WordPad. Unit 8 features the program Paint, which is for creating and editing pictures. Unit 9 covers HyperTerminal, used for data communication. Unit 10 presents other Windows accessories, such as Fax, Calculator, Clock, Notepad, Character Map, Phone Dialer, and Multimedia. Finally, Unit 11 introduces other members of the Microsoft family of Office 95 products: Word for Windows, Excel, Project, and PowerPoint.

WordPad

Microsoft WordPad is a word processor that allows you to create memos, reports, and letters. It permits you to include pictures as part of your text. It supports most printers using any font that has been installed for your specific printer. WordPad is another Windows application that incorporates WYSIWYG (what you see is what you get) technology. You can format paragraphs flush left, flush right, or centered, and can choose from three line-spacing options.

Although WordPad is not as powerful a word processor as a full-feature application like Microsoft Word for Windows, using it offers a good introduction to word processing in a graphical environment. Documents that you create with WordPad can be transferred through Clipboard to other Windows applications.

Learning Objectives

At the completion of this unit you should know

1. how to start and exit WordPad,

2. how to create a document in WordPad,

3. how to save and retrieve a document in WordPad,

4. how to edit a document in WordPad,

5. how to format characters, paragraphs, and pages in WordPad,

6. how to use online Help in WordPad,

7. how to print a document in WordPad.

Starting WordPad

Start WordPad, from the Programs/Accessories menu. Click on WordPad. The WordPad window shown in Figure 7.1 will open.

FIGURE 7.1
Microsoft WordPad

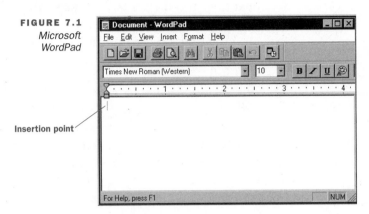

Insertion point

At the top of the WordPad window a menu bar lists the commands File, Edit, View, Insert, Format, and Help. Other elements to the WordPad window include *smarticons* for Fonts, Font Size, Bold, Italics, Underline, Color, Align Left, Center, Align Right, and Bullets. Each of these gives you document attributes that can enhance your document. If you position the mouse pointer on the smarticon, you will get a description for that particular icon. The attribute is selected by merely clicking on its icon. In addition, you will see:

- The *insertion point*, which indicates where the text appears (the upper-left corner of the window when you first open WordPad).

- The *mouse pointer*, which appears as an *I-beam* (if you have a mouse connected to your computer), as shown in Figure 7.2. It indicates where the mouse is pointing inside the WordPad window and where the insertion point will move to if you click the button (except that you cannot move the insertion point beyond the end of the document).

The remaining parts of the WordPad window screen include the familiar minimize-maximize buttons, close button, full page, and menu bar. You can also have a "ruler" at the top of the screen, as discussed later in this unit.

FIGURE 7.2
Untitled document

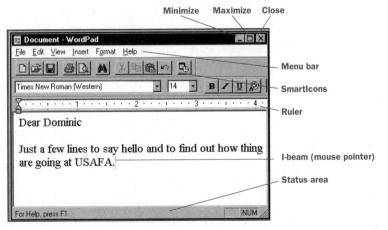

Minimize   Maximize   Close

Menu bar

SmartIcons

Ruler

I-beam (mouse pointer)

Status area

Using WordPad

Entering text in WordPad is simplicity itself. When you are ready to begin, just start typing. The text that you enter will appear at the insertion point. As you reach the end of a line, WordPad uses *word wrap*, which automatically jumps text to the next line. You do not have to press the ⏎Enter key to start a new line. If a word is too long to fit on the line, WordPad automatically moves the entire word to the next line.

Hard returns (created by pressing ⏎Enter) are used to create paragraphs. To start a new paragraph, press ⏎Enter twice, which will leave a blank line between the paragraphs, as shown in Figure 7.3. Or, if you prefer indented paragraphs, press ⏎Enter once, and then Tab for the indent.

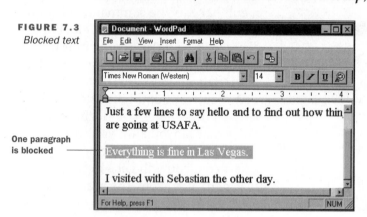

FIGURE 7.3
Blocked text

One paragraph is blocked

Editing Text

Editing in WordPad is performed very much the same as editing in any other Windows application. If you make a mistake while typing, press Backspace to erase the mistake. You can also use Del and Ins when editing.

Pressing the Ins key will shift to *overstrike* mode. To replace text, position the cursor with the mouse (or use the arrow keys on the keyboard) on the text you want replaced; then type in the new text. As you do this, notice how the old text disappears as the new text takes its place.

If you want to erase a small portion of text, position the cursor at the insertion point, either before or after the text you want erased. Then, press Del or Backspace. The Backspace key erases text to the left of the insertion point, while Del erases text to the right. In the event that you need to erase a large amount of text, you can mark the text that you want erased. To mark text with the mouse, position the cursor on (or to the left of) the first character to be deleted and drag the mouse pointer to highlight all the characters, words, or lines you want to delete. (Using the keyboard, hold down Shift and use arrow keys to highlight the text.) You will notice that the block of text will be shaded in black, as shown in Figure 7.4. Press Del to erase this block of text. If you delete too much, immediately use the Edit Undo comand.

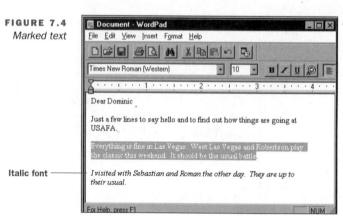

FIGURE 7.4
Marked text

Italic font

Formatting a Document

After your document has been created, you probably will want to format it. Making your document appear professional entails choosing a suitable type style, ample spacing, legible alignment of lines, and an attractive overall page layout. The WYSIWYG (what you see is what you get) concept applies to formatting, since "what you see on the screen is what you get on the printer."

To format, you must first mark the text you want to format, as in Figure 7.4, and then select the desired attribute from the smarticons. In the figure, italic is selected (the Italic button appears pushed in and the words have an italic slant).

You can use Bold, Italic, or Underline. Each of these choices can be invoked with a single click. In addition, you can use the Strikeout or Underline feature from the Format Font command, which is discussed in the next section.

WordPad saves character formats when you save your document. Also, WordPad transfers character formats if you copy or move formatted text either to another location in the document or to another WordPad document.

Using Fonts

Just as you are able to change character styles in WordPad, you can also change the font. Recall that a font is the design or shape shared by a set of alphanumeric characters. The fonts that are available to you will depend on the type of printer being used. For example, a dot-matrix printer may not contain the same fonts as a laser printer. Figure 7.5 lists several different fonts. Normally, printed versions of the fonts look better than the screen versions do.

FIGURE 7.5
Sample fonts

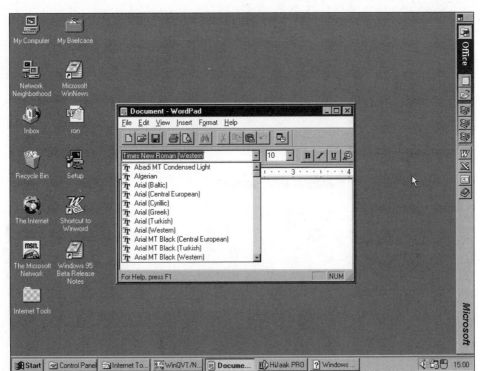

Fonts can be changed in a couple of ways. First, you can click on the box just above the ruler. The default Font might read "Times New Roman (Western)," or some other font depending on your setup. A single click on the down-pointing arrow will produce a listing of other available fonts. Use the scroll bar to review other fonts (Figure 7.6) installed on your computer. The second method for changing fonts involves the Format command from the menu bar. Click on Format, and then mouse to Font. You will then be presented with the Font dialog box where you can make changes. You can either select the font you want or press [Alt][F] to enter the font list. The list of fonts may be different on your computer, depending on the fonts that have been installed.

Point size can be selected from the Fonts dialog box. A point equals 1/72 of an inch and describes the height of a character. The point size is selected with the scroll bar, or you can place the pointer on the list and click the mouse button. You may wish to scroll through the fonts listed to find one that is suitable.

Font and style of text permit you to enlarge or reduce text as well as to add special effects to your document. For instance, if you want to create a memo letterhead, the size of your company name can be set at point size 24. The subject line can be underlined, and the sender's name can be in bold.

Formatting Paragraphs

You can change the format of paragraphs to achieve a more professional look for your document. *Text alignment* can be set to left-aligned, centered, or right-aligned. You may align part or all of your text. WordPad automatically aligns your text flush with the left margin as you type. A paragraph that is left-aligned (also called flush

FIGURE 7.6
Additional fonts

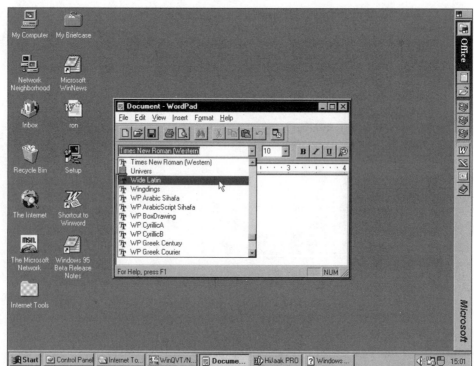

FIGURE 7.7
Text alignment

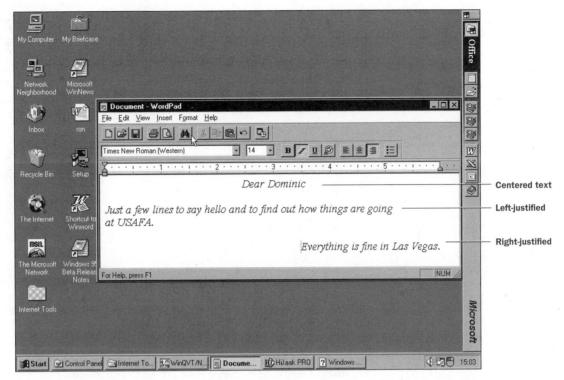

left) will show a straight edge on the left margin, but the right margin will be uneven or jagged. Text can also be centered on the page. Titles are usually centered. Right alignment (flush right) is the opposite of left alignment, in that the right edge is even and the left margin is jagged. Figure 7.7 shows examples of these formats.

You can use Paragraph commands on the Format menu to change the format in each paragraph of a document.

You can display the ruler to see how your text lines up relative to the paper's edges. To show the ruler, click Ruler from the View command and the ruler will appear as shown in Figure 7.8.

Retrieving, Saving, and Printing a Document

To retrieve or open a WordPad file, select Open from the File menu as shown in Figure 7.9, and then select the file name from the Open dialog box displayed in Figure 7.10. In most educational settings, you will save your work on a floppy disk (normally in drive A: or B:). If that is so, click on the drop-down list for Save In: to make the A: or B: drive the default drive. You can also save, retrieve, or print from My Computer, the C: drive, the D: drive, or the Network Neighborhood. The Open dialog box lists all possible file types to include Word for Windows 6.0 (*.doc), Windows Write (*. wri), Rich Text Format (*.rtf), Text Document (*.txt), Text Documents - MS-DOS (*.txt), or All Documents (*.*). Click the Open button, select the Look In: directory, the file type, and then highlight the name of the file you want to retrieve, double-clicking to complete the action.

FIGURE 7.8
WordPad ruler

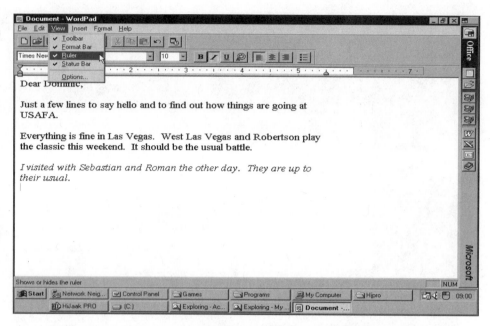

After you have created or modified a document, you will want to save your changes.

To save a file, select the Save or Save As command from the File menu. Be sure to save to the proper disk (or folder): usually you will have to designate the proper disk (or folder) by clicking on the Save In drop-down list for drives (your instructor might give you different instructions). Use Save after the first time, unless you want to change the name or file format. When you use Save As, the dialog box in Figure

FIGURE 7.9
File menu

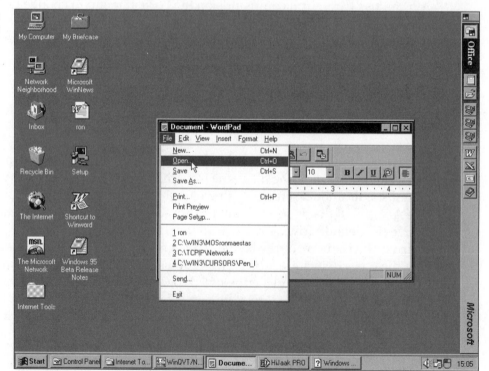

FIGURE 7.10
Open dialog box

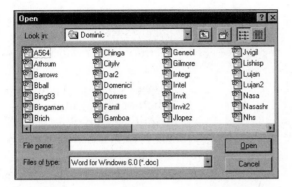

7.11 appears, where you can type the file name of the document that you want saved. When you are using WordPad for a long document, you should save your work often. A good rule of thumb is to save about every 15 minutes or less, and every time you get up from your chair or answer the phone.

FIGURE 7.11
Save As dialog box

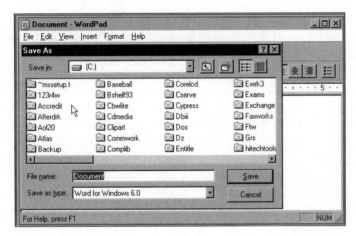

CAUTION   *Power failures or other unexpected occurrences can result in the loss of your data unless it is saved.*

WordPad allows four formatting options when you save a document. Choose the option you desire from the Save as Type list box in the Save As dialog box.

Format	Result
Word for Windows 6.0	A *.doc* extension is added to the file name.
Rich Text Format	An *.rtf* extension is added to the file name.
Text Documents	A *.txt* extension is added to the file name.
Text Doc - MS-DOS Format	A *.txt* file is created with no text formatting, only the words.

To print a document, select the Print command from the File menu. Printing in WordPad is very similar to printing in other Windows applications. Once you select the Print command, the Print dialog box appears (Figure 7.12). Select the print

FIGURE 7.12
Print dialog box

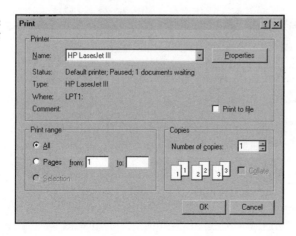

options that you want, and then click OK to start printing. Of course, you can Cancel the command if you wish to do so.

The print options include the Number of Copies you want to print or whether you want to print All pages or print From a certain page To a specific page. Quick printing can be done by clicking the Printer icon in the smarticon section of the desktop.

Inserting an Object or the Date and Time

Date and Time as well as Objects can be inserted in a WordPad document by selecting Insert from the menu bar and mousing down to your particular choice. For example, when you select Date and Time, the dialog box (Figure 7.13) will appear. You will notice the different date formats that are available. Double-click on the for-

FIGURE 7.13
Date and Time dialog box

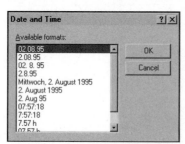

mat you want. Objects can be included in your document in the same way. Select Insert, and then mouse to Object; the Object dialog box will appear (Figure 7.14). Some objects that can be inserted on the document are: Bitmap files, Freelance graphics, Microsoft ClipArt Gallery, Microsoft Excel Chart, Microsoft Organization Chart, Microsoft PowerPoint Slides, Paint images, Pocket CD, and Video Clips.

FIGURE 7.14
Object dialog box

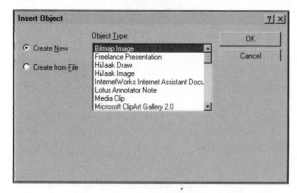

✎ **NOTE** *You may wish to refer to Unit 6 for assistance in printing.*

Exiting WordPad

When you are finished creating, editing, or printing a document in WordPad, you will need to save the document and exit. To exit or quit WordPad, select the Exit command from the File menu. If you have made any changes in your document without saving, a dialog box will appear, asking you to confirm your choice (Figure 7.15).

FIGURE 7.15
Confirm your changes

You can select Yes, No, or Cancel to complete the process.

GUIDED ACTIVITY 7.1

Creating a Document

1. Open WordPad from the Accessories submenu.

2. Type a short letter to "Mom" or a friend.

3. Click on File and then on Save As. Click on the drop-down list for drive A: (under "Save In:," you might have to scroll up the list to select drive A:). Click File Name, enter MOM, and then click on Save.

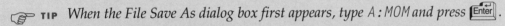

☞ **TIP** *When the File Save As dialog box first appears, type A : MOM and press* ⏎ *.*

4. Edit the file for the following changes (highlight the text using the mouse by going to the first letter of the text, pressing and not releasing the mouse button, moving the mouse to the last letter of the text, and releasing the mouse button):

   a. Add or delete phrases.

   b. Using the smarticon, change the salutation to bold.

   c. Using the smarticon, change your name to italic.

   d. Using Fonts in Format, change the font size to 14.

   e. Save the file again (click on File and then on Save).

5. Click on File and then on Print. Click on OK to print the file.

6. Close WordPad.

Review Questions

1. Briefly explain the following terms: insertion point, page status area, mouse pointer, and word wrap.

*2. How is a large area of text erased most efficiently?

*3. In WordPad, do character formats transfer if formatted text is copied or moved to another location and/or WordPad document?

4. What is a font?

*5. What is meant by text alignment being left-aligned, centered, right-aligned?

6. Review the command(s) to do the following: save, retrieve, and print a document.

7. Briefly identify and describe the four formatting choices that WordPad invokes when saving a document.

Key Terms

End mark	Mouse pointer	Text alignment
Hard return	Overstrike	Word wrap
I-beam	Point size	
Insertion point	Smarticon	

Paint 8

Microsoft Windows Paint is a graphics program that allows you to create and edit a variety of drawings. Using Paint, you can prepare greeting cards, newsletters, letterheads, text banners, line diagrams, or sophisticated art. Your imagination is the only limit to Paint!

Learning Objectives

At the completion of this unit you should know

1. the anatomy of Paint,

2. the differences between raster and vector graphics,

3. how to start and exit Paint,

4. how to use the toolbox,

5. how to create simple drawings.

Introduction to Paint

Paint is a computer-aided drawing program. As you progress through this unit, you will understand and be able to use the "tools" that Paint offers. Paint is easy to use because its icons are very descriptive and easily understood. You do not have to be an artist to be able to use and understand Paint. This unit gives a brief introduction to Paint and its capabilities; you will have to experiment and use the online Help.

Paint makes extensive use of the mouse. As you can well imagine, a mouse is much easier and more efficient to use than the keyboard when creating drawings.

Understanding Graphics Formats

Paint and many other "paint" programs deal with each "dot" on the screen, affecting its color by altering the amount of red, green, and blue used in its composition. These programs are called *raster graphics* because they are based on the movement of the raster (the electric beam that paints any cathode ray screen, such as that on a personal computer monitor). The files are saved in *bitmap* or similar format, using various coding schemes that remember the color of each dot (or bit). Depending on your monitor and software setup, you might see these images in 16 or 256 (or up to 16 million!) colors or shades of gray. Bitmap graphics files are easy to create and save, although it is difficult to change the size of a bitmap image.

Other graphics programs deal with objects such as lines, arcs, and polygons. These are described to the computer as vectors, which can be *scaled* (sized) as necessary. Although *vector graphics* files are more complex than raster graphics files, it is easier to manipulate discrete objects (such as the image of a chair or table) in this format.

Programs like Paint are usually preferred for artistic endeavors, while vector programs are preferred for technical drawing such as in architectural or engineering work. The understanding of raster versus vector graphics is not vital to your use of Paint, but it *is* useful to know which class of images Paint produces.

Starting Paint

To start Paint, click on the Paint option on the Programs/Accessories menu. The opening screen is illustrated in Figure 8.1.

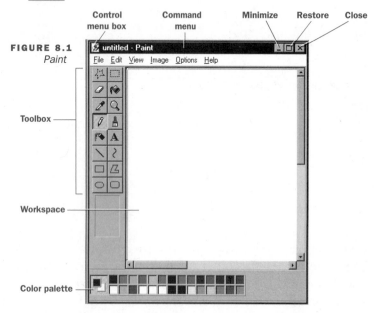

FIGURE 8.1
Paint

NOTE *The figures in this unit are black-and-white. On a color monitor, you will see the color palette on the screen instead of the shades of gray boxes as portrayed in the figure.*

Elements of the Paint Window

Paint makes use of the following elements:

- The *workspace* is the area where you will create your drawings.

- The *cursor* indicates where a line or other object will be placed when you start your drawings. The cursor shape differs, depending on the tool that is being used.

- The *toolbox* contains the tools that you use to create drawings. These tools include fill, airbrush, erase, enter text, pencil, and so forth.

- The *palette* contains the colors and patterns available.

- The *line size box* contains the available drawing widths.

Cursor Shapes

Paint uses different cursor shapes, depending on the drawing or editing tool that you are using. Normally, the default tool is the brush.

The cursor shapes represent a box, crosshairs (dotted and filled), ink bottle, eye dropper, magnifying glass, pencil, air can, as well as other shapes depending on the specific drawing tool in use. When you use text, the cursor will appear as an insertion point and an I-beam. You may recall using the I-beam and insertion point in WordPad. The mouse pointer (also called the "arrow") is used as a cursor as well. When you place the mouse outside the drawing area, the pointer resumes its normal arrow shape and is used to select commands and operations.

The Color Palette

Paint normally offers 28 different colors in the palette at the bottom of the screen. On some systems you might see as many as 256 colors or shades of gray. In Paint you will use both a *foreground color* and a *background color*. Choose the foreground color by pointing to the desired color and pressing the left mouse button. Choose the background color by pointing to the desired color and pressing the right mouse button. The foreground color is used for most drawing operations, the background color for backgrounds and some special effects.

Using the Toolbox

Paint uses the toolbox for its drawing *tools*. These tools can be grouped into three categories: graphic, text, and editing. Graphic tools are used for drawing shapes (line, circle, box, brush, and the like). Text tools enable you to add labels to your drawing; text is represented by the "A" icon. The final category, editing tools, permits you to change portions of your drawing. The Free Form Select, Select, and Eraser/Color icons are used to make changes.

Table 8.1 lists the name of the tool, its icon, and a short description of each tool.

TABLE 8.1
Drawing tools

NAME	ICON	DESCRIPTION
Free Form Select		To select an irregularly shaped cutout
Select		To select a rectangular cutout
Brush		To create a "spray paint" effect
Text		To add letters, numbers, and words in various typefaces, sizes, and styles
Eraser/Color Eraser		To change the foreground color to the background color in a portion of the drawing
Air Brush		To fill enclosed areas with the foreground color
Curve		To draw smooth curves
Line		To draw straight lines
Fill with Color		To fill object
Pick color		To select color
Magnifier		To zoom in
Pencil		To do free-form writing
Rectangle		To create a rectangle
Rounded Rectangle		To create rectangles with rounded corners
Ellipse		To create unfilled circles and ellipses
Polygon		To create irregular closed shapes

The Line Size Box

FIGURE 8.2
Line size box

This box allows you to select the width of the line and curve tools, the width of lines, and the size of the border around filled objects. With a mouse, click on the desired tool and the width box will appear (Figure 8.2).

Simple Drawings

FIGURE 8.3
*Freehand
drawing*

To use a graphic tool, click on the tool that you want and move the pointer first to the workspace and then to the position where you want to begin the drawing. If you want to do some freehand drawing, your name for example, select the Pencil tool from the toolbox, move the cursor to the workspace, and begin drawing, as shown in Figure 8.3. With the mouse, press and hold the left button as you "paint" the screen. Your initial efforts may be a bit shaky, but with practice you will soon become more skilled at using the various tools.

Entering Text

To enter Text, click on its icon (the "A" icon), position the cursor in the workspace where you want to begin, and enter the text. Paint allows you to select the Fonts, Size, Bold, Italic, or Underline characteristics of the text by selecting the View command from the menu bar. Mouse to Text Toolbar from the menu. Another dialog box will appear listing the available styles and fonts installed on your computer (Figure 8.4). A sample of the chosen typeface is shown in Figure 8.5. Usually, it is a good idea to choose fonts that have the TrueType symbol next to them (such as Times New Roman in Figure 8.6). This symbol indicates a TrueType font. TrueType fonts give the best results on both screen illustrations and printed output. Clicking the top line evokes the regular style (neither bold nor italic).

FIGURE 8.4
View command

Fonts —

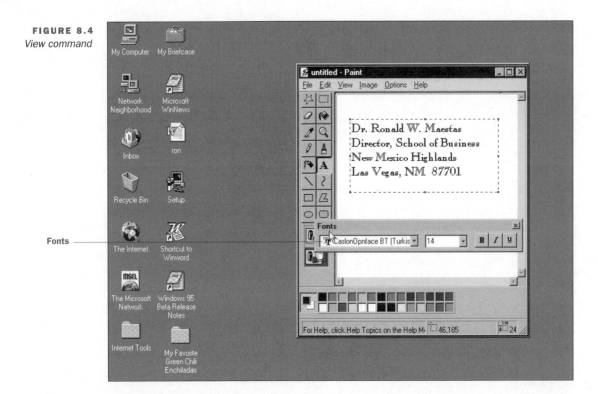

FIGURE 8.5
Sample typeface

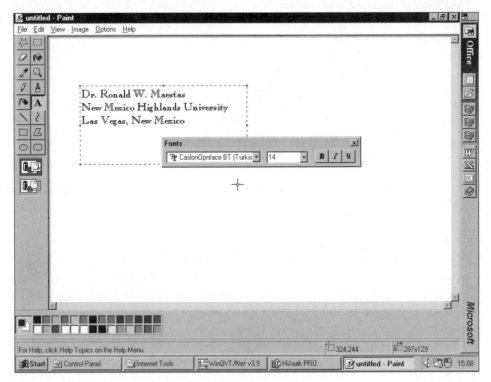

FIGURE 8.6
TrueType fonts

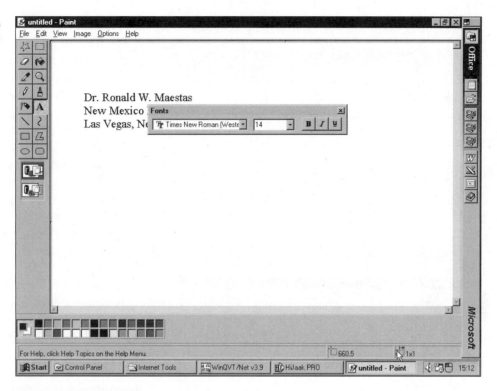

Using Drawing Tools

FIGURE 8.7
Paint toolbox

Before you begin working in the drawing area (workspace), you must select a tool from the toolbox at the left of the Paint window, shown in Figure 8.7. To select a tool, click the mouse button on it.

To draw with the tool you have selected, move the cursor to the drawing area workspace and position it where you want to start drawing. Press the mouse button, and drag around the drawing area. When you are finished with the drawing, release the mouse button.

You can edit any mistakes with the Undo command in the Edit menu or with the Eraser tool in the toolbox. If you are using the keyboard, press [Alt] [Backspace]. You may want to experiment with drawing and editing. It takes some practice to become familiar with the toolbox, as well as with the drawing area. This experience is much like learning to ride a bicycle. After a few falls, you are able to straighten the wheels and enjoy the ride!

Saving Your Work

Work that has been created with Paint can be saved very easily. Use the Save and Save As commands from the File command (Figure 8.8). Use Save As the first time you save the file, and Save for subsequent saves. Save As also allows you to save the file under a different name or format.

FIGURE 8.8
File command

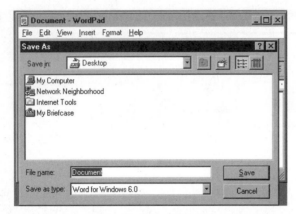

If you select Save As, the File Save As dialog box (Figure 8.9) will appear. You will be prompted to enter a file name or a directory. Save as Type has a list of available formats for saving your work. Figure 8.10 illustrates some of the options that are available when the Save as Type command is selected. These formats support compatibility with other graphics software.

Paint will save each completed drawing as a *.bmp* file (bitmap format is used by many Windows programs). The formats include Monochrome bitmap, 16 Color bitmap, 256 Color bitmap, and 24-bit bitmap. Your instructor may provide you with some additional information regarding the graphic format that you are using. Generally, you will save your work in the *.bmp* file format.

FIGURE 8.9
File Save As dialog box

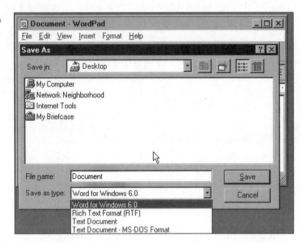

To complete the saving process, click or choose OK. You can, of course, cancel the command prior to your final selection. Remember to select the appropriate drive from the drop-down drive list. A word of caution while saving a drawing to drive A:—since bitmap files are normally quite large, you might not be able to save a file (*.bmp*) on a 360KB disk. You often need a ***high-capacity disk*** with 1.2MB or 1.44MB of disk space.

Exiting Paint

To exit Paint is a very simple process, as with most other Windows GUI programs: select Exit from the File menu as shown in Figure 8.11, or double-click on the control menu on the top left of the desktop.

GUIDED ACTIVITY 8.1

Practicing Fundamental Paint Operations

1. Open Paint from the Programs/Accessories menu.

2. Click on the color black in the color palette at the bottom of the screen. Click on the Pencil tool and move the mouse pointer to the center of the workspace.

FIGURE 8.10
*File Save as
Type options box*

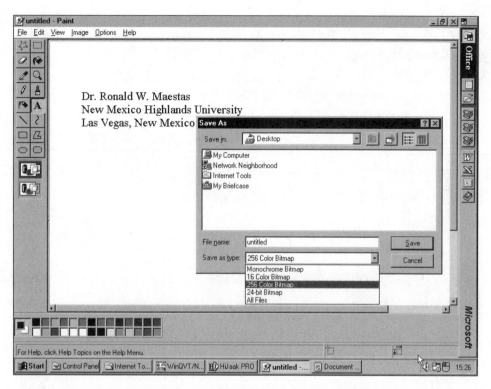

FIGURE 8.11
Exit Paint

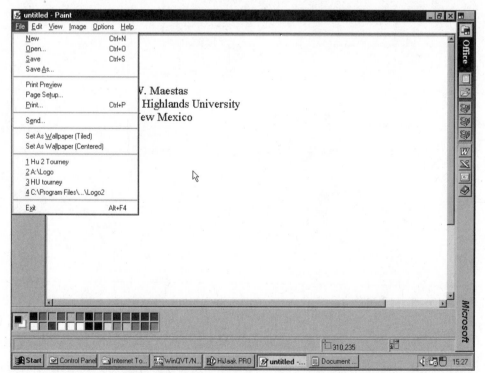

3. Draw some circles by clicking and not releasing the left mouse button and moving the mouse in a circular motion. Release the mouse button when you are finished.

4. Click on the Pencil tool and "write" your name in the workspace.

5. Clear the workspace by clicking on New from the File menu. You will be asked if you want to save changes to untitled, as shown in Figure 8.12; click on No.

FIGURE 8.12
*Save changes
message*

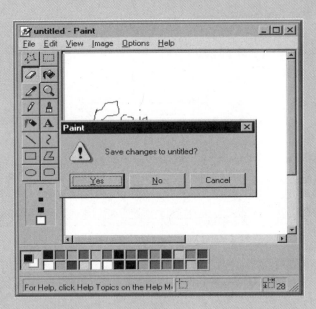

6. Draw a line from the center of the workspace to the top using the Line tool from the toolbox. Notice that it is difficult to draw a perfectly vertical line. Pressing Shift and then dragging the line pointer will give you a straight vertical line. Draw several other lines.

7. Clear the workspace by clicking on Undo from the Edit menu or on New from the File menu.

8. Click on the Rectangle tool from the toolbox. Draw a box by placing the mouse pointer near the upper-left corner of the workspace, dragging it near the lower-right corner, and releasing the mouse button. Make several more rectangles.

9. Experiment with the other tools, such as circle/ellipse and filled shapes. Use Shift to draw perfect circles.

10. Clear the workspace.

11. Click on the Text tool. Click on a spot in the upper-left part of the workspace; choose a font and size, and then enter your name, date, and class.

12. Close Paint by clicking on the Control Menu box and then on Close. Do not save the changes.

Printing a Paint Drawing

Printing a drawing is similar to printing in WordPad. When Paint prints a drawing, it preserves the proportions of the drawing. It maintains squares and circles as they were originally drawn and does not change them to rectangles and ellipses. To print, select or choose the Print command from the File menu; a drop-down dialog box will appear (Figure 8.13).

FIGURE 8.13
Print command

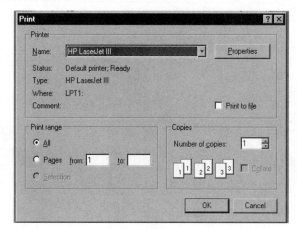

The Print dialog box is used to specify the printer source, the number of copies, range of pages, or From starting page To ending page. In addition, you can specify Print Properties. These properties allow you to select the paper size, orientation (portrait or landscape), graphics resolution, dithering, intensity, and so forth. To complete the print process, choose or click OK. Keep in mind that the quality of the printout will depend on the printers installed on your system and on whether or not you are using a network. You should particularly keep in mind that printing through a Novell network may present some noticeable differences.

The Page Setup command on the File menu is used to change the margins (left, right, top, or bottom) on your drawing. When Page Setup is selected, the Page Setup dialog box will appear as shown in Figure 8.14.

The Printer properties are used to identify the Paper Source, Paper Size, and Orientation of layout—***Portrait*** (taller than wide) or ***Landscape*** (wider than tall).

Paint Wallpaper

To use a picture as the desktop background to cover the screen with repetitions of your bitmap, click the File menu, and then click Set as Wallpaper (Tiled). To put your bitmap in the center of your screen, click the File menu, and then click Set As Wallpaper (Centered).

✎ **NOTE** *You must save a picture before you can use it as wallpaper.*

Other Paint Commands

Windows 95 Paint has additional commands on the menu bar. You will notice the View, Image, and Options commands. View allows you to enable/disable (turn on-off) the Tool Bar, Text Toolbar, Color Box, Status Bar, Zoom, and View Bitmap (Figure 8.15). You may wish to try the effects of these View commands. Image allows you to Flip/Rotate, Stretch/Skew, Invert Colors, and Change Attributes (Figure 8.16). If you

FIGURE 8.14
*Page Setup
dialog box*

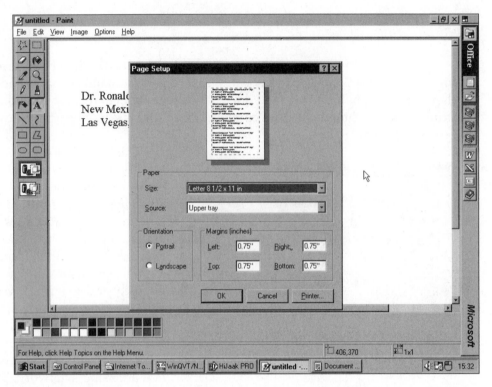

have created a Paint image, you may wish to try each of these commands. You can of course Undo each of the operations prior to saving your document. Finally, Options allow you to Edit Colors, Save Colors, and Draw Opaque (Figure 8.17).

FIGURE 8.15
View command

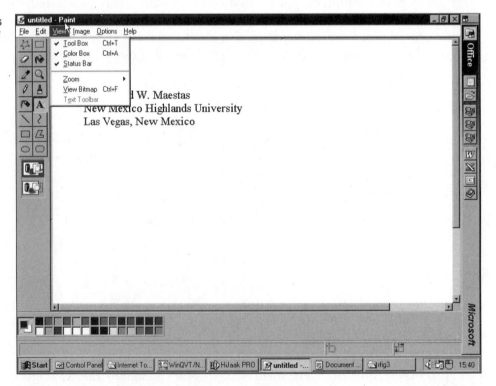

FIGURE 8.16
Image command

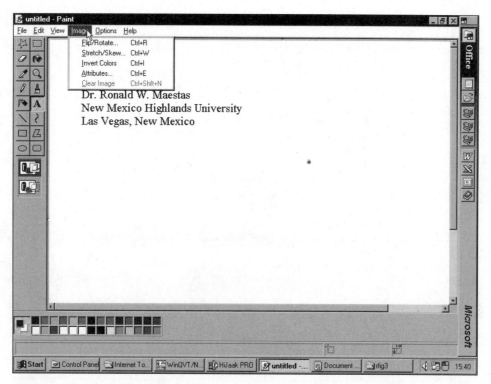

FIGURE 8.17
Options command

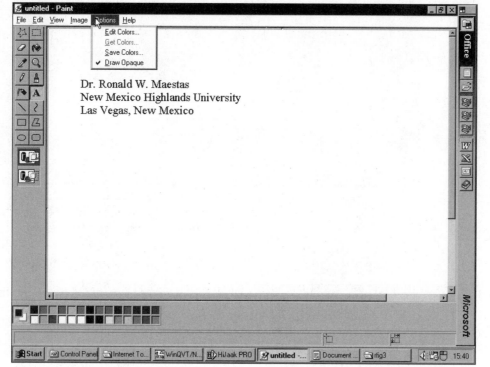

GUIDED ACTIVITY 8.2

Creating, Saving, and Printing a Drawing

1. Open Paint.

2. Maximize the workspace by clicking on the maximize button in the upper-right corner of Paint.

3. Create a sample floor plan for your future "office," using the various tools in the toolbox. Use Figure 8.18 as inspiration. Remember, to use a particular tool, click on that tool, enter the workspace, and begin to "draw."

FIGURE 8.18
Sample floor plan

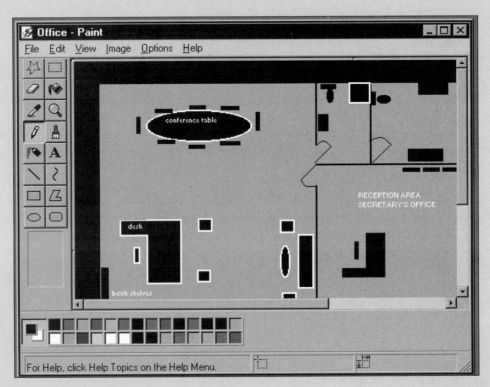

4. Save the file by clicking on File and then on Save As. Click [- a -] under Save In:. The following will appear in the Filename box: untitled. Highlight untitled (*), and then type a name for the drawing, for example FLOORPLN. You should see A:FLOORPLN.BMP in the Filename box; click on Save to save the file.

☞ TIP *When the File Save As dialog box first appears, type A:FLOORPLN and press* Enter.

5. Click on Print from the File menu. Click on OK to print the file.

6. Close Paint.

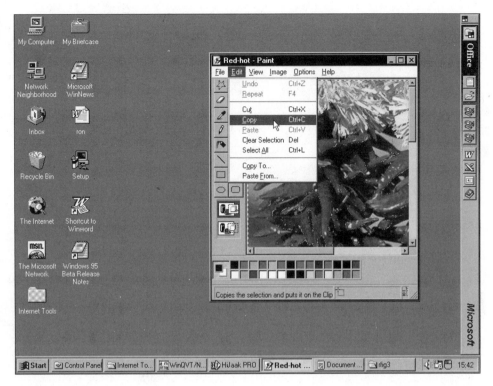

FIGURE 8.19
Edit command

Transferring Artwork

Artwork or diagrams created with Paint can be transferred to a WordPad document and to other word processors, such as Word for Windows 7.0, that are compatible with Windows operations. This process is known as *cut and paste*. While you are in Paint, Open the file containing the work that you want to transfer. Using the Select tool from the toolbox, position the cursor in the upper-left corner of the artwork, drag the mouse pointer to the lower-right corner of the diagram, and release the mouse button. You will see the broken-line outline around the diagram, as shown in Figure 8.18. Select Copy or Cut from the Edit menu shown in Figure 8.19. Normally you would select Copy because you want to leave the original art intact.

Minimize Paint to its button. Open WordPad or Word for Windows 7.0 and select the destination file. Position the mouse pointer at the insertion point (where you want the diagram to appear), and select Paste from the Edit menu.

GUIDED ACTIVITY 8.3

Cutting and Pasting a Diagram to a WordPad Document

1. Open WordPad from the Accessories program group.

2. Type a letter to "Dad" telling him about your new position. Minimize WordPad by clicking on the minimize button in the upper-right corner of the window.

3. Copy the "office" floor plan that you created in Guided Activity 8.2:

   a. Open Paint from the Programs/Accessories menu.

   b. Click on File and then on Open. Double-click on the name of the "office" file that you created in Guided Activity 8.2.

   c. Click on the Select tool from the toolbox. Move to the upper-left corner of the diagram. Click and do not release the mouse button. Drag the pointer to the lower-right corner of the diagram. Release the mouse button. A broken gray box will show the part of the diagram that is marked.

   d. Click on Edit and then on Copy.

   e. Minimize Paint by clicking on the minimize button.

4. Restore WordPad by clicking on its button at the bottom of the dektop. Position the mouse pointer (I-beam) at the point where you want to insert the diagram and click once. Click on Edit and then on Paste.

5. If the diagram that you have just pasted appears too small, you will need to enlarge the picture. Click on the picture. Drag the mouse on a corner sizing handle to enlarge the picture. An outline box will indicate the size of the picture as it is being enlarged. Clicking the mouse button will complete the sizing.

6. Save the file by clicking on File and then on Save. (Remember to choose drive A:.)

7. Click on File and then on Print. Click on OK to print the document with the diagram.

8. Close WordPad and Paint.

Review Questions

*1. Explain the difference between raster and vector graphics.

2. Name the two categories in which images can be grouped. Identify the category of images produced by Paint.

*3. Briefly identify and describe the elements of the Paint window.

4. Give an example of each of the following types of tools: graphic, text, and editing.

*5. What is the major difference between the Copy and Cut commands in Paint?

6. If a mistake is made in Paint, what are the options available to correct the mistake?

*7. Describe the process required to select a tool from the toolbox using the mouse.

8. Review the processes to print and save a drawing and to exit Paint.

9. What is the name of the process that transfers artwork or diagrams created in Paint to a WordPad or Word for Windows document?

Key Terms

Background color	Landscape	Toolbox
Bitmap	Line size box	Tool
Cursor	Palette	Vector graphics
Cut and Paste	Portrait	Workspace
Foreground color	Raster graphics	
High-capacity disk	Scaled	

HyperTerminal

The Microsoft Windows 95 HyperTerminal connects your computer to other computers. Its data communication capability enables you to dial remote sites (whether mainframes or other personal computers) so that you can receive or send files via telephone lines. National databases and online bulletin boards are readily available to personal computer users. With HyperTerminal, you can use your computer to obtain financial investment data from the Dow Jones News/Retrieval service; shop at home with CompuServe; make reservations for air, lodging, or rental car; connect to *Microsoft Network*; use the *Internet* and the *World Wide Web (WWW)*; or send electronic mail with MCI. Other possible business applications for *telecommunications* include order entry, credit checking, inventory control, cash management, administrative messages, and resource management.

Before you can use HyperTerminal, however, you must possess certain hardware. You must have a modem installed in or connected to your computer, and you must have a telephone (analog, not digital) line available. You will not be able to talk on the phone line while the computer is using it (a circumstance that causes great distress to our teenage children).

This unit is designed to give you the basics of HyperTerminal's terminology, concepts, and procedures. If the subject of telecommunications is new to you, you might want to obtain additional reference materials. Because communications capabilities vary so much among organizations, we have not included a Guided Activity in this unit. If your school or organization has the appropriate facilities, your instructor or supervisor will provide you with further instruction on the use of HyperTerminal.

Learning Objectives

At the completion of this unit you should know

1. the anatomy of telecommunications,

2. the purpose and characteristics of a modem,

3. communications protocols,

4. how to start and exit HyperTerminal,

5. how to establish HyperTerminal settings,

6. how to establish communications settings,

7. how to save and retrieve settings,

8. how to dial a call,

9. how to transfer files through a modem using HyperTerminal,

10. how to send and receive files,

11. how to copy and paste received text.

Introduction to HyperTerminal

Telecommunications systems are fast becoming critically important assets to organizations, whether academic or corporate. They can help coordinate the activities of many people in various locations; they can reduce the costs of more traditional methods of communication and routine clerical activities; and they can improve sales through faster and better customer services.

As you probably are aware, we are surfing the "information superhighway." Increasingly, vast amounts of information are readily available through "electronic libraries." In an era when timely information can give a competitive edge, businesses as well as entrepreneurs and the self-employed are relying heavily on telecommunications for their day-to-day operations. The wealth of information available to them is easy for you to access as well, but only if you know where and how to ask for and retrieve it. HyperTerminal provides the means to put this vital information at your fingertips.

Telecommunications Concepts

Before you start working with HyperTerminal, you should be aware of some basic telecommunications concepts and terms regarding both your computer and the remote computer with which you will be communicating. These concepts include: modem, baud rate, data bits, stop bits, parity, and data flow control. When you subscribe to an online service, you will receive the necessary information for these settings. The settings, which will vary from service to service, are often referred to as the *communications protocol*.

Figure 9.1 illustrates a connection made between two computers. A *modem* (short for modulator/demodulator) is a hardware device that converts digital signals (data from the computer) to analog signals (sounds that travel over telephone lines) at the sending end. At the receiving end, analog signals are converted back into digital signals used by HyperTerminals and computers. The digital signal must be modulated (converted) into an analog signal so that it can travel over the phone lines. Many computers have built-in modems instead of the external modems illustrated in Figure 9.1.

FIGURE 9.1
Telecom-munications

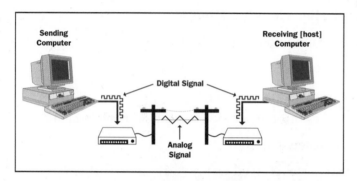

Baud rate is the measure of the speed at which data is sent or received over a telephone line. The higher the rate, the faster the data can be sent. Modems are commonly available in 9600, 14,400, and 28,800 baud. If you try to connect to a 9600-baud modem from a 14,400-baud modem, the 14,400-baud modem will automatically switch to the 9600-baud rate. The transmission speed of a modem in characters per second is estimated by dividing the baud rate by 10; thus, a 9600-baud modem sends approximately 960 characters per second.

Data flows through the modem in a series of ones and zeros (digits). The number of *data bits* equals the number of ones and zeros in each piece of data, such as a single character. Both computer systems must use the same number of data bits. Two choices are available: 7 bits (which represents all the letters of the alphabet, numbers, punctuation marks, and some special symbols), and 8 bits (which is large enough for the entire IBM-PC character set). Both choices include one start bit and one stop bit. The *stop bit* is used as a signal to tell the receiving computer where one character ends and another begins. The most common setting is 8 data bits.

Parity is a method of detecting errors in the data being transmitted. By adding a one or a zero after the data, the telecommunications system alters the total number of ones to an even or odd number. Therefore, the choices for parity checking are Odd, Even, or None. The most common setting when communicating with mainframes and online information services is 7-E-1 (seven data bits, Even parity, and one stop bit). Public bulletin boards (*BBS*) usually operate as 8-N-1 (eight data bits, No parity, and one stop bit).

The *buffer* area is a portion of memory used to hold incoming data until it can be stored on disk. *Data flow control* is designed to notify the remote computer when HyperTerminal's buffer capacity has been reached. HyperTerminal needs to be able to notify the remote system to pause momentarily before sending any more characters;

otherwise, incoming data could be lost while previously received data is being written to a disk file. When HyperTerminal is ready to receive again, it sends another signal to the sending computer. These "pause" and "resume" signals are known as *handshaking*.

Starting HyperTerminal

Hypertrm

To start HyperTerminal, press the Sart button and click on Programs/Accessories. Then click on HyperTerminal (see Figure 9.2). Mouse to the HyperTerminal icon (shown in the margin) and double-click.

FIGURE 9.2
HyperTerminal
screen

HyperTerminal Settings

To set up a new connection, click on the File menu and mouse to New Connection. Type a name that describes the connection, and then click an appropriate icon. Then click OK. Enter the information for the call and then click OK. To dial the call, click Dial.

Calling a Remote Computer

On the File menu, click Open, and then double-click the connection you want to use (Figure 9.2). On the Call menu, click Connect. Click Dial.

Changing the Settings for Making a Call

In the HyperTerminal Connections folder, double-click the connection you want to change. On the File menu, click Properties to activate the Properties box (Figure 9.3). Click the Phone Number tab, and then make the changes you need. To change settings such as the terminal type, click the Settings tab, and then make the changes you need.

To initiate a HyperTerminal session, you must indicate the settings for the remote computer, as well as any other settings you may want to use. You can use the settings from a previous communications session if you saved them in a ***Properties dialog box***. Files are saved with an *.ht* extension. The attributes of the New Connection dialog

FIGURE 9.3
*HyperTerminal
properties*

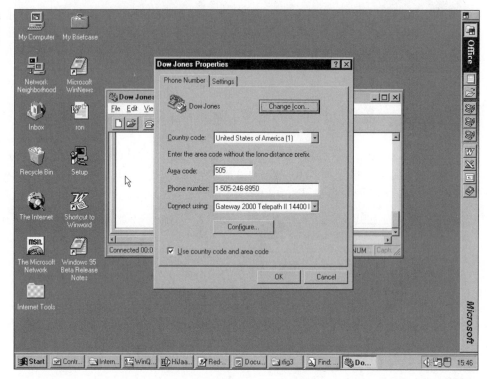

box, shown in Figure 9.4, will become HyperTerminal's settings, which can be recorded in a file. The file is automatically saved when you enter a name for the new connection (for example, DJNR for Dow Jones News/ Retrieval, or perhaps DOW).

FIGURE 9.4
*HyperTerminal
settings*

Phone Number

The first setting is the Phone Number of the computer you want to reach. Select HyperTerminal Properties from the File command (Figure 9.5).

In the Phone Number tab, type the phone number that you want the modem to dial; if appropriate, include a 1 and the area code (for example, 1-505-454-3104). Parentheses or hyphens are not required (they are ignored by HyperTerminal), but you can use them to make the number more readable. Use commas to provide any delays needed by your telephone system. A comma represents approximately a two-second delay. If your organization uses an outside line system, you might need to enter a 9, followed by one or more commas before the phone number (for instance, 9,,1-505-454-3584). If you have "Call Waiting" on your phone, you should disable it by adding *70,, to the beginning of the number. You can also change the Country, Area Code, or Icon from the Phone Number tab.

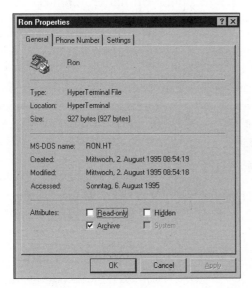

FIGURE 9.5
File command

The other tab is Settings. Use Settings to change terminal emulation, backscroll buffer lines, and so on.

Set the options that appear in the bottom half of the dialog box as necessary. These include: Timeout If Not Connected In (which many users set to 60 seconds), Redial After Timing Out, and Signal When Connected. To complete the Phone Number setting, click or choose OK.

HyperTerminal Emulation

The HyperTerminal Emulation setting is designed to reflect the type of Hyper-Terminal that the remote computer expects. Information on HyperTerminal type is available from the online service to which you are connecting. To select the type of Hyper-Terminal, right-click or choose HyperTerminal Properties from the File menu. Mouse to the Settings tab (Figure 9.6).

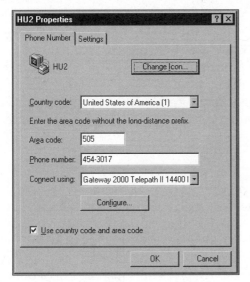

FIGURE 9.6
Settings tab

The HyperTerminal types appear in the Emulation drop-down list in the dialog box. The choices for HyperTerminal type include Auto Detect, TTY , VT-100, Minitel, View Data, and VT-52. The default HyperTerminal type depends on which modem is installed, as detected by Windows 95. It varies with the user. To change the HyperTerminal type, place the cursor on the HyperTerminal of your choice, and click the mouse button. If you are not sure which HyperTerminal type to use, select TTY.

HyperTerminal Preference

The HyperTerminal Preference setting contains several choices that affect how your computer will respond during a communications session. These choices include

HyperTerminal Modes, Translation, Columns, Cursor, HyperTerminal Font, CR to CR/LF, Show Scroll Bars, and Buffer Lines.

When you are finished selecting the HyperTerminal Preference settings, click or choose OK.

Communications Protocol

Setting the Communications protocol will determine how your data files are packaged and sent over the telephone line. The telephone line must be an analog line. (Some parts of the country, especially downtown business districts, are being converted to digital phone services. Most personal lines are still analog.) Ask your instructor or laboratory supervisor whether your local telephone system will accommodate telecommunications using HyperTerminal.

FIGURE 9.7
Configure

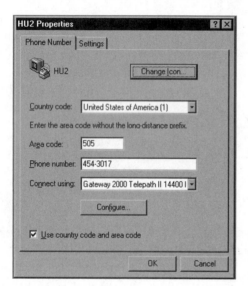

To change the port settings for a modem connection in the HyperTerminal Connections folder, double-click the connection you want to change. On the File menu, click Properties. Click the Phone Number tab, and then click Configure (Figure 9.7). Click the Connection tab, and then make the changes you need. To change settings such as flow control and error correction, click Advanced, and then make the changes you need. The changes that you make to the port settings affect only this connection.

The Connection tab contains the choices for Connection and Call Preferences where you can set Data Bits, Stop Bits, Parity, Flow Control (Hardware RTS/CTS or Software XON/XOFF), and Modulation type.

You can make the appropriate communications setting changes for your computer, as well as the remote computer. When you are finished, select or choose OK.

Modem

The Modem Commands dialog box tells HyperTerminal what signals it needs to initiate a call, as well as how to receive a call, dial the telephone, and hang up the telephone. The default settings for the modem depend on the system you are using. For example, this book was prepared on a Gateway 2000 computer with a Telepath II 14,400 baud internal modem. Check with your instructor or laboratory system's supervisor to determine if another type of modem is installed in or onto your computer and what settings it requires.

Saving and Retrieving HyperTerminal Settings Files

After you have entered settings, you can save the *settings file* using the File menu (Figure 9.8). Saving a file in Hyper-Terminal is done the same way you save files in other Windows applications.

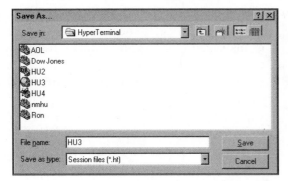

You can select Save or Save As, and type the file name. HyperTerminal will automatically add the *.ht* extension. The selections that you made in the Settings menu are now saved in a file. You are ready to dial a call.

Dialing a Call

Once you have established your communications protocol (settings), you can initiate a call to a remote system. To initiate a call, click on Open from the File menu and then double-click the connection you want to use (HUVAX). From the Call menu, mouse to Connect and then click on Dial. If you have not established or retrieved a settings file, you can still initiate a call by choosing Dial from the Call menu. You will be prompted to enter the telephone number, as shown in Figure 9.9. To proceed with the call, choose Dial.

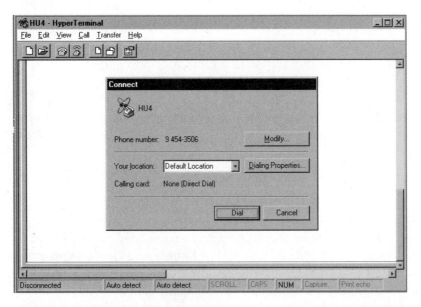

While HyperTerminal is dialing and awaiting an answer, your screen will appear as in Figure 9.10. The phone number that you have dialed and the time remaining in seconds (until HyperTerminal stops waiting for an answer) appear in the Hyper-Terminal application window.

When the remote system that you are calling receives your call, the message box will disappear. If the system does not answer, HyperTerminal leaves the line open for the amount of time you specified in the Phone Number dialog box. Once the time has lapsed, the phone hangs up. You can cancel the call at any time before it is answered by choosing Cancel. If for some reason your hardware is not properly installed, you will get an error message in the HyperTerminal dialog box. Check with your instructor or laboratory system supervisor for help. You may also need to refer to the User's Guide for equipment setup instructions.

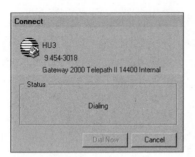

FIGURE 9.10
HyperTerminal waiting screen

Logging On to a Remote System

Once the call is answered by the remote system, you must perform a *log-on* procedure to verify to the system that you are a legitimate user and that you have access to some or all of the system's features. Log-on procedures vary substantially from one system to another. At a college or university, your instructor will tell you how to log on. If you subscribe to a commercial service such as America Online, Prodigy, CompuServe, or the Microsoft Network, your membership packet will include log-on instructions for various locations. The remainder of this unit deals with procedures performed after you have logged on to the remote system.

Communicating with a Remote System

In some cases, you will log on to a remote system and interact directly with the system to learn about cyberspace, weather, football scores, or stock trading. Most of these systems provide a menu of choices from which to choose, sending the results to you as plain text. The text received from the remote computer and your responses are kept in a buffer in your computer that can be copied to the *Clipboard*, pasted into WordPad or another Windows application, or saved as a file.

Transferring Files

When you have connected to the remote computer, you can send or receive *text files* (such as unformatted documents) or *binary files* (such as programs or formatted documents). However, before you can send or receive files, you have to indicate the manner in which the transfer will be accomplished.

Text files prepared with a word processor (such as WordPad or Word) should be saved to the disk as unformatted. Unformatted text is saved as an *ASCII* file and contains both printable ASCII characters and control codes, such as carriage returns and line feeds. Binary files consist of ASCII characters plus the IBM-PC extended-character set.

The two methods of transfer—text and binary—differ in some ways. It is best to send *both* text and binary files in binary, because binary transfers check for errors and loss of data. If, however, you do not need to send formatting codes and are not concerned about loss of data, text transfer is faster. Some systems will not accept binary file transfers, and you can only use the text file mode in such cases.

Sending Files

To send a file to a remote computer, prepare the file transfer software on the remote computer to receive the file, if necessary. On the Transfer menu (Figure 9.11), click Send File. In the Filename box, type the path and name of the file. To change the protocol you will use to send the file, use the Protocol box to select it. To send the file, click Send. In most cases, you also need to prepare the remote computer's file transfer software to receive the file. For more information, contact the remote computer's administrator.

You can also send a text file to the remote computer by clicking Send Text File on the Transfer menu.

Receiving Files

To receive a file from a remote computer, use the software on the remote computer to send (download) the file to your computer. On the Transfer menu, click Receive File (Figure 9.12). Type the path of the folder in which you want to store the

FIGURE 9.11
Transfer menu

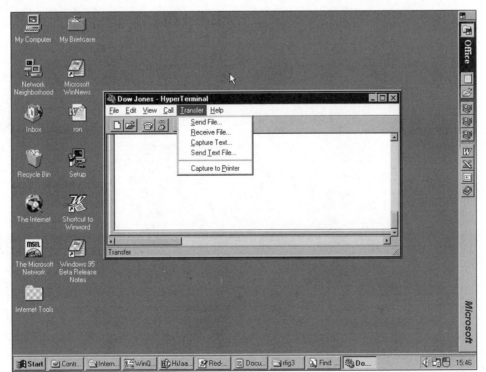

FIGURE 9.12
Receive File

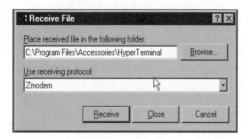

file. In the Use Receiving Protocol box, click the protocol the remote computer is using to send your file.

Copying Text to the Clipboard

You can use the Edit menu, as shown in Figure 9.13, to modify the contents in the HyperTerminal window. You can save or print the contents of a file that has been received. Once you save the text, you can cut and paste any of it into a WordPad or Word document file. To do this, select (highlight) the text that you want to copy and select Copy from the Edit menu. The selected copy is placed in the Clipboard, from which you can insert it in a new position or file in either WordPad or Word.

FIGURE 9.13
Edit command

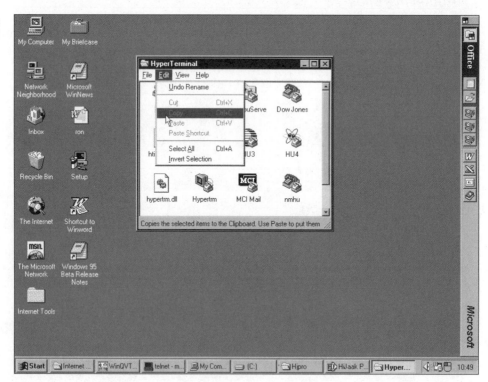

HyperTerminal Problems[1]

HyperTerminal troubleshooter (located in Help) will help you identify and solve modem problems. Problems that may arise when using HyperTerminal may include the following:

- I don't know how to install my modem.
- Dialing doesn't work correctly.
- The wrong number is being dialed.
- I can't make a local call to a different area code.
- I can't make a long-distance call to the same area code.
- I can't connect to another computer, or the connection doesn't work properly.
- Does your telephone line have Call Waiting?
- Can't transfer a file to or from another computer.
- Dial-Up Networking doesn't work correctly.
- Cannot connect to the remote computer; the remote computer hangs up right after answering the phone.
- The remote computer hangs up unexpectedly.
- I get a different message.
- I can't dial international calls.

Review Questions

*1. Explain each of the following terms:

a. modem

b. baud rate

c. data bits

d. stop bits

e. parity

f. data flow control

g. handshaking

2. Summarize the steps (commands) used to create a new settings file. What is (are) the command(s) required to use an established settings file?

---

1 Adapted from the online help for the Windows programs. Portions of the following are Copyright © 1990–1995 by Microsoft Corporation.

3.   Describe the process to enter the phone number 427-1234 (in area code 206). Assume that you are calling from an office at work that requires a "9" to gain access to an outside line.

*4.   What does the HyperTerminal Emulation setting do? If you are not sure which HyperTerminal type to use, which type should you select?

*5.   State what communications settings and modem settings accomplish.

6.   What must be established before a call can be placed using HyperTerminal? What is (are) the command(s) to place a call? How long does it take Hyper-Terminal to hang up the phone if the remote system does not answer?

7.   What types of files can be sent and received using HyperTerminal? What are the differences between the different types?

Key Terms

ASCII	Data flow control	Properties dialog box
Baud rate	Handshaking	Settings file
BBS	Internet	SLIPP
Binary file	Log-on	Stop bit
Buffer	Microsoft Network	Telecommunications
Clipboard	Modem	Text file
Communications protocol	Parity	World Wide Web (WWW)
Data bit	PPP	

Other Windows Accessory Programs

In previous units, you have been working with Windows' primary applications. As you recall, Windows allows you to arrange your electronic "desktop" in very much the same way you organize your desk at work. The items you can use on your windows desktop are Fax, Calculator, Multimedia, System Tools, Notepad, and Phone Dialer.

In this unit, we will discuss how to use most of these additional Windows accessories.

Learning Objectives

At the completion of this unit you should know

1. the features available in Windows Accessories applications,

2. how to start and close Calculator,

3. how to perform calculations with Calculator,

4. how to start and close Multimedia,

5. how to start and close System Tools,

6. how to open and close Notepad,

7. how to enter text in Notepad,

8. how to start and close Phone Dialer,

9. how to start other accessory programs.

FIGURE 10.1
Start button

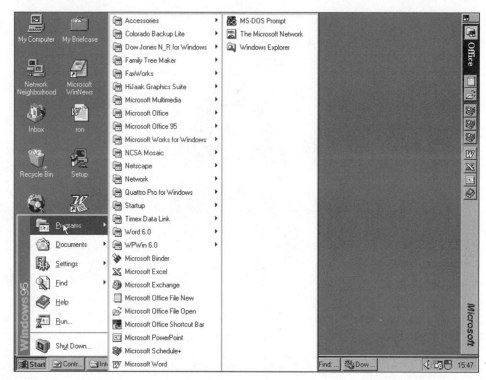

Calculator

Calculator

Windows Calculator is an electronic calculator that includes a standard 10-key calculator as well as a scientific calculator. Calculations derived from Calculator can be transferred into any Windows applications program (Word, WordPad, Excel, and so on) by using the Clipboard. The Calculator icon is shown to the left.

Starting Calculator

FIGURE 10.2
Calculator

Calculator can be started from the Programs/Accessories menu window. Remember, to open Accessories you will need to go through the Start button, shown in Figure 10.1. From the Accessories, click on the Calculator selection.

Calculator will appear as in Figure 10.2. By choosing View from the Calculator menu (Figure 10.3), you can switch from the scientific calculator to a standard calculator (Figure 10.4).

FIGURE 10.3
View command

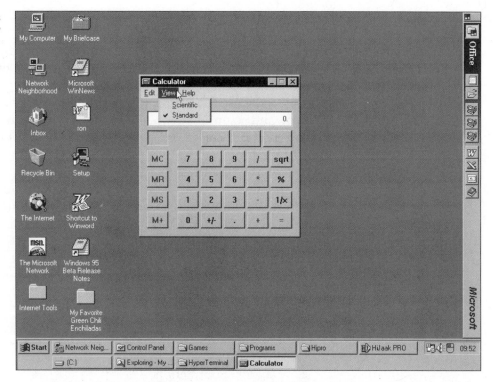

The first time Calculator is started, the standard mode will appear. When Calculator is started again, the last calculator mode that was used will appear. Calculator's window cannot be resized, but can be minimized to the taskbar. The icon will appear at the bottom of the screen and is available to you when you want to perform calculations.

FIGURE 10.4
Standard calculator

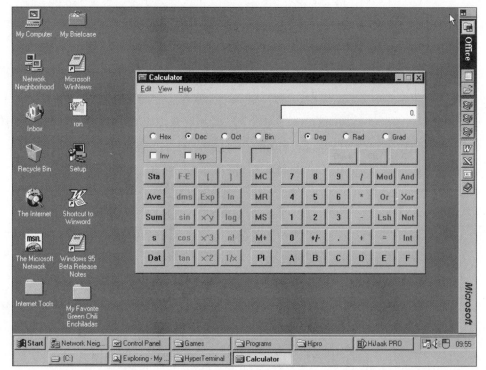

Performing Calculations

Calculator is best operated with a mouse, and therefore is slower than using a pocket calculator. Using a mouse, point to a Calculator button and click the mouse.

To perform calculations, click on the first number in the calculation. The number will appear in the display area of Calculator. Select the operator (addition, subtraction, multiplication, division, and so on) that you want in the calculation. Enter the next number in the calculation. If you make a mistake entering either number, you can click on the Back key or the CE (Clear Entry) button to clear the entry. Finally, click on the equal sign key (=) to complete the calculation.

Calculator uses its own memory to store a value or provide an answer for future use. The MR key displays the value stored in memory; MC clears any value stored in memory; MS stores the displayed value in memory, while M+ adds the displayed value to any value currently stored in Calculator's memory. If you are using Calculator's memory function, an "M" will appear in the box directly above the MC key. The following table describes each key on the standard calculator, its keyboard equivalent, and its function:

Button	*Keystroke*	*Function*
+	+	Addition
−	−	Subtraction
*	*	Multiplication
/	/	Division
sqrt	@	Square root of displayed value
%	%	Percentage
1/x	[R]	Reciprocal of displayed value
=	= or [Enter]	Performs the operation between two numbers
+/−	[F9]	Changes the sign of displayed value
.	. or ,	Inserts a decimal point in displayed value
BACK	[Backspace] or [←]	Deletes the right-most digit of displayed value
CE	[Del]	Clears the displayed value
C	[Esc]	Clears the calculation
MC	[Ctrl][L]	Clears the value stored in memory
MR	[Ctrl][R]	Displays the value stored in memory
MS	[Ctrl][M]	Stores the value in memory
M+	[Ctrl][P]	Adds the displayed value to the value stored in memory

The scientific calculator is capable of doing simple programming calculations. In addition, it can be used for exponential and logarithmic operations; calculations in binary, octal, and hexadecimal number systems; and trigonometric calculations. Its statistics window calculates sum, average, and standard deviation, as discussed later in this unit.

GUIDED ACTIVITY 10.1

Using Calculator

1. Select Accessories from the Program menu.

2. Click on the Calculator icon to open it. You should use the standard calculator. If the scientific calculator is present, switch to the standard calculator by clicking on View and then on Standard.

3. Perform the following calculation by clicking on the specific keys. If you make a mistake, choose Back to correct a few digits, or click on CE to clear the entire number.

    2 * 3 + 4

    Press Enter or click on = to get the answer. Your answer should be 10. Click on C to clear the equation.

4. Perform the following calculation:

    3 + 3 * 2

    Your answer should be 12. Press Esc or click on C to clear the equation.

5. Calculate the following percentage:

    400 * 25%

    Your answer should be 100. Clear the equation.

6. Click on View and then on Scientific to switch the standard calculator to scientific. Calculate the sine of 5 by clicking on 5 and then on Sin. Your answer should be .08715574274766.

7. Minimize Calculator to an icon by clicking on its minimize button in the upper-right corner of the calculator. The calculator should now appear as an icon button in the lower portion of the desktop.

8. Close Calculator by clicking on the Calculator button to bring the calculator into view, click on its icon, and then on Close when its Control menu appears.

Using a Statistics Window

To calculate sums, averages, and standard deviation for groups of numbers, click on the Sta button. The **Statistics Box** will appear, as illustrated in Figure 10.5, superimposed on the scientific calculator. The dialog box is used to record and delete the

FIGURE 10.5
*Statistics
dialog box*

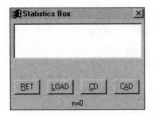

numbers you have entered. Use the mouse or the Move command from the Control menu to move the box to the side so that you can view both it and the calculator. You can switch from one active area to the other as you enter data and compute results. Do this with the mouse by clicking on the one you want.

To perform a statistical calculation:

1. Choose Sta. The Statistics dialog box will appear, as discussed above.

2. Enter the first value in the set. If you click Calculator buttons with the mouse, the focus returns to Calculator and the value appears in the display area. If you are using the keyboard, press [Alt][R] (for the RET button) before entering the number.

3. Choose Dat or press [Ins] to enter the value in the Statistics Box. You will see the value displayed.

4. Enter the remaining numbers in the set, choosing Dat (or pressing [Ins]) each time to enter the number in the Statistics Box.

5. Use the Statistics Box buttons to edit the data set. Click on the Statistics Box or press [Ctrl][S]. The last-entered number will be highlighted. Use the arrow keys to select a different number. The buttons have the following effect:

Button	Keyboard	Function
RET	[Alt][R]	("Return to calculator") Switches to the main calculator and retains the Statistics Box entries
LOAD	[Alt][L]	("Load this number into the calculator") Copies the selected number in the Statistics Box to the calculator display
CD	[Alt][C]	("Clear datum") Deletes the selected number from the Statistics Box
CAD	[Alt][A]	("Clear all data") Deletes all numbers from the Statistics Box

6. When all numbers have been entered into the Statistics Box, you can perform the following calculations:

Statistic	Mouse Action	Keyboard
Sum	Click the Sum button	[Ctrl][T]
Sum of Squares	Click Inv, Sum	[I], [Ctrl][T]
Mean	Click Ave	[Ctrl][A]
Mean of Squares	Click Inv, Ave	[I], [Ctrl][A]

Statistic	Mouse Action	Keyboard
Standard Deviation (sample)	Click s	[Ctrl][D]
Standard Deviation–3 (population)	Click Inv, s	[I], [Ctrl][D]

GUIDED ACTIVITY 10.2

Doing Statistics

1. Open Calculator and put it into Scientific mode. Open the statistics window by clicking on Sta.

2. Move the Statistics Box to another part of the screen so that it does not overlap the Calculator, by placing the mouse pointer in the title box and dragging it to a new location.

3. Activate the calculator by clicking on its window.

4. Enter the following test scores: 55, 87, 99, 100, 75. Use the following procedure:

   a. Enter a number.

   b. Click the Dat button. Notice that the number is displayed in the Statistics Box.

   c. Repeat steps a and b for each number.

5. After you have entered all test scores, calculate the following:

   a. Sum: Click the Sum button. (Answer: 416)

   b. Sum of Squares: Click Inv, Sum. (Answer: 36020)

   c. Mean: Click Ave. (Answer: 83.2)

   d. Mean of Squares: Click Inv, Ave. (Answer: 7204)

   e. Sample standard deviation: Click s. (Answer: 18.76699230031)

   f. Population standard deviation: Click Inv, s. (Answer:16.78570820669)

6. Minimize Calculator to its icon.

Copying Calculator Results to the Clipboard

The result of a calculation can be copied to the Clipboard for use in a spreadsheet or word processing document. Simply choose Copy from the Edit menu. The result can then be pasted into another application. (That is how we transferred the precise results of the Guided Activities into the Word for Windows document that became this unit.) Similarly, a number from a spreadsheet or document can be copied to the Clipboard in that application and then pasted into the Calculator display window.

Closing Calculator

When you are finished using Calculator, minimize it to the taskbar. As mentioned earlier in this unit, you cannot resize a Calculator window; you can only minimize it to the taskbar. When you have minimized Calculator to the taskbar, the icon will appear at the bottom of the screen. To close the Calculator, click once on the icon; Calculator's dialog box will appear. Select Close to finish working with Calculator for this session.

A second method is available to close Calculator. Click once on Calculator's Control menu box. From the menu that appears, as shown in Figure 10.6, select Close. The keyboard combination Alt F4 is another fast and easy way to close Calculator.

FIGURE 10.6
Control menu box

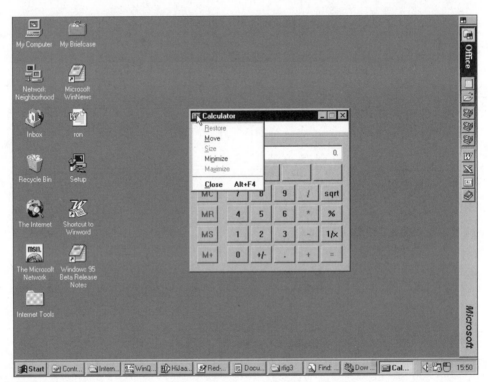

GUIDED ACTIVITY 10.3

Closing the Calculator

1. If Calculator is not minimized, click on the Control Menu box (upper-left corner) and then on Close.

2. If Calculator has been minimized to its button at the bottom of the desktop, click on the button, and then click on its icon. The Control menu will appear; click on Close.

Notepad

Notepad

Notepad is included in the Accessories program. Notepad is different from WordPad. Notepad is intended for brief notes, whereas WordPad is intended as a basic word processor.

FIGURE 10.7
Notepad

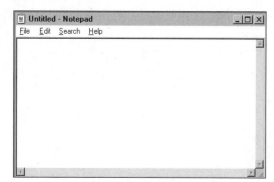

To start Notepad, mouse to Notepad. Remember, the Notepad icon must be highlighted to perform this procedure. The Notepad window (untitled) will appear as in Figure 10.7.

Entering Text

Text that you enter will start at the upper-left corner (insertion point) of the Notepad window. Text can be entered directly in the Notepad window. If you are entering long sentences or paragraphs, check Word Wrap. This option automatically wraps text to the next line when you reach the right border of the window. Word Wrap can be set from the Edit menu shown in Figure 10.8. Word Wrap remains on until you execute the command again—toggle it on, toggle it off.

FIGURE 10.8
Edit menu

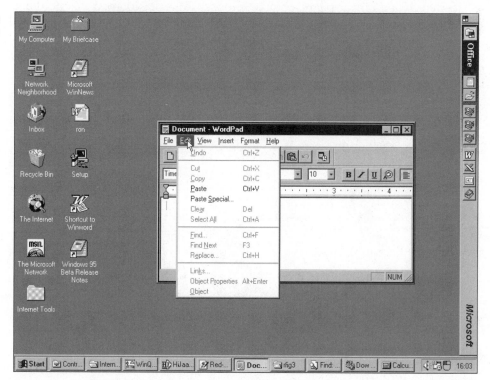

FIGURE 10.9
*Control
menu box*

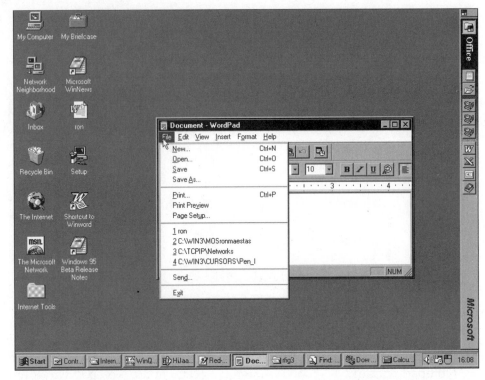

Closing Notepad

If Notepad has been minimized to the taskbar, single-click its button at the bottom of the screen. Single-click on the icon to get the Control menu box. When the drop-down dialog box appears, click or choose Close. If Notepad has not been minimized, single-click the Control menu box. Choose Close. You can also close the file by selecting Exit from the File menu, as shown in Figure 10.9.

GUIDED ACTIVITY 10.4

Writing in Notepad

1. Open Notepad from the Accessories group in Programs.

2. Type the following text. *Do not press* Enter after each line; instead, enter the text as a single long line.

   ```
   Notes from Dr. Maestas's Information Analysis Class July
   16, 1994. Topic: Systems Development Life Cycle, review
   each step.
   ```

3. The notes will be hard to read because the lines extend beyond the right edge of the screen, so click on Word Wrap in the Edit menu. The text will fit within the borders of the window, and you will be able to read it.

4. The cursor will rest at the beginning of the document. For practice, check to make sure you typed the word systems. To search for the word, click on Find in the Search menu. Enter the word systems in the Find What box. Click on Find Next. You will see the word highlighted in Notepad. Close the dialog box.

5. Click on Print in the File menu to print the document.

6. Click on Save As in the File menu to save the document. Type NOTES in the Filename box. Be sure that you save the file on your data disk. Click on Save to complete the process.

7. Click on Exit in the File menu to leave Notepad.

Creating a Time Log File

By entering .LOG in capital letters at the beginning of a Notepad file, as shown in Figure 10.10, you can create a log to keep track of how you spend your time. When you open this file again, Notepad automatically adds the current time and date to the end of the file. You can keep a log of how you spend your day by entering notes after each time and date.

FIGURE 10.10
Time log file

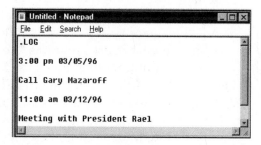

GUIDED ACTIVITY 10.5

Creating a Time Log File

1. Start Notepad.

2. In the empty Notepad window, type .LOG.

3. Click on Save As in the File menu and give the file name TIMELOG. Remember to save the file on your data disk.

4. Click on Open in the File menu to reopen the file you just saved. Below the word .LOG, you will see the current date and time.

5. Below the date and time stamp, type a list of tasks that you will perform today. For example, enter your class, study periods, work schedule, or any important appointments for the day.

6. Save the file again. Click on Save in the File menu. Click on Exit in the File menu to leave Notepad.

7. When you are finished with your tasks, start Notepad again and open your file. Notepad places the current date and time at the end of the file. You can now subtract the first time from the second to determine the amount of time you spent on this task.

8. Save the file again.

9. Close Notepad.

Other Windows 95 Accessories

Multimedia

Multimedia (its icon is shown in the margin) adds the capabilities of audio to the primarily visual world of Windows. You must have special hardware attached to your system that allows the recording and playback of specially coded sound files. With the right hardware, you can add your own voice or a measure from your favorite symphony to a Windows document. Most computers these days are equipped with CD-ROM drives that allow you to take advantage of your CD music collection. To start Multimedia, select Programs/Accessories from the Start button, then mouse to Multimedia (Figure 10.11). Multimedia contains CD Player, Media Player, Sound Recorder, and Volume Control (Figure 10.12). To play a CD, make sure the CD is in the CD-ROM drive, and then click the right-pointing triangle (Figure 10.13). To stop playing your CD, click the box. To eject your CD from the drive, click the up arrow icon. If you want to specify individual tracks to play, you can create a Play List. Your CD continues to play even if you minimize CD Player.

FIGURE 10.11
Accessories

FIGURE 10.12
Volume control

FIGURE 10.13
Play CD

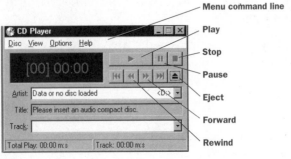

Microsoft Fax

Windows comes with a fax program you can use to send and receive faxes directly within Windows.

Microsoft **Fax** enables you to send and receive fax messages. You can also send faxes directly from programs you create them in, such as Microsoft Word. Fax messages appear in Microsoft Exchange, where you can view them online or print them. Microsoft Exchange provides you a universal in-box that you can use to send and receive electronic mail (**E-mail**). In addition, you can use the in-box to organize, access, and share all types of items from online services. To start Microsoft Exchange, double-click the Inbox icon on your desktop. If the Inbox icon is not on the desktop, you will need to install it. To open Microsoft Exchange to send or receive a fax, double-click the Inbox icon on your desktop. If the Inbox icon is not on your desktop, then Microsoft Exchange is not installed. You must install both Microsoft Exchange and Microsoft Fax to send and receive fax messages. For information on how to use Microsoft Fax, click the Help menu in Microsoft Exchange, and then click Microsoft Fax Help Topics.

Customizing CD Player

To customize CD Player, click the View menu (Figure 10.14), and then click the settings you want.

To specify preferences, click the Options menu, and then click Preferences. For Help on an item, click the **?** at the top of the dialog box, and then click the item.

FIGURE 10.14
View menu

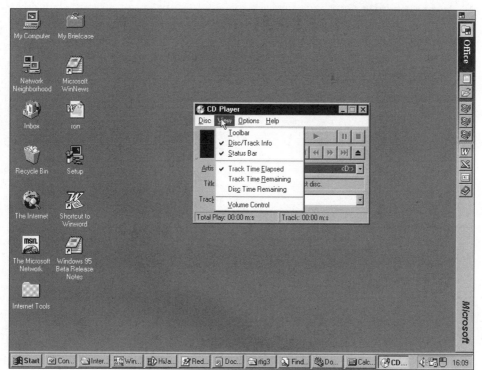

Specifying Which Tracks to Play and in Which Order

Make sure your CD is in the drive. On the Disc menu, click Edit Play List. Specify the artist's name and the title of your CD. In the Available Tracks box, click the track you want to add as the first track in your Play List, and then click Add. Repeat this procedure for each track you want to add to the Play List.

To clear the default Play List, click Clear All. To remove a track on the Play List, click the track, and then click Remove. If you click Reset, the Play List matches the contents of the Available Tracks box.

Storing the Track Titles of Your CD

Make sure your CD is in the drive. On the Disc menu, click Edit Play List. Specify the artist's name and the title of your CD. In the Available Tracks box, click the track whose name you want to store. In the Track box, type the title of the track, and then click Set Name. You can specify which tracks should be played and in which order by modifying the Play List.

Media Player

The Media Player accessory gives you the opportunity to utilize video, sound, MIDI Sequence, and CD Audio with your documents. To start Media Player, click on the Start button, mouse to Accessories, and select Multimedia (Figure 10.15). Multimedia is the third option from this menu. To play a multimedia file, select the Device

FIGURE 10.15
Multimedia

FIGURE 10.16
Device command

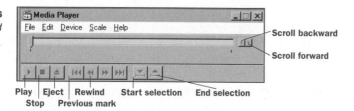

command (Figure 10.16) from the menu and click the device you want. For example, if you select Sound, double-click the file you want to play and click the right arrow to play the multimedia file. File types for sound include: Chimes, Chord, Ding, Tada, or The Microsoft Sound. You will notice the *.wav* extension for each of these files. Of course, you could add additional *.wav* files to use other sounds.

To play a portion of a multimedia file, click at the starting point, click End Selection to end the selection, and then click Play. Windows includes some sample multimedia files in the Media folder.

Sound Recorder

To play a sound, click Open on the File menu (Figure 10.17). Open the folder containing the sound file you want to play, and then click Open. Windows usually places sound files (*.wav*) in the Media folder. You can start playing the sound or stop playing the sound. You can move to the beginning or move to the end.

FIGURE 10.17
File menu

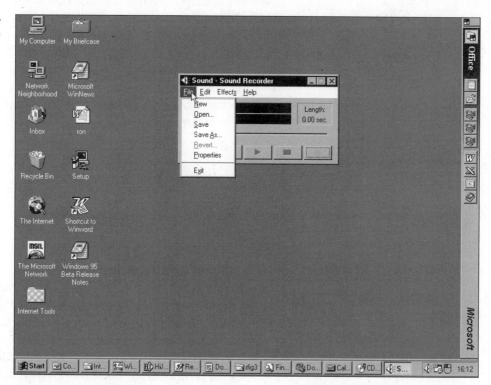

Volume Control

To adjust the playback volume, drag the Volume Control (Figure 10.18) slider up to raise the volume and down to lower it. To change the balance between the left and right speakers, drag the Balance slider. If your computer has more than one device (for example, a **MIDI** or **Wave device**), you can set the volume for each device.

FIGURE 10.18
Volume control

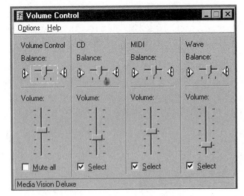

To adjust the recording volume on the Options menu, click Properties, and then click Recording. Make sure the device you want to adjust the volume for is checked, and then click OK. Drag the Volume Control slider up to raise the volume and down to lower it. To change the balance between the left and right speakers, drag the Balance slider. To turn off sound in the Volume Control area, click Mute All.

System Tools

FIGURE 10.19
System tools

The System Tools accessory (Figure 10.19) can be used to back up files and folders, rearrange files and any unused space on your hard disk, compress both hard and floppy disks to create more free space for files, check your hard disk for logical and physical errors and repair the damaged areas, or see what is currently using resources on your computer. The system tools include Disk Defragmenter, DriveSpace, Inbox Repair Tool, ScanDisk, and WinBug.

Disk Defragmenter

To speed up your hard disk by using **Disk Defragmenter**, click on the shortcut in Help to start Disk Defragmenter (Figure 10.20). Click the drive you want to defragment, and then click OK. If you want to change the settings that Disk Defragmenter uses, click Advanced. Click Start. While Windows defragments your disk, you can safely use your computer to carry out other tasks. However, your computer will operate more slowly. To temporarily stop Disk Defragmenter so that you can run other programs at full speed, click Pause.

FIGURE 10.20
*Disk
Defragmenter*

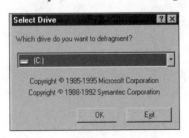

DriveSpace

Using DriveSpace increases disk space. You can use DriveSpace to compress both hard and floppy disks to create more free space for files. You can also use it to configure disk drives that you have already compressed by using DoubleSpace or DriveSpace. To start DriveSpace (Figure 10.21), click on the shortcut in Help or select System Tools in Accessories. A compressed drive is not a real disk drive, although it appears that way to Windows and your programs. The contents of a compressed drive are stored in a single file, called a compressed volume file (*CVF*), which is located on an uncompressed drive, called a *host drive*. For example, suppose you want to compress your hard disk, drive C. The first thing DriveSpace does is assign a different drive letter to your disk, such as H:. Drive H: will be the host for drive C:. DriveSpace then compresses the contents of your hard disk into a compressed volume file stored on drive H:. To Windows and your programs, the compressed volume file on drive H: will appear to be your original drive C:, but drive C: will magically have more free space than it originally had.

FIGURE 10.21
DriveSpace

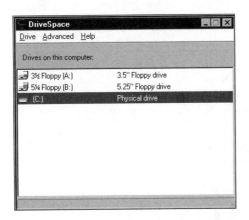

When you view the contents of your computer by using My Computer or Windows Explorer, the host drive is hidden unless it contains more than 2MB of free space. If it contains more than 2MB of free space, it will be visible and you can work with it as you would any other drive. In addition to compressing the contents of an entire drive, DriveSpace can use the free space on an uncompressed drive to create a new, empty compressed drive. For example, instead of compressing drive C:, you could use 10MB of the free space on drive C: to create a new drive, drive G:. Drive G: will contain approximately 20MB of free space.

DriveSpace for Windows supports drives that were compressed using Double-Space (which was included in MS-DOS versions 6.0 and 6.2) as well as DriveSpace for MS-DOS (which was included in MS-DOS version 6.22). You can use DriveSpace and DoubleSpace drives interchangeably. For example, you can use floppy disks that were compressed using either DoubleSpace or DriveSpace. However, such floppy disks can be used only in computers that have DriveSpace for Windows or Double-Space installed.

If you have drives that were compressed using either DoubleSpace or DriveSpace, you can configure them by using DriveSpace for Windows.

To compress a drive, click the drive you want to compress. On the Drive menu, click Compress. Click Start. If you have not backed up your files, click Back Up Files, and then follow the instructions on your screen. When you are done, proceed to Compress Now. If Windows prompts you to restart your computer, click Yes. To uncompress a drive, click the drive you want to uncompress. On the Drive menu, click Uncompress. Click Start. If you have not backed up your files, click Back Up Files, and then follow the instructions on your screen. When you are done, click

Uncompress Now. You may want to consult the instructor or the lab manager before you compress a drive. Double-spacing a drive has occasionally proven to cause problems.

 CAUTION   *Be sure you know the what and why of DriveSpace before attempting to compress a drive!*

ScanDisk

ScanDisk

To check for disk errors when your computer starts, click on the shortcut in Help or select the ***ScanDisk*** icon (shown in the margin) from System Tools in Accessories. You may wish to add a ScanDisk icon to your Startup folder. After you have added a ScanDisk icon to your StartUp folder, use your right mouse button to click the icon. Click Properties, and then click the Shortcut tab. After the text in the Target box, specify one or more of the following:

`drive:`	to specify the drive(s) you want to check
`/a`	to check all your local, nonremovable hard disks
`/n`	to start and close ScanDisk automatically
`/p`	to prevent ScanDisk from correcting any errors it finds

For example, to check drive D: and to start and close ScanDisk automatically, the text in the Target box should look similar to the following:

`c:\windows\scandskw.exe d: /n`

To check all nonremovable hard disks but prevent ScanDisk from correcting any errors it finds, the text in the Target box should look similar to the following:

`c:\windows\scandskw.exe /a /p`

To check your disk's surface, files, and folders for errors, click the shortcut icon in Help to start ScanDisk from the System Tools in Accessories. Click the drive you want to check. Select Thorough.

If you want to change the settings ScanDisk uses when checking the disk's surface, click Options. If you want to change the settings ScanDisk uses when checking files and folders, click Advanced. Click Start.

If you want to specify how ScanDisk repairs any errors it finds, make sure the Automatically Fix Errors box is not checked. For Help on an item in the main Scan-Disk screen, use your right mouse button to click the item, and then click the What's This? command. For Help on an item in the Surface, select Scan Options or ScanDisk Advanced. To check files and folders for errors, start ScanDisk. Click the drive that contains the files and folders you want to check. Click Standard. If you want to change the settings ScanDisk uses when checking files and folders, click Advanced. Click Start. If you want to specify how ScanDisk repairs any errors it finds, make sure the Automatically Fix Errors box is not checked.

Phone Dialer

 Windows Accessories contains a ***Phone Dialer*** program (icon shown in the margin). To dial your phone, make sure your modem and modem cables are connected correctly. Type the number in dialable format or international format, or click a number you've already dialed. Click Dial. If you dial the same number frequently, you can store it on a speed-dial button. To see a log of calls, click the Tools menu, and then click Show Log. To dial a number in the log, double-click the log entry. To store frequently dialed numbers, click an empty speed-dial button. Fill in the requested information. Click Save or click Save and Dial. To edit all of your speed-dial buttons at once, click the Edit menu, and then click Speed Dial. To dial a stored phone number, click the speed-dial button for the number. To log telephone calls, select Tools from the menu, and click Show Log. To select the types of calls to log, click the Log menu, and then click Options. To dial a number from the log, double-click the name or number. To purge log entries, select the entries, click the Edit menu, and then click Delete.

Review Questions

*1. Which command(s) would be used to switch from a standard calculator to a scientific calculator?

2. State the Calculator key and keyboard equivalent used to perform each of the following functions:

   a. Perform a mathematical operation between two numbers.

   b. Clear the calculation.

   c. Display the square root of the displayed value.

   d. Delete the right-most digit of the displayed value.

3. When you are using the Statistics window, the Statistics Box will overlap the calculator. How do you switch from one active area to the other, using a mouse? Using the keyboard?

*4. If you are using Notepad to create a memo, what should be done to prevent the text's going beyond the right edge of the window?

*5. How is a time log file created?

Key Terms

Clipboard	Fax	Phone Dialer
CVF	Host drive	ScanDisk
Disk Defragmenter	MIDI	Statistics Box
E-mail	Multimedia	Wave device

The Windows Family of Products

This unit deals with four Microsoft software packages that you will probably encounter sometime in your work with the Windows environment. These products—Word for Microsoft Windows 95 version 7.0, Microsoft Excel for Windows 95 version 7.0, PowerPoint, and Project for Windows 95—have been designed to work with each other to provide a substantial "tool kit" on a personal computer. This unit focuses on the features of the products and gives a small demonstration of how they combine to support a decision-making task. Unlike other units in this book, this unit focuses on *what* can be done, rather than on *how* to do it. Books in the WEST MICRO-COMPUTING SERIES provide instruction in the use of Word for Windows 95, Excel for Windows 95, PowerPoint for Windows 95, Access for Windows 95, Microsoft Project for Windows 95 version 7.0, and Microsoft PowerPoint for Windows 95 version 7.0, and can be purchased from your favorite bookstore.

Learning Objectives

At the completion of this unit you should know

1. the names and features of four prominent members of the Microsoft family of Windows products—Word for Windows, Excel, PowerPoint, and Project,

2. the three primary methods of sharing data among Windows applications,

3. which of the products to use for a given application.

The Problem

To illustrate these software packages, we developed a simple problem. We have decided to build a cabin in the woods and want to plan our time to accomplish that feat. To solve our problem, we must plan a schedule to accommodate the tasks of building the cabin, which must be accomplished in a specific order. Microsoft Project for Windows 95 version 7.0 will enable us to plan the schedule. Once the schedule is complete, we would like to produce a pie chart showing the proportion of time spent on each phase of the project. We will use Microsoft Excel for Windows version 7.0 to develop the chart. We plan to use the chart in two places: a letter to our father (created in Microsoft Word for Windows 95) and a set of overhead transparencies (created in Microsoft PowerPoint 7.0).

To begin, we list the steps to be accomplished and the relationship of these steps to other steps. You might do this on paper (as we did), or you can enter them directly into Project. Table 11.1 contains the task information. Some of the durations are in weeks (which, by definition, consist of five eight-hour days) and others are in days. The most complex part of this example is the constraints. Note that some tasks start after others are finished (for example, bidding cannot start until a week after the plans are finished, to give contractors time to study the plans), while other tasks start a certain number of days after another task has started (electrical work cannot start until after five days of framing). The most complex constraint is that for finishing, which cannot start until framing, electrical, and plumbing have reached certain stages of completion. Given the July 25th starting date, can you predict when the task will be finished?

TABLE 11.1
Task List

STEP	TASK	DURATION	CONSTRAINTS
1	Engineering Design	2 weeks	Start on 7/25/96 at 8:00 a.m.
2	Bidding	2 days	Start 1 week after completion of task 1.
3	Construction – Frame & Mech.	3 weeks	Start 4 days after completion of task 2.
4	Construction – Electrical	8 days	Start 5 days after start of task 3.
5	Construction – Plumbing	1 week	Start 7 days after start of task 3.
6	Finishing	2 weeks	Start after the following, whichever is latest: ...3 days before completion of task 3; ...2 days before completion of task 4; ...completion of task 5.

Microsoft Project for Windows 95

The first step in analyzing our project requires using the software package Microsoft Project for Windows 95. We can enter information such as that contained in Table 11.1, whereupon Project will determine the starting and ending dates and times for each task. It will also determine a *critical path*, the sequence of tasks that must be completed on time for the project as a whole to be completed on schedule.

Task information is entered on a multiwindowed screen in Project. The upper-left window contains a list of the tasks. The upper-right window contains a special type of bar chart, called a *Gantt chart* (named after the inventor), that shows the starting and ending times of each task. The bottom window is used for entering information about a task. Constraints are entered in the lower-right corner of this window. Unless you make a different entry, Project assumes that the constraint is a "finish before start" (FS) type of constraint. A negative number means that the current task can start that many days (or weeks, months, and so on) before the previous (antecedent) task ends. A positive number indicates a delay from the finish of the antecedent task to the start of the current task.

Project also allows the entry of resources that are associated with a task. Often, specific personnel must be scheduled for specific tasks, further complicating the planning process. We did not use the resource feature in this example, assuming that resources needed to build the cabin would be available from the contractors.

Once the tasks are entered, you can ask Project to display and print several items. Figure 11.1 contains the full Gantt chart. Tasks on the critical path are indicated by the diagonal hatching pattern. Figure 11.2 contains a diagram called a *PERT* (project evaluation and review technique) *chart*. Notice that information about the task is displayed in the box and that the relationship among tasks is displayed by their arrangement on the page. From both diagrams, we see that the scheduling of the electrical work is not critical, but that all other tasks *are* on the critical path and must be closely monitored if we are to finish our cabin on September 23.

This illustration of Microsoft Project for Windows 95 has visited only a few of its capabilities. One feature of the graphical user interface (GUI) that project planners will appreciate is the ability to enter and edit information directly on the Gantt or

FIGURE 11.1
Gantt chart

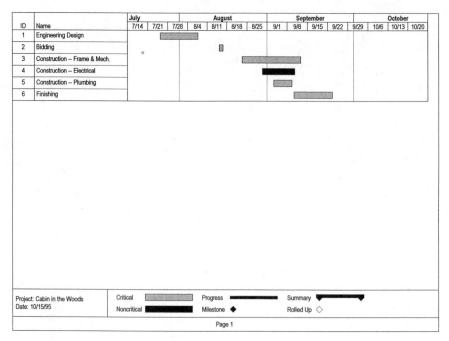

FIGURE 11.2
PERT chart

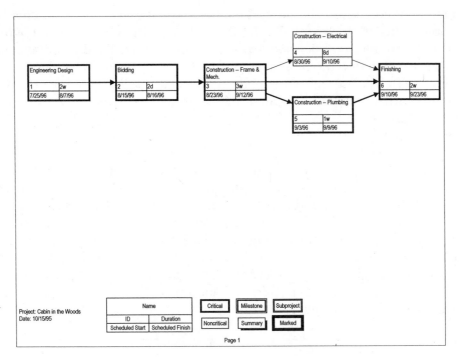

PERT charts. Use the mouse to change the duration of a task on the Gantt chart, and all other parts of the project schedule adjust accordingly.

Sharing Information with Microsoft Excel for Windows 95 Version 7.0

Once the project is planned, we want to use the spreadsheet package Microsoft Excel for Windows 95 version 7.0 to create a graph. One of the methods for sharing information between Project and Excel is to *save in a different format*. Normally, Project saves information in a special format with an *.mpp* file extension. However, Project can also save the data in a file format that is directly transferable to Excel, the *.xls* format. Once the data are saved in an Excel file, we can move to the next step of our project: creating a graph.

Microsoft Excel for Windows 95 Version 7.0

Excel is the state-of-the-art spreadsheet package from Microsoft and the first popular PC package to use the graphical user interface extensively. Users familiar with other spreadsheet packages report that they are pleased with the power of Excel, the ease with which powerful models can be constructed, and the attractive output available using Excel's broad range of formatting options.

With Excel, you can display and link multiple spreadsheets on your screen. You can record macros as you work, store them on separate sheets, and apply them to any worksheet. You can check your figures with an array of advanced, built-in auditing tools as well. Excel has the capacity of 256 columns by 16,384 rows. In addition, it has 131 built-in worksheet functions and 224 macro functions. Excel operates with user-defined menus, dialog boxes, and online help for creating easy-to-use shortcuts and custom applications. Furthermore, Excel is compatible with Lotus 1-2-3 and Symphony, dBASE III Plus, and Microsoft Multiplan. For graphic display of numbers, a gallery of 14 major chart types plus customization is available in Excel. Further, Excel provides complete laser printer support for annual report-quality output, with multiple fonts, borders, shading, custom number, formats, and color.

Creating the Graph

After starting the Excel program, we opened the spreadsheet (*.xls*) file saved by Project. To create the graph, we highlighted 12 spreadsheet cells containing the 6 task names and durations, and used Insert Chart on This Sheet to access the Chart Wizard to create a chart of the data. The 3-D pie chart was selected on step 2 of the Chart Wizard. To produce the *pie chart* illustrated in Figure 11.3 took fewer than ten mouse clicks and no typing! Adding the *legend* explaining the shading patterns used is included in step 5 of the Chart Wizard. We did have to type the text of the title, but all other aspects of creating the graph and formatting the spreadsheet for printing were accomplished using the mouse.

FIGURE 11.3
Printed copy of Excel spreadsheet

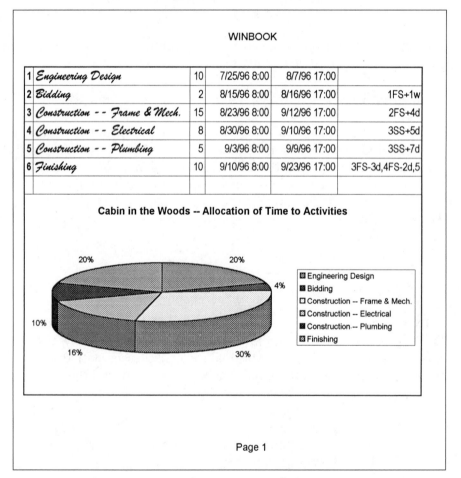

WINBOOK

1	Engineering Design	10	7/25/96 8:00	8/7/96 17:00	
2	Bidding	2	8/15/96 8:00	8/16/96 17:00	1FS+1w
3	Construction - - Frame & Mech.	15	8/23/96 8:00	9/12/96 17:00	2FS+4d
4	Construction - - Electrical	8	8/30/96 8:00	9/10/96 17:00	3SS+5d
5	Construction - - Plumbing	5	9/3/96 8:00	9/9/96 17:00	3SS+7d
6	Finishing	10	9/10/96 8:00	9/23/96 17:00	3FS-3d,4FS-2d,5

Cabin in the Woods -- Allocation of Time to Activities

20%   20%
4%
10%
16%   30%

☒ Engineering Design
■ Bidding
☐ Construction -- Frame & Mech.
☒ Construction -- Electrical
■ Construction -- Plumbing
☒ Finishing

Page 1

Figure 11.3 contains the printed output we created using Excel. Both graph and spreadsheet data are printed on the same page. We used formatting features available in Excel to *highlight* (shade) the task number and task name columns, to draw the lines separating cells, and to specify a script typeface for the task name. The formatting was readily accomplished using the graphical user interface. The WYSIWYG (what you see is what you get) display on the screen provides the feedback that assures you that you are making the changes you intend to make.

The total time required to convert the file created by Project to the output displayed in Figure 11.3 was about 15 minutes. The next step, discussed in the following section, was to copy the chart to the Clipboard for insertion into a Word for Windows document.

Sharing Information with Microsoft Word for Windows

We will use the technique called *Dynamic Data Exchange (DDE)* to share information between an Excel chart and a Word for Windows document. Before we leave the Excel program, we select the chart and copy it to the Clipboard. Selecting the chart is easy: place the mouse pointer in an open area of the chart (for example, between the word `Cabin` and the `20.00%` notation) and click once. Small hollow boxes appear around the perimeter of the chart: its titles and legends. Copying to the Clipboard is almost as easy: issue the menu command Edit | Copy. The chart will stay on the Clipboard until you exit Windows or cut or copy something else to the Clipboard. Linking the chart to the word processing document is covered in the next section.

Microsoft Word for Windows 95

Word for Windows is the word processing package developed by Microsoft for the Windows environment. A similar package, Microsoft Word, exists for those users who are not using Windows.

Word for Windows is a sophisticated program that includes a *spell checker*, a *thesaurus*, *mail merge* capability, and other utilities. Other features of Word include *annotation*, which allows you to add comments to a document; *automatic numbering*, which permits numbering and renumbering of headings in outlines or renumbering of items in a series in the body of a document; *autosave*, which preserves changes in your document at intervals you specify; and *bold*, *italic*, and other *character formats*, which add emphasis to text. Single and double underlining, strike-through, superscript, subscript, and hidden text are additional character formats that Word supports.

Word contains a number of paragraph formats, which are helpful in setting up your text. A document can contain multiple formats to permit you to have a standard format, say double-spaced and justified, while reserving a special format for headings and important paragraphs. These special formats can have left, center, or right alignment; a unique typeface; extra spacing before, after, or in the middle of the paragraph; and numerous other characteristics. The possibilities for arranging text are almost as limitless as your imagination.

Indexing is another helpful Word capability. Word can locate text that you have marked for index entries and then generate an index from these entries. The index can be created in multiple-column format, with continuous page referencing, special capitalization and indentation, and any other formatting feature you want. Clearly, such features are very useful in performing desktop publishing.

Word permits the importing of pictures, charts, and stylized text directly into a document. The *graphics* capabilities of Word enable you to include layout features within text. For example, you can create a company logo using Paint, and then import it into every page of your text. Or, as we shall do here, an Excel graph can be put in a Word document and linked to the original spreadsheet.

Linking the Chart to the Document

Once we started Word, we immediately pasted the chart into our document. (We could have waited until we typed the letter, but the chart was already on the Clipboard, so we decided to paste it before starting on the text of the letter.) To accomplish the Dynamic Data Exchange, we chose the Edit Paste Special, Paste Link command in Word, and indicated that the link should be updated automatically. This *dynamic* data exchange means that the chart in the word processing document will change whenever the data in the spreadsheet file changes. If we desired a *static* data exchange, we would have used the Edit | Paste command. The benefit of a *static data exchange* is that it is faster to accomplish initially; it also permits a more rapid opening of the file in the future because there is no link between the document and the spreadsheet. A dynamic link requires that the spreadsheet program (Excel) be started whenever the document is opened. By contrast, a static link preserves the values of the data at the time the link is made. Subsequent updates to the data will not be reflected in the word processing document unless you redo the cut and paste.

Once the chart was in place, we typed the remainder of the letter. After typing, we used the mouse to highlight words and then boldface or italicize them. We also changed the typeface of two phrases to emphasize them. As with Excel, this is an easy process, requiring jsut a few mouse movements. A portion of the letter as printed appears in Figure 11.4.

Microsoft PowerPoint

PowerPoint for Windows provides a fast, easy way for you to create and manage high-quality overhead transparency and 35mm slide presentations. With Power-Point, you do not need to be an artist to create professional-looking overheads and slides. Because PowerPoint uses the WYSIWYG technology of Windows, you see your material on the screen exactly as it will appear when printed or converted to 35mm slides. Changes can be viewed instantly, as well.

Creating the Slides

We created three slides for our presentation. Figure 11.5 contains the first two slides, printed in a *handout* format. Figure 11.6 shows a full-page version of the third

FIGURE 11.4

Part of the letter printed by Word for Windows

Dear Dad,

The following chart shows the allocation of time to the various activities involved in building our *Cabin in the Woods*.

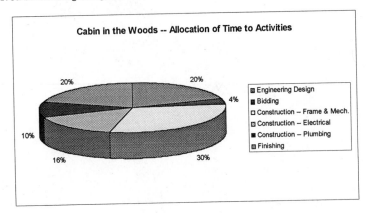

We will start the engineering design on **July 25** and expect to finish the cabin on **September 23**. We're hoping that you will come up to visit us during the "fall colors" festival in October. Our cabin should be the *perfect* base for your activities.

...

Love,

The Kids

slide, the one with our famous graph. Notice that a consistent pattern is printed on the left side of the slide and that the slide titles are in the same type style—but different sizes—and in a shaded box. PowerPoint makes it easy for you to design a *master slide* that carries common design elements from one slide to the next. The effects in black-and-white are interesting, but the effects in full color are fantastic!

The text on slide 2 was copied to the Clipboard from the Excel spreadsheet, and then pasted onto the slide. The diamond-shaped *bullet* characters were added after the paste. The chart on slide 3 required more sophisticated treatment. We wanted to be able to edit the chart if necessary while we were working on the PowerPoint presentation. The chart was copied to the Clipboard in Excel and then brought into the PowerPoint slide with the command File | Edit | Paste Special, Paste Link. As explained below, this command links both the chart and the program that created it to the slide.

Some Windows products support a technique called *object linking and embedding*, or *OLE* (pronounced *oh-lay*). The premise of OLE is that an object (here, the chart) will appear as part of the receiving program (PowerPoint), but that all editing of that chart will be done using the originating program (Excel). OLE goes beyond the Dynamic Data Exchange (DDE) method we used to link the chart to the Word document. Not only will the chart change when the original data are changed in Excel (common to both DDE and OLE), but with OLE we can initiate editing of the

FIGURE 11.5
*Two slides in
handout format*

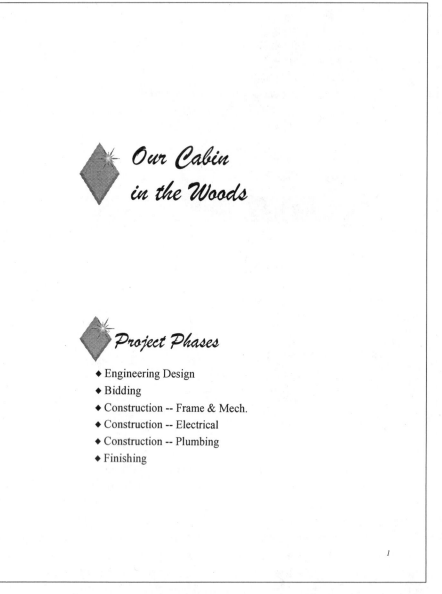

chart from within PowerPoint. By contrast, with DDE we would have to leave Word and enter Excel to edit the chart. With OLE, we simply initiate editing of the chart from within PowerPoint, by double-clicking the object to be edited. If Excel is not open, it will be started, the appropriate spreadsheet and accompanying chart will be loaded, and editing can commence. When we are finished editing the chart (changing the legend, for instance), we are taken back to the PowerPoint slide.

OLE as demonstrated in the PowerPoint/Excel link might not seem such a big deal, but future Windows software, both from Microsoft and from other companies, will make great use of this feature to further integrate their products. OLE is one example of *object-oriented programming* (*OOP*), a new technique that enables objects to contain both data (such as the numbers behind the chart) as well as the procedures necessary to display the data (for instance, Excel's charting program). You

FIGURE 11.6
A full-page slide

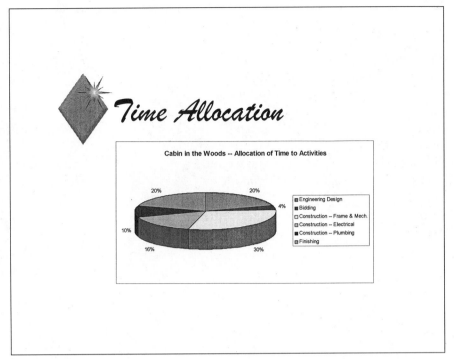

will see OOP techniques applied more and more in Windows as well as other operating systems as programmers become more familiar with their use.

Review Questions

*1. Increasing numbers of users are starting to benefit from the Windows family of products. Identify those products that are mentioned in this unit, and give a brief description of each.

2. Describe the three methods of transferring data from one Windows application to another. What are the advantages and disadvantages of each?

*3. Identify the product associated with each set of terms:

    a. macros, columns, spreadsheets

    b. slide creation, WYSIWYG technology, overheads

    c. spell checker, superscript, annotations

    d. PERT chart, Gantt chart, critical path

Key Terms

Annotation
Automatic numbering
Autosave
Bold
Bullet
Character format
Critical path
Dynamic Data Exchange
   (DDE)
Gantt chart
Graphics

Handout
Highlight
Indexing
Italic
Legend
Mail merge
Master slide
.mpp file
Object linking and
   embedding (OLE)

Object-oriented
   programming (OOP)
PERT chart
Pie chart
Save in a different format
Spell checker
Static data exchange
Thesaurus
.xls file

Advanced Windows Applications

III

■ **PART THREE** In this section we discuss advanced Windows applications. Such applications include Internet and The Microsoft Network, PIF Editor, Control Panel, and Clipboard. While the last two topics have been presented earlier, here we provide additional information on the advanced features of each.

Unit 12 covers the Windows 95 application of Internet and The Microsoft Network; we have not included any Guided Activities in this unit. Unit 13 introduces PIF editor, which allows you to edit program information files to use non-Windows applications that have been written for MS-DOS while you are in the Windows environment. Units 14 and 15 cover advanced topics in customizing and fine-tuning Windows. Finally, Unit 16 explains how to use Clipboard to transfer information between applications (this was also discussed in Unit 11).

Internet and The Microsoft Network

Internet is the largest electronic network in the world and the widest lane on what is termed the *"information superhighway."* It is really a global network of networks. Some sources estimate that the Internet currently interconnects more than 11,000 different networks in 100+ countries. It is believed that some 1.7 million computer hosts take part in the Internet and provide service for between 25 million and 40 million users worldwide. Essentially, Internet could be considered the world's largest library. It is very hard to pin down the actual numbers to describe how large the Internet really is. No one runs the Internet. There is no central office that you sign up with. There is no regulatory body making up the rules with the power to enforce them. Also, the Internet is growing at an ever-increasing rate. It is easier to talk about how much the Internet has grown in the years since its introduction than it is to put solid numbers to its current growth.

Learning Objectives

At the completion of this unit you should know

1. how to connect to the Internet,

2. the significance of the "information superhighway,"

3. how to access the Microsoft Network,

4. how to use Internet, the world's largest library,

5. how to exchange E-mail messages with others,

6. how to open an account with The Microsoft Network.

The Information Superhighway

The "information superhighway" is an international conglomeration of computer networks that offers access to data through FTP, Gopher, and the World Wide Web. It also supports written communications through electronic mail (*E-mail*) and various forms of electronic conferencing. Those building, cruising, and studying the information superhighway predict it will have profound effects on society, education, and language itself by effectively altering our definitions of reading and writing, perhaps even knowledge itself. It is felt that the information superhighway will change dramatically the way people work and communicate.

Internet

The beginning of the Internet dates back to the year 1969. A network was developed by Bolt, Beranek, and Newman (*BBN*) for the Advanced Research Projects Agency of the U.S. Department of Defense. This network became known as *ARPANET*. This new network connected university, military, and defense contractors who were working on ARPA projects. The intent was to allow researchers at these organizations to share information. From this early research network the Internet traces its history.

In 1973, ARPA, renamed *DARPA* for Defense Advanced Research Projects Agency, started a program called Internetting Project. This project was to study how to link various packet networks to each other. This Internetting Project evolved into what is known today simply as the Internet. In 1985, there were only 100 networks within the Internet. Four years later, in 1989, the number of networks had risen to more than 500. The Defense Data Network Information Center reported that 2,218 networks were connected by January 1990. The National Science Foundation's Network Information Center estimated that some 4,000 networks were connected by June of 1991. Paul Gilster, author of *The Internet Navigator*, estimates that by the end of 1995 the Internet could reach more than 40 million people. If that growth rate continues, the Internet would top 100 million by 1998.

The Internet can be used to connect to other protocols and software. Examples of these services include E-mail, *TCP/IP*, *Telnet*, *FTP*, *Gopher*, *Archie*, *Veronica*, *WAIS*, and *WWW*. The Internet could be considered the largest library in the world! Telnet allows users to log in to remote computer systems. To gain access to a remote host, a user needs to have an account on that computer. FTP (file transfer protocol) allows users to exchange files between two computer systems. These systems do not have to be alike or even running the same operating system. There are two basic ways one uses FTP. First, you can use FTP under your own *userid* on the remote system. This would place you in your home directory. You can then transfer files to and from both computers you are connected to.

The second method for using FTP is known as *anonymous* FTP. This is the most common way files are exchanged. In this method, a user does not need an account on the remote computer. Guest log ins are permitted with the user's E-mail address being used as a password. Under anonymous FTP you are able to access files placed in a public directory. Gopher is a relative newcomer to the Internet. Borrowing from its animal counterpart, Gopher tunnels through the Internet to help users locate the information they need. Gopher understands and works with both Telnet and FTP. Finally, WWW or the Wide World Web is also available through the Internet. The big difference between Gopher and WWW is that Gopher is linear in its approach to information retrieval. WWW uses hypertext links to allow the user freedom in choosing the links they wish to explore. Another important difference is that the Web works with sound, video, and still images. You can download files, images, or sound from the Web.

Internet Utilities

Some of the utilities you can find on the Internet include:

FINGER used to retrieve information about users registered on a particular computer system

NETFIND used to provide a type of Internet "white pages" user directory

NSLOOKUP used to query Domain Name servers for IP addresses

PING used to determine if a particular host is up

WHOIS "official" list for registered network names

Internet Tools

Some of the tools you can find on the Internet include:

ARCHIE used to locate files to anonymous FTP sites by file name search

FILE SERVICE PROTOCOLS (FSP) a connectionless protocol for transferring files

JUGHEAD used to get menu information from Gopher servers

TELNET used to log in to remote computers

VERONICA used to locate titles of Gopher items by keyboard searches

Internet Systems

Some of the systems you can find on the Internet include:

GOPHER used to locate and retrieve resources using a graph of menus

WIDE AREA INFORMATION SERVICE (WAIS) used to retrieve resources by searching indexes of databases

WORLD WIDE WEB (WWW) used to retrieve resources by hypertext browsers

Internet Interfaces

Some of the interfaces you can find on the Internet include:

CELLO MS-Windows–based WWW browser that incorporates WWW, Gopher, FTP, Telnet, and News

HYTELNET provides Internet access info by hypertext

MOSAIC FOR X/MS-WINDOWS/MAC-WWW   interface that incorporates WWW, Gopher, FTP, Telnet, WAIS, Archie, and News

LYNX   provides an ASCII terminal browser for WWW

Windows 95 includes a fast, robust, 32-bit TCP/IP protocol stack (TCP/IP is the language used by the Internet) as well as PPP or "dial-in" support. Windows 95 supports the large number of tools used to connect to the Internet, such as Mosaic, Netscape, WinWAIS, and WinGopher, through the Windows Sockets programming interface. Windows 95 also includes standard Internet utility support, such as Telnet and FTP. In addition, the Microsoft Exchange mail client included with Windows 95 provides a mail driver that supports Internet electronic mail standards, including STMP and POP, to make it easy to send and receive mail over the Internet.

E-Mail over the Internet

Access to The Microsoft Network, a new online service, is a feature of Windows 95. With The Microsoft Network, you can exchange messages with people around the world; read the latest news, sports, weather, and financial information; find answers to your technical questions; download thousands of useful programs; connect to the Internet, and more! To start The Microsoft Network, double-click The Microsoft Network icon on your desktop. For more information, click the Help menu in The Microsoft Network.

There are many ways you can connect to the Internet using Windows. Here are two ways you can connect: you can sign up for The Microsoft Network online service; or you can create a Dial-Up Networking connection to an Internet access provider.

Getting an Internet Account

When you call an Internet access provider to sign up for an Internet account, make sure you get the following information: User name, Password, Access phone number, your host name and domain name, and Domain Name Server (DNS) server address. The access provider may also provide the following information: IP address and subnet mask, DNS search order (if required), and Gateway address. Use a PPP account if your provider offers it. If your organization has a direct connection to the Internet, you can skip this step.

You need a modem (9600 bps or faster is recommended) to connect to the Internet. Or, if your organization has a direct connection to the Internet, you can use a network adapter card instead of a modem. If you haven't set up your modem, refer to Unit 9. Make sure you have Dial-Up Networking installed. Double-click the My Computer icon on your desktop. If you do not see a Dial-Up Networking icon, then go to Add/Remove Programs from the Control Panel on your desktop. Under Windows Setup, click Communications and then click Details. Check Dial-Up Networking and then click OK.

Install the Windows 95 TCP/IP protocol by selecting Network properties (Figure 12.1). Click Add (if the Windows 95 TCP/IP protocol is already installed). Click

FIGURE 12.1
*Network
properties*

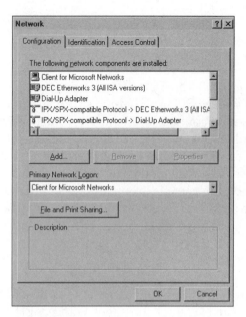

Protocol, and then click Add. Click Microsoft and then click TCP/IP. Click OK. Click Dial-Up Adapter and then click Properties. Or, if your organization has a direct Internet connection, click your network adapter and then click Properties.

Click the Bindings tab and then make sure the TCP/IP check box is checked. If prompted, restart your computer. When you install TCP/IP, it is bound to all of your adapters by default. If you have a network card and don't use TCP/IP with it, you should go to Properties for the network card, click the Bindings tab, and then remove TCP/IP.

Display Network properties, again. Click TCP/IP (if there is more than one TCP/IP entry, click TCP/IP → Dial-Up Adapter) and then click Properties. On the IP Address tab, if your provider gave you an IP address, click Specify an IP Address, and then type your IP address and subnet mask. If your provider did not give you an IP address, click Obtain an IP Address Automatically. If you are using a direct network connection to the Internet, type your IP address and subnet mask. If your network uses a DCHP server to assign IP addresses, click Obtain an IP Address Automatically. On the Bindings tab, it is recommended that you clear the File and Printer Sharing box.

You can set up a connection to your access provider by selecting Make New Connection in Dial-Up Networking (if it is your first Dial-Up Networking connection, you'll be prompted automatically). Follow the instructions on your screen. Using your right mouse button, click the connection icon, and then click Properties. If your provider requires a terminal window to log in, click Configure. Click the Options tab, make sure Bring Up Terminal Window After Dialing is checked, and then click OK. In the Properties for the connection, click Server Type, and then make sure the type of server is set to PPP.

You can decrease the time required to connect by making sure that the following options are *not* checked:

Log On to Network NetBEUI IPX/SPX Compatible. If you have a SLIP account, you need to install SLIP support. This is available on the Windows 95 CD-ROM or from the Windows 95 Resource Kit. After SLIP support is installed, go to the properties for your connection, click Server Type, and make sure SLIP is installed.

To dial your Internet access provider, double-click the connection, enter your name and password, and then click Connect. Follow the instructions provided by your Internet access provider for browsing the Internet, reading E-mail, and accessing information. Information transfer on the Internet is bidirectional, meaning that while you are connected, other people can gain access to your computer. For this reason, it is recommended that you disable file and printer sharing before connecting. People who send you mail over the Internet must specify your address as `member ID@msn.com`. Replace `member ID` with your MSN member ID. You receive Internet mail in your Inbox, just as you would from other MSN members. You can identify

Internet E-mail by looking at the From address. An Internet address has the following format: `name@domain`, such as `RonMaestas@Merlin.NMHU.Edu`. The From address from another MSN member is just the member's name. To send E-mail over the Internet in MSN Central, click E-mail. Click Compose, and then click New Message. In the To field, specify an Internet E-mail address instead of an MSN address. If you communicate with certain people often, you can add their Internet addresses to your personal address book.

The Internet Center

Growing and changing every day, the Internet Center contains updates of popular *newsgroups* and file libraries, and the always-hopping Internet Cafe. The *.alt* groups are now available, and you'll be able to post to them in the very near future. If you have questions about the Internet or want to swap stories with other Net surfers, you should definitely stop by.

The Microsoft Network

The Microsoft Network is a new online service that Microsoft is developing to bring the rapidly expanding world of electronic information and communication to mainstream PC users. The Microsoft Network (*MSN*) will bring all Windows 95 customers affordable and easy-to-use access to electronic mail, bulletin boards, chat rooms, file libraries, and Internet newsgroups. Microsoft Windows 95 customers worldwide will be able to access MSN with just a local phone call.

Microsoft has long believed in "Information at your Fingertips" and MSN is the vehicle to deliver that vision. The online service business has great promise to provide consumers with easy communication and information access, but it is still in the infancy stage and many factors must come together to make it a mainstream phenomenon. Online services must offer a more compelling multimedia-rich set of publications, shopping services, games, and the like, that will attract and retain a large audience. This will require both investments by the providers of information and services, and investments by the online service companies in new tools and infrastructure.

When you dial into MSN, you're calling a network provider. Network providers have local nodes or junctions in cities and towns all over the world that allow you to make a local phone call to connect to MSN.

The network provider then connects you to the MSN Data Center over a very-high-speed network. This network is much faster than connecting over phone lines, so at any time during your session on MSN, the slowest link in the chain is between your modem and the network provider's modem.

The MSN Data Center is where all of the actual information exchange takes place, whether you're chatting with someone in another city or another country, reading messages on your favorite bulletin board, or scanning the day's headlines.

To sign up to become a member, double-click the MSN icon (Figure 12.2) on your desktop. Once you've completed signup, you can begin using MSN immediately.

FIGURE 12.2
MSN Sign In

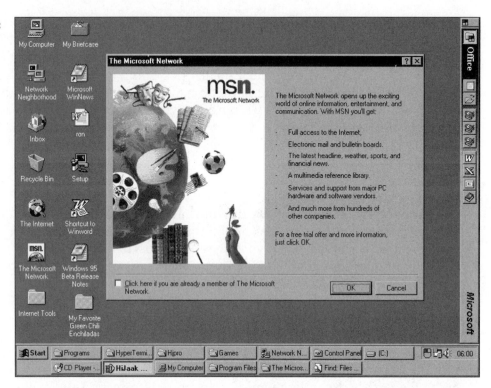

You have full use of MSN as soon as you sign up. However, your membership information will not be available in the address books for up to 24 hours.

To sign up more than one member on one computer on the desk-top, double-click My Computer, and double-click the icon for your hard drive where Windows 95 is installed. Double-click the *Program Files* folder, and then double-click *The Microsoft Network* folder. Double-click the Signup icon. Follow the directions, providing information about the new member. Each member is billed as a separate account.

To connect to MSN, double-click the MSN icon on the desktop. Type your member ID and password (unless they appear automatically), and then click Connect (Figure 12.3). To keep your account secure, the password doesn't appear when you type it. To disconnect from MSN, click the File menu, and then click Sign Out. You can also use the connection indicator to sign out. On the Windows taskbar to the left of the time, use the right mouse button to click the connection indicator, and then click Sign Out. To disconnect from MSN automatically, use MSN Central, click the View menu, and then click Options.

Set the number of minutes MSN can be idle before it is automatically disconnected from your computer.

MSN Central

MSN Central (Figure 12.4) is the main MSN window that appears immediately after you sign in. You can go anywhere on MSN from MSN Central. Click Categories (Figure 12.5) to browse through the available forums and services. To return to MSN Central (if you've closed the MSN window), double-click The Microsoft Network icon on your desktop or select the Edit menu of the current window, point to Go To,

FIGURE 12.3
Connect to MSN

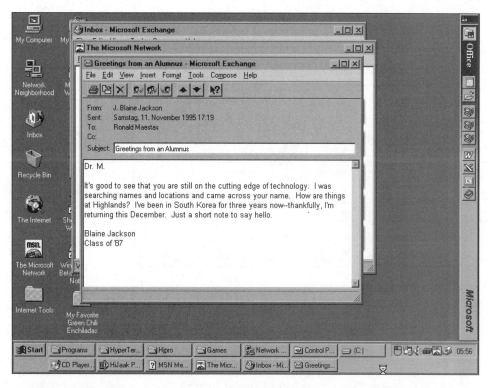

and then click MSN Central. You can also use the right mouse button to click the connection indicator, and then click View MSN Central.

FIGURE 12.4
MSN Central

FIGURE 12.5
MSN Categories

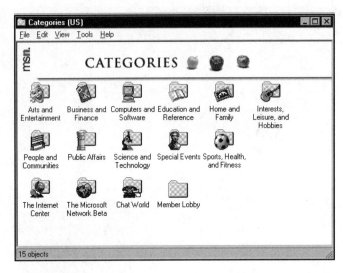

Member ID and Password Guidelines

Your member ID is the name other members will see when you send E-mail or participate in a chat room or bulletin board. It becomes your online identity.

A password is a code you specify when you connect to MSN. Keep your password secret to prevent others from signing in as you add accumulating charges on your account. You can change your password at any time.

 CAUTION *Once you've chosen a member ID and MSN has approved it, you can't change it. You might prepare a list of alternate names before you sign on, in case your first choice is taken.*

Guidelines for Communicating Online

Good manners are as important online as they are in person. The impression you make online will depend on how well you know the rules. You can read the guidelines for communicating online by clicking Member Assistance in MSN Central.

You can express emotions, gestures, and other physical cues by using special characters and abbreviations. To see some common gestures, read the following with your head turned toward your left shoulder:

Gesture	Symbol
Crying	:'-)
Grin	:-D
Hug	{},[]
Kiss	*
Smile	:.)

Gesture	Symbol
Wink	;.)
Yelling	:-O

Abbreviation	Meaning
BTW	By The Way
IMHO	In My Humble Opinion
IOW	In Other Words
LOL	Laughing Out Loud
ROFL or ROTFL	Rolling on the Floor Laughing
WRT	With Regard To

Sometimes these gestures and abbreviations have been referred to as *emoticons*.

Using MSN Chat

Chat enables you to converse with other MSN members by computer. A chat session on MSN (Figure 12.6) is like a conference call. However, instead of speaking aloud, you type your messages and MSN displays them for other people to read. Each member in the chat session is either a participant or a spectator. A chat session may also have one or more hosts, who are designated by the forum manager. The host facilitates the conversation and determines whether members are participants or spectators.

FIGURE 12.6
MSN Chat session

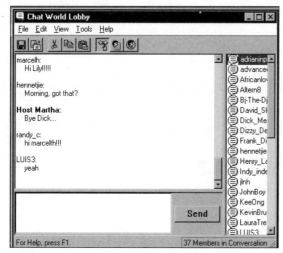

To join a conversation, you go to a chat room whose subject interests you. Before you contribute to the chat, you can observe it for a while to see if you'd like to join in. If you have participant status, and you want to contribute, you can send a question, answer, or comment to the other members.

Chat Window

The Chat window in MSN consists of three panes, all of which can be resized or hidden. The Chat window also has a toolbar and status bar designed to help you complete tasks more quickly. You display or hide the toolbar and status bar by using commands on the View menu. The Chat History pane is the upper-left pane. It displays all of the participants' messages from the time you join the chat line to the time you leave, provided that you don't clear the chat line. The Compose pane is below the Chat History pane. It is where you type the message that you want to send to the chat room. The Member List pane appears to the right of the Chat History and the Compose panes, displaying a list of members in the chat and identifying whether they are participants, spectators, or hosts. When you ignore members, their names appear with a line through them.

MSN Categories

In MSN Central, click Categories (Figure 12.7), and double-click the category (subject) you're interested in. Double-click any icon or folder until you see the information you want (Figure 12.8). You can use this approach to find forums, chat rooms, and bulletin boards (including those with files you can copy) in addition to other MSN services.

FIGURE 12.7
MSN Categories

FIGURE 12.8
MSN folders

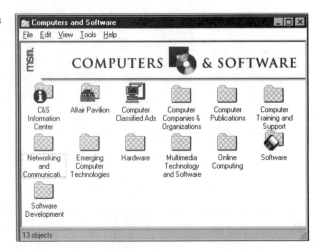

Favorite Places and Shortcuts

Favorite Places are a feature of MSN and can be used only for MSN services. Only you can be placed in the Favorite Places folder. It can't be shared with other people. To add an icon to your *Favorite Places* folder, find the service or folder you want to add to your *Favorite Places* folder. Click the service or folder, click the File menu, and then click Add to Favorite Places. If you are already in the service or folder, click the File menu, and then click Add to Favorite Places. You can't add a shortcut to your *Favorite Places* folder. To delete an icon from your *Favorite Places* folder, click the icon you want to delete. Click the File menu, and then click Delete. When you delete an icon from your *Favorite Places* folder, you delete only the icon, not the item itself. The service or folder that the icon represented still exists on MSN. To go to one of your Favorite Places, click the Edit menu, point to Go To, and then click Favorite Places; or in MSN Central, click Favorite Places. Double-click the icon for the place you want to go. If there is no icon for the place you want to go in your *Favorite Places* folder, you must add it to the folder.

Member Assistance

The following services are available in the *Member Assistance* folder:

- Netiquette and member guidelines
- MSN Lobby for meeting new members
- Customer support

It is a good idea to learn about network etiquette (*netiquette*) and read the member guidelines. To report inappropriate online behavior in MSN Central, click Member Assistance. Double-click the MSN Member Support folder. You can also report problems by calling the customer service number for your area, or by contacting the forum manager for the forum where the problem is occurring.

At times, you may want to exercise control over which bulletin boards, newsgroups, and chat rooms your account can access. For example, parents might want to prevent children from using their account to open adult-only areas on MSN and in certain Internet newsgroups. In some cases, you will be notified before entering an area that contains explicitly adult material. However, opinions differ about what qualifies as "adult" material. You may come across material that you consider adult that isn't designated as such. If you are offended by this material, you should avoid the area. If you want to prevent your children from accessing the material, it's strictly up to you to do so.

Meeting New MSN Members in MSN Central

To meet new member of MSN, click Member Assistance, and then double-click MSN Lobby (Figure 12.9). Double-click the MSN Member Lounge. Type your message

FIGURE 12.9
MSN Lobby

in the Compose pane at the bottom of the Chat window, and then click Send or press the [Enter] key.

Member Support

If you can't find an answer to your question in the *Member Assistance* folder (click Member Assistance in MSN Central), call Customer Service for questions about your account, general product information, or assistance connecting to The Microsoft Network. For questions on using The Microsoft Network after installation, call Technical Support. The phone numbers are located in the *Member Assistance* folder. Customer Service numbers are subject to change. You can download the latest numbers from the *Member Assistance* folder.

Review Questions

*1. Who developed the Internet?

*2. List five Internet services or protocols.

 3. What type of services are available on The Microsoft Network?

*4. Give three examples of emoticons.

 5. Explain the term netiquette.

*6. How can you join a chat session?

Key Terms

Anonymous	FTP	TCP/IP
Archie	Gopher	Telnet
BBN	Information	Userid
ARPANET	superhighway	Veronica
Chat	MSN	WAIS
DARPA	Netiquette	WWW
E-mail	Newsgroup	
Emoticon	SLIP	

Program Information Files

Windows 95 uses properties dialog boxes to replace PIF Editor used in earlier versions of Windows. PIF was necessary to run MS-DOS applications (non-Windows programs). Some MS-DOS–based programs cannot run in Windows.

Learning Objectives

At the completion of this unit you should know

1. how to change properties of non-Windows applications programs,

2. what a program information file is.

Program Information Files

Each "Windows" application program—such as WordPad, Paint, Word, Excel, and others that we have discussed to this point—contain instructions to Windows as to how the program is to be treated. These instructions include the amount of memory required to run the program, the size of the window, the video display requirements, and so on. "Non-Windows" applications programs, such as Lotus 1-2-3 (version 3.4 and lower), Quattro Pro, or WordPerfect (version 5.1 and lower) do not contain such information. The *PIF Editor* is used to instruct Windows on how to deal with an MS-DOS application that you want to run in the Windows environment. The settings are saved in a *program information file* (**PIF**) that has a *.pif* extension. Normally, you will create a PIF file for each program (some program publishers furnish a PIF file with their software). MS-DOS programs that do not have an associated PIF file will be assigned to use the file named _Default.pif_ (the underscore is part of the file name).

FIGURE 13.1
*MS-DOS
properties*

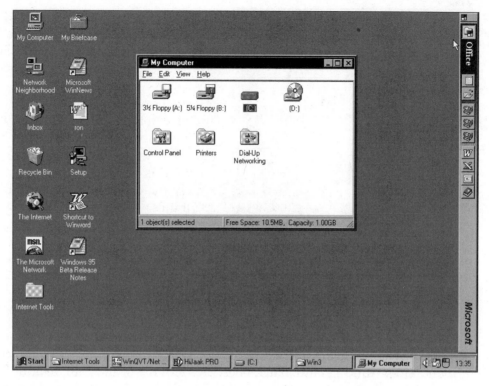

PIF Properties

To optimize an MS-DOS program, select My Computer and click the icon for the drive where the non-Windows program resides. On the File menu, click Properties (Figure 13.1). The settings you specify in the Properties dialog box will be used each time you start the program by double-clicking its icon. If you start the program from an MS-DOS window within Windows, however, these settings won't be used.

FIGURE 13.2
Run properties

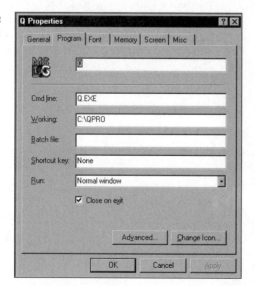

To specify whether MS-DOS starts in a full screen or in a window, change the Run properties (Figure 13.2) on the Program tab. Note that some MS-DOS–based programs cannot run in a window. The Properties dialog box replaces the PIF Editor used in earlier versions of Windows.

For example, if you wanted to inspect or change the settings of the non-Windows application Quattro Pro version 4.0, you would double-click on My Computer on the desktop. Mouse to the C: drive icon and then choose the directory where Quattro Pro 4.0 resides. Double-click this icon and you will get the full program listings for this directory. Next, you will need to click on the executable file for Quattro Pro, which is *Q.exe*. From the File

FIGURE 13.3
*Properties
command*

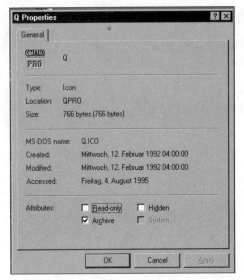

menu, select Properties (Figure 13.3). The Q Properties dialog box will appear. You will notice the various tabs, which include General, Program, Font, Memory, Screen, and Misc. The General Properties tab gives you information concerning the Type, Location, and Size of the non-Windows application. In addition, you will see additional information regarding the MS-DOS name, plus the dates the file was Created, Modified, and Accessed. Finally, the General Properties tab lists the Attributes as Read-only, Archive, Hidden, and System. Notice that the Archive box is checked.

🖐 CAUTION *Do not change these settings unless directed to do so by your instructor.*

The Program tab in Properties includes information on the current Icon, Command Line, Working Path, Batch Files, Shortcut Keys, and Run. In addition, the Program tab includes an Advanced Button and Change Icon Button. If you click on Advanced you will see the PIF name with a check box marked Suggest MS-DOS mode as necessary.

FIGURE 13.4
Font tab

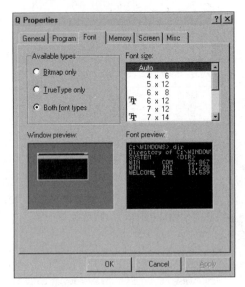

The Font tab (Figure 13.4) allows you to inspect or change Font properties for Available Types (Bitmap Only, TrueType Only, or Both Font Types) and Font Size. You may wish to experiment with each of these properties. The Windows Preview and Font Preview will give you an example of how these properties can be changed.

Memory Properties (Figure 13.5) include the ability to specify or change Conventional, Expanded (EMS), Extended (XMS), or MS-DOS Protected mode (DPMI) memory.

🖐 CAUTION *Consult the* User's Manual *or check with your instructor or lab manager before you make any changes to Memory Properties.*

FIGURE 13.5
Memory properties

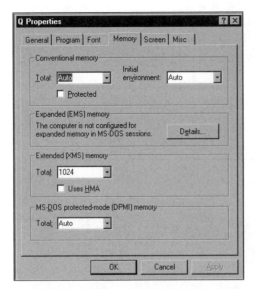

Screen Properties (Figure 13.6) enable you to change Usage (Full Screen, Window, or Initial Size). If you wish to change Initial Size (Figure 13.6) click on the arrow. You will see the available choices as Default, 25, 43, or 50 lines. In addition, the other screen properties include Window (Display Toolbar and Restore Settings on Startup). Each of these have a check box where you can enable/disable your preference. Finally, the last screen property is Performance. Performance allows you to operate in Fast ROM Emulation and Dynamic Memory Allocation.

Misc Properties (Figure 13.7) permit you to make changes on Foreground, Background, Idle Sensitivity, Windows Shortcut keys, Mouse, Termination, and Other, which includes Fast Pasting. Foreground lets you use screen savers; Background allows suspend. Idle Sensitivity detects when your machine is not in use. It can be adusted to High or Low. Mouse properties provide for Quick Edit or Exclusive Mode.

FIGURE 13.6
Screen properties

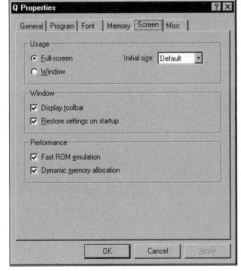

NOTE *PIF settings in your system may be different from those illustrated here. Your system manager may have established a different PIF file for Quattro Pro, or it may not be on your system. Ask your instructor about the settings in your system.*

GUIDED ACTIVITY 13.1

Using the Properties Dialog Box for Non-Windows Applications

(TO BE DONE ONLY AT THE DIRECTION OF THE INSTRUCTOR!)

1. Locate a non-Windows application such as WordPerfect Release 5.1, using My Computer.

FIGURE 13.7
Misc properties

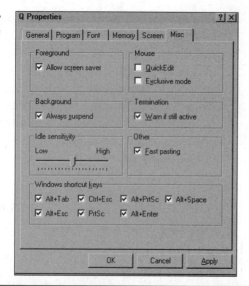

2. In the File menu, select Properties.

    This entry is intended only as an example. Your entry will depend on the non-Windows application that you wish to install.

3. Do not change any of the other settings. This Guided Activity is intended for you to inspect the Properties dialog box only.

Specifying an Environment

To allocate all system resources to an MS-DOS Program, select My Computer and click the icon for the program. On the File menu, click Properties. On the Program tab, click Advanced and then click MS-DOS Mode. You can specify the environment you want your program to run in by providing alternative *Config.sys* and *Autoexec.bat* files. Either type the commands you want in the spaces provided, or create a basic configuration by clicking Configuration and selecting the options you want.

Review Questions

*1. What is a program information file (PIF)?

2. What type of application utilizes PIFs? Explain why.

Key Terms

Dynamic Memory
Allocation

Fast ROM Emulation
PIF Editor

Program Information File

Customizing Windows

You can customize Windows to your particular taste using the Control Panel from the Settings menu. The default settings in Windows are recorded in a file called *Win.ini* (for *Windows ini*tialization). With earlier versions of Windows you would make changes directly in the *.ini* file using Notepad, Write, or some other text editor. You can still use this approach to customize Windows 95.

Control Panel was presented in Unit 5. You may wish to review that unit before proceeding. In addition to the changes (color, desktop, keyboard speed, and the like) presented in Unit 5, you can use Control Panel for more advanced customization of Windows.

Learning Objectives

At the completion of this unit you should know

1. how to select background patterns,

2. how to choose a custom wallpaper,

3. how to define country options,

4. how to select or deselect sound.

Customizing the Desktop

The **desktop** consists of that area of the Windows screen that is outside any particular window or icon. It is also the background area where you create and work with

Windows applications. Control Panel is used to change or customize the appearance of your desktop. You can do all of the following:

- Add a language or keyboard layout
- Add a program to the Start or Program menu
- Put additional items in your *Network Neighborhood* folder
- Adjust the rate at which your cursor blinks
- Adjust the double-click speed for your mouse
- Adjust the speed of your mouse pointer
- Assign sounds to program events
- Calibrate your display to actual dimensions
- Change the appearance of your mouse pointer
- Change the background of your desktop
- Change the number of colors your monitor displays
- Change screen resolution
- Customize the taskbar or Startup menu
- Enable multiple users to personalize settings
- Protect your files by assigning a screen-saver password
- Protect your screen by setting up a screen saver
- Remove programs from the Start or Programs menus
- Reverse your mouse buttons
- Start a program each time Windows starts
- Personalize Windows
- Turn on and adjust mouse trails

Adding a Language

Windows 95 includes a new feature that allows you to customize the keyboard by adding a language. To add a language, click on the Start button and select Settings; mouse to Control Panel. Once Control Panel is open, double-click on the Keyboard icon. The **Keyboard Properties** dialog box (Figure 14.1) will appear. Click on the Language tab (Figure 14.2). A new dialog box will appear. In the section entitled Installed Keyboard Languages and Layouts you will see a listing of installed languages. If this box is empty, then you will need to Add/Remove Programs from Control Panel. For example, Figure 14.3 illustrates the various languages and keyboard layouts installed. They include English, German, Spanish (Mexican), Russian, and

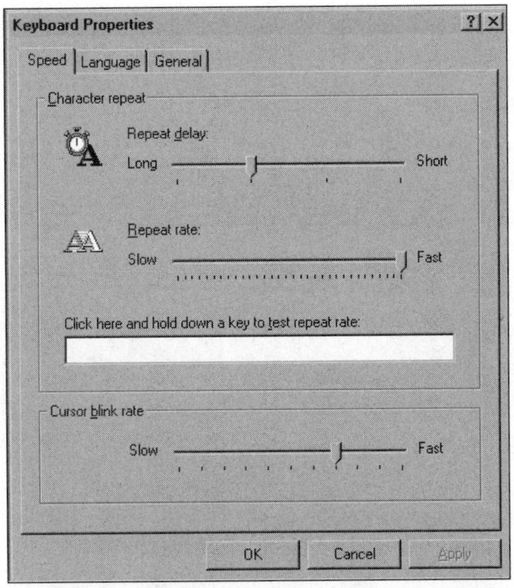

FIGURE 14.1
Keyboard Properties

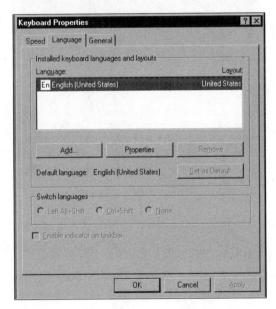

FIGURE 14.2
Language tab

Afrikaans. You can add a language by choosing the Add button. You can also inspect the Properties or Remove the language. When you are satisfied with the language, select OK, Cancel, or Apply.

GUIDED ACTIVITY 14.1

Adding a Keyboard Language

1. Click on the Keyboard icon in Control Panel.

2. Click on the Language tab. Then click Add.

3. Select the language—for example, French (standard)—and then click OK.

4. Make sure Enable Indicator on Taskbar is checked.

5. Insert the Windows 95 CD-ROM or requested disk into the appropriate drive to copy the necessary language files.

FIGURE 14.3
Various languages available

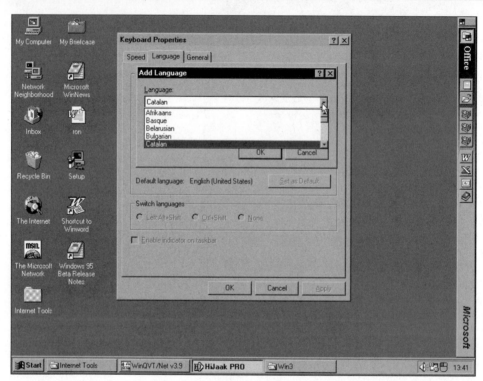

FIGURE 14.4
Language indicator on taskbar

Language indicator for English

When Enable Indicator on Taskbar is checked, and you have two or more languages installed, an indicator representing the default language appears on the taskbar (Figure 14.4). To quickly switch between languages (say, to write a short paper in Spanish), click on the indicator and then click on the language you want to use.

GUIDED ACTIVITY 14.2

Changing the Keyboard Layout

1. Click on Start button, select Settings, and mouse to Control Panel.

2. Double-click on the Keyboard icon.

3. Click on the language—for example, French (standard)—you want to change, and then click Properties.

4. Select the French keyboard layout.

Multilanguage Support

Windows 95 has a special feature that allows you to use various languages as well as keyboard layouts for them. By default, only a limited set of languages is installed during Windows setup. For more languages refer to the *Add/Remove Programs* in Control Panel. Click on the Add/Remove Programs icon in Control Panel. You will see the Add/Remove Programs Properties box (Figure 14.5) appear. Select the Windows Setup tab and scroll down to Multilanguage Support. If you did not install Multilanguage Support when you first installed Windows 95, you will notice the check box is blank. Place a check mark on this box. You will be prompted to insert your Windows 95 CD. When Windows is finished installing Multilanguage Support, you will then need to add the language keyboard from Control Panel. For example, assume that you wish to write a letter to your new pen pal in Russia. Using WordPad, Figure 14.6 illustrates this multilanguage support. You may wish to try this feature; however, you may need to check with your instructor or laboratory manager to find out if it is OK to install multilanguage support.

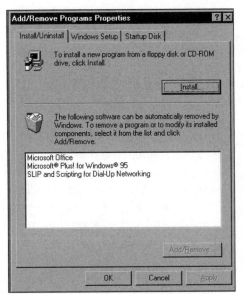

FIGURE 14.5
Add/Remove Programs Properties box

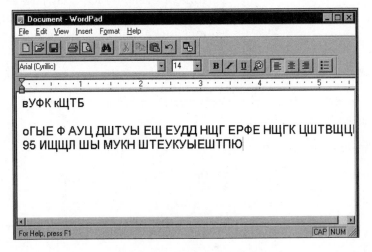

FIGURE 14.6
WordPad showing a foreign language

Starting a Program Each Time Windows Starts

If you want to start a program each time Windows itself starts, click the Start button and mouse to Settings. Click on Taskbar and then click the Start Menu Program tab. Click Add and then click on the Browse button. Locate the program you want to start and then double-click it. Click on the Next button and double-click the *StartUp* folder. Finally, type in the name that you want to see on the StartUp menu and click on the Finish button. If Windows prompts you to choose an icon, click one, and then click Finish. For instance, let's say that you want Microsoft Word 7.0 to appear in the StartUp menu. Every time you launch Windows 95, this choice will be added to the StartUp menu.

Adding a Program to the Start or Program Menus

By customizing the Start button or Program menu, you will be able to quickly bring up those items that you use most frequently. To add a program to the Start or Program menus, click on the Start button and mouse to Settings. Mouse to Taskbar; the **Taskbar Properties** dialog box (Figure 14.7) will appear. Select the Start Menu Programs tab. Notice the Add, Remove, and Advanced buttons (Figure 14.8). Click Add, and then click Browse. Locate the program you want to add and double-click it. Finally, click on Next and select the *Start menu* or *Program menu* folder. Click on Next. Type the name that you want to see on the menu and click on Finish. You can quickly add a program to the top of the Start menu by dragging the program's icon onto the Start button.

You can also customize the taskbar. In the Taskbar Properties dialog box, click on the Taskbar Options tab (see Figure 14.7). You can set the various options, which include Always on Top, Auto Hide, Show small icons in Start Menu, or Show Clock. Each of these options has a check mark that you can enable/disable (turn on/off).

FIGURE 14.7
Taskbar Properties dialog box

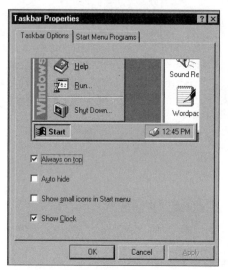

GUIDED ACTIVITY 14.3

Adding a Program to the Start Menu

1. Click the Start button.

2. Point to Settings.

3. Click Taskbar and click the Start Menu Programs tab.

4. Click Add, and then click on Browse.

5. Locate the program you want to appear (for example, *Msoffice\Winword\Word*). Double-click on the program name. Click on Next.

6. Select the Start menu and click on Next.

7. Type in the name of the program and click on Finish.

GUIDED ACTIVITY 14.4

Customizing the Taskbar

1. Click on the Start button.

2. Point to Settings.

3. Click on Taskbar.

4. On the Taskbar Options tab, change the setting you need (for example, Show Clock).

Removing a Program from the Start or Program Menus

FIGURE 14.8
Taskbar options

Items that you have placed on the Start or Program menus can also be removed. Simply click on the Start button and point to Settings. Mouse to Taskbar and click on the Start Menu Programs tab (Figure 14.8).

Click Remove and choose the program that you wish to remove. Click on the program (for example, Microsoft Binder) and click on the Remove button. Even though you are deleting this program from the shortcut list on the Start menu, the original program remains on your computer. This is *not* a permanent deletion.

Changing the Desktop

The options available for customizing the desktop include Background Pattern, Sceen Saver, Appearance, and Settings.

Pattern lets you cover your desktop with a repeating dot pattern. You can create the pattern yourself or use a pattern furnished by Windows.

You can add an interesting *wallpaper* background to your desktop for a more artistic design. Windows is furnished with many wallpaper choices and also allows you to design your own wallpaper.

You can specify a *screen saver*, a moving pattern or picture that displays after you have not used the computer for a period of time. This avoids damage to the screen from displaying the same image for extended periods.

Starting Display

Display

To customize your Display, open the Control Panel through the Start button, click on the Control Panel, and then double-click the Display icon. The Display Properties dialog box will appear as in Figure 14.9. The standard (default) settings for Pattern Name and Wallpaper File appear as (None) until you make a change.

FIGURE 14.9
Display Properties dialog box

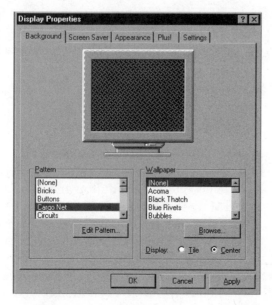

GUIDED ACTIVITY 14.5

Looking at the Display

1. Open the Control Panel by double-clicking on its icon from the Settings menu on the Start button.

2. Double-click on the Display icon.

3. Observe the Background tab of the Display Properties dialog box. The Pattern box may read as (None), or may list one of the other available patterns installed on your version of Windows.

4. If the Wallpaper reads (None), proceed with this Guided Activity. If it does not:

   a. Scroll up or down the Wallpaper list of choices and click on (None). You might have to scroll to the top of the list to find this selection.

   b. Choose OK to exit the Display dialog box.

Customizing the Background Pattern

To customize the background pattern on your desktop, scroll through the list of available patterns in the Pattern box as shown in Figure 14.10.

Patterns that are available in Windows 95 include Bricks, Buttons, Cargo Net, Circuits, Cobblestones, Colosseum, Dizzy, Field Effects, Live Wire, Rounder, Waffles Revenge, and so forth. If you want to view any pattern without actually selecting it, click on the Edit Pattern button in the Pattern box (visible in Figure 14.9). A Pattern Editor dialog box will appear as shown in the figure.

Press the down arrow, and you will see the pattern list, as well as a sample of each. For example, the illustration in Figure 14.11 contains the *Cobblestones* pattern. To complete the pattern selection, click on Done and then click on OK.

You can edit a background pattern, as well as add a new background pattern. Using the mouse, click on a spot where you want to add or remove a dark dot. You cannot edit the pattern using the keyboard. If you create a new pattern, select the Add button, and the pattern will be included on the list. Double-click the mouse to apply this pattern to your desktop.

FIGURE 14.10
Pattern Editor

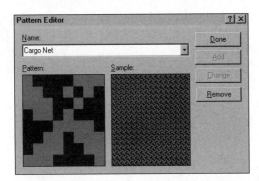

FIGURE 14.11
Cobblestones

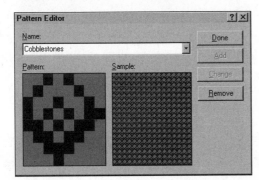

GUIDED ACTIVITY 14.6

Selecting Patterns for the Desktop

1. Open Control Panel from the Start button. Double-click on the Display icon.

2. Change the Name in the Pattern box to Cobblestones by clicking on the down arrow that is to the right of the Name box. When the list appears, click on Cobblestones. You can see a sample of your choice by clicking on the Pattern Editor box. The pattern will appear in the Sample box. Click on Done when you want to continue.

3. Click on OK to complete the choice. You will return to the Control Panel.

4. Minimize Control Panel to the taskbar by clicking on the minimize button in the upper-right corner. Your desktop should have a pattern of cobblestones on it. (You have to use some imagination to see them.)

Customizing Wallpaper

If you want to change the desktop to a different background, use the Wallpaper option. This option allows you to display a picture as a backdrop to everything you do in Windows. Figure 14.12 shows an example of the Acoma background. Several other choices are available, including Black Thatch, Blue Rivets, Carved Stones, Circles, Clouds, Forest, Gold Weave, Houndstooth, Metal Links, Pinstripes, Red Blocks, Sandstone, Stitches, Straw Mat, Tiles, and Triangles. To customize the desktop with a wallpaper option, click on the Display icon on the Control Panel. When the dialog box appears, scroll through the list in the Wallpaper box. Each wallpaper file has a *.bmp* extension, which means that the file's contents "maps" the position of each visible bit in the image. To complete your choice of wallpaper, select OK.

If the picture is large enough, the wallpaper will cover the entire screen. If the picture is large, click on the Center option box to display one copy of the picture in the center of the screen; otherwise, click on Tile to display side-by-side as many copies as will fit on the screen.

Even More Custom Wallpaper

If you want to get really fancy, you can make your own wallpaper using Paint or any other program that creates *.bmp* files. Or you might acquire a wallpaper file from a friend, as **shareware**, or from a public bulletin board. The ultimate thrill is to take a color photograph or picture to a copy shop that has a color scanner (we went to the Kinko's in our town) and ask the operators to create a scanned image. Tell them you

FIGURE 14.12
Acoma wallpaper

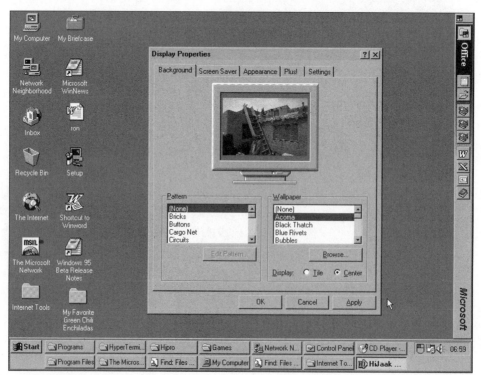

want the image to be 640 by 480 (or whatever your screen resolution is) and ask them to save it in *.bmp* image format, if possible. If they can't do this, ask for *. pcx*. You can retrieve the *.pcx* image in Paint and Save As a *. bmp* file. Make sure you get a disk in an IBM-PC format, not Apple Macintosh format.

Regardless of how you obtain the *. bmp* file, put it on your hard disk in the *Windows* folder. It will then appear among your choices when you select wallpaper.

GUIDED ACTIVITY 14.7

Applying Wallpaper to the Desktop

1. Restore Control Panel from the taskbar by clicking on it. Double-click on the Display icon.

2. View the list of wallpaper images by scrolling throught the list in the Wallpaper section.

3. Select Blue Rivets.*bmp* from the list in the File box. To cover your entire screen with a small wallpaper image, click Tile. To center a wallpaper image, click Center. You can use patterns and wallpaper simultaneously. However, if Tile is selected, you will not see the pattern. By default, only a limited set of wallpapers is installed during Windows setup. For more wallpapers, refer to the Add/Remove Programs in Control Panel. Choose Tile or Center by clicking on the particular option.

4. Click on OK to complete the choice.

5. Close Control Panel.

Customizing the Mouse

FIGURE 14.13
*Mouse
Properties*

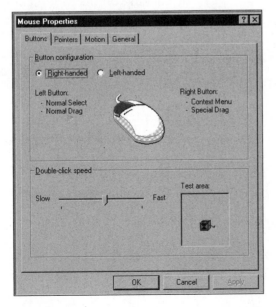

Windows 95 gives you several options for customizing the mouse. For example, you can change the appearance and speed of the mouse pointer, the double-click speed of the mouse, the kind of mouse trails left when you move the mouse, and you can also reverse the mouse buttons. To change the appearance of the mouse pointer, double-click on the Mouse icon in Control Panel. The *Mouse Properties* dialog box (Figure 14.13) will appear. Click on the Pointers tab. Click on the Scheme list box to display the available pointers (Figure 14.14). When you first installed Windows 95, you may have installed only a limited set of mouse pointer schemes. You can Add/Remove Programs in the

FIGURE 14.14
Scheme list box

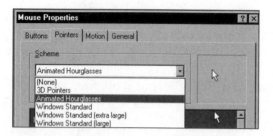

Control Panel if you wish to install additional mouse pointers. You can customize as many pointers as you want, and then save them as a new scheme by clicking Save As. To remove a pointer scheme, click it in the Scheme list and then click Delete.

To adjust the speed of your mouse pointer, click on the Motion tab (Figure 14.15). In the Pointer Speed area, drag the slider. Changing the speed of your mouse pointer causes the pointer to respond more quickly or slowly to the movements of the mouse itself. You should be careful not to adjust it too high because the speed will be too fast. You will notice that you will not be able to click the mouse fast enough to execute a command. If you notice that the double-click does not work, or perhaps that someone set the speed too high, highlight the Mouse icon in the Control Panel and press ⟦Enter⟧ to bring up the Mouse Properties dialog box.

FIGURE 14.15
Motion tab

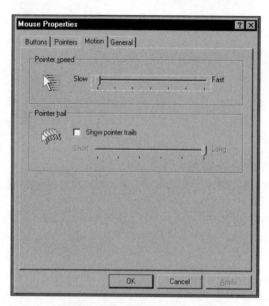

The double-click speed for your mouse is adjusted in the same manner. In the Mouse Properties dialog box, drag the slider in the Double-Click Speed area. To test the speed, double-click the image in the Test Area.

Mouse trails can also be customized, by clicking on the Motion tab (Figure 14.16). In the Pointer Trail area, make sure the Show Pointer Trails box is checked. To adjust the length of the pointer trail, drag the slider. This option is especially useful if you are using an LCD (liquid crystal display) screen. The mouse pointer is easier to see on laptop computers if you turn on pointer trails. Finally, from the Buttons tab, you can reverse the mouse buttons in the Button Configuration area of Mouse Properties (Figure 14.13). This is helpful for left-handed as well as right-handed users.

FIGURE 14.16
Mouse trails

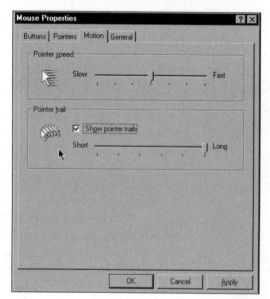

Customizing Sounds

Windows sounds a warning beep when you select a command that is not valid. Sound can be turned on or off. If you do not hear the warning beep (providing you have a sound card in your computer), you may need to turn the sound on.

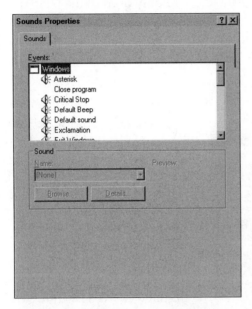

FIGURE 14.17
Sounds Properties

Sounds can be assigned to program "events" in Windows. Program events include the following: Critical Stop, Default Beep, Exclamation, Start/Exit Windows, Minimize/Maximize, Menu Command, and others. From the Control Panel, the Sounds Properties dialog box (Figure 14.17) lists the various other Events that can be customized. In the Events list, click on the *event* you want to assign a sound to. In the Name list, select the sound you want Windows to play whenever the selected event occurs. For instance, you can assign The Microsoft Sound to any event. Figure 14.18 lists the other options in the Name list.

Finally, you can select Schemes from its list box. Additional schemes include Jungle, Windows default, Musica, Robotz, and Utopia. Experiment with each of these. Make sure your instructor or laboratory manager approves

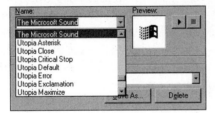

FIGURE 14.18
The Microsoft Sound event

that you do so. You can test a sound by clicking its name and then the Preview button. By default, not all sounds are installed during Windows setup. To install additional sounds, click on the Add/Remove icon in Control Panel and then click on the Windows Setup tab.

Using Sound

If you do not have a sound card installed in your computer, which is usually the case as we write this text, then most of the features on the Sound dialog box are unavailable to you and will appear gray (dimmed) when you invoke this item. If you have a sound card installed, then you can assign different sounds (stored in *.wav* files) to different events. The new Compaq DeskPro computers contain a feature called Business Audio that allows the easy recording and playback of sounds. In the future, expect to see more computers equipped with sound capabilities.

Customizing Regional Settings

The **Regional Settings** icon in Control Panel allows you to customize your system for a wide variety of countries. You can customize Windows for international currency symbols, dates and times, or even measurement systems.

Windows 95 default settings are those commonly used in the United States. However, with the Regional Settings you can change these other settings as desired. Perhaps you will find yourself corresponding with an international associate. You can customize your desktop to accommodate your needs.

Starting Regional Settings

FIGURE 14.19
Regional Settings Properties dialog box

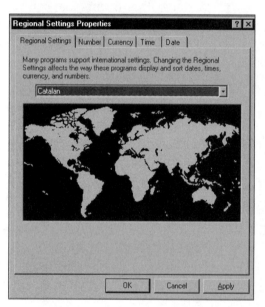

To change Windows 95 Regional Settings, double-click on the Regional Settings icon in the Control Panel. The Regional Settings Properties dialog box will appear (Figure 14.19. This dialog box contains individual tabs to change Number, Currency, Time, and Date.

To customize Windows, choose the Language drop-down list box. The default language is English (United States). Other language choices include Swedish, French, German, Italian Swiss, and English (British), to name a few. After you select a particular language, the Control Panel automatically adjusts the settings of Measurement, Date Format, Time Format, Currency Format, and Number Format.

GUIDED ACTIVITY 14.8

Going International

1. Open Regional Settings by double-clicking on its icon from the Control Panel in the Settings menu from the Start button.

2. Change the current country setting (English-United States) to Swedish. You will have to scroll down the list to see this choice. After you restart your computer, you will notice how the numeric formats change for date, time, and currency.

3. Click on OK to complete the action. You might be asked to insert one of the Windows Setup disks. Do so, or click Cancel.

4. Before you close the Control Panel, be sure to change the setting back to its original value—by default, English (American) language. Then close Control Panel.

Customizing a Screen Saver

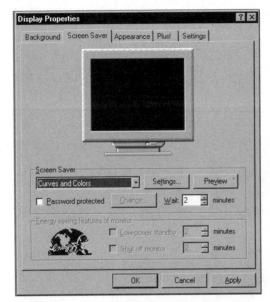

FIGURE 14.20
Display Properties dialog box

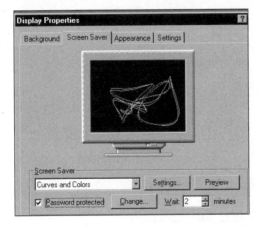

FIGURE 14.21
Change password

A screen saver is used when your computer is idle for a specified number of minutes. Select Display from the Control Panel and the Display Properties dialog box (Figure 14.20) will appear. Select the Screen Saver tab; you will notice the list box for Screen Saver. Click on the arrow in the box to see the available screen savers (Blank Screen, Curves and Colors, Starfield Simulation, Flying Windows, Mystify Your Mind, and Scrolling Marquee). You can specify the amount of time (in minutes) before the screen saver will start. After you select a screen saver, you can Preview it. If you are satisfied with your choice, click on the Apply button to select that particular choice. To customize the screen saver, click Settings. By default, only a limited set of screen savers is installed during initial Windows 95 setup. To change Screen Saver, click on the Display icon in the Control Panel. To protect your files by assigning a screen-saver *password*, make sure *Password Protected* is checked and then click Change (Figure 14.21). Type your password and then confirm the password by typing it again.

☞ **TIP** *Use a password you won't forget, such as your ATM banking password.*

If you assign a password to a screen saver, people who do not have access to the password can't clear the screen saver and therefore can't easily gain access to your computer when you leave it for the specified idle time (say, to go to lunch).

Allowing for Multiple Users

You can customize your computer to enable multiple users to personalize settings. Click on the Password icon in Control Panel. The Passwords Properties dialog box (Figure 14.22) will appear. You will notice the three tabs in this dialog box,

FIGURE 14.22
*Passwords
Properties
dialog box*

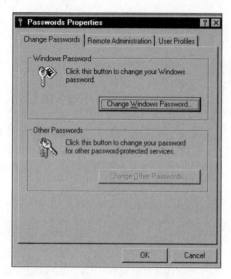

FIGURE 14.23
User profiles

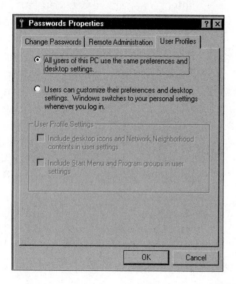

Change Password, Remote Administration (only if you are on a network), and User Profiles. Click on User Profiles (Figure 14.23). Select the second option, that users can customize their own desktop settings. The next person who logs on to Windows 95 can change settings without affecting the settings you prefer. The next tme you log on, your settings will be restored.

Review Questions

*1. What is the desktop?

*2. List and briefly describe the options available for customizing the desktop.

3. What command(s) will allow you to view a pattern without actually selecting it?

4. What can be done to the Regional Settings section of Control Panel?

5. What are the boxes used when customizing the Regional Settings?

*6. What indicates that Sound is off?

7. What are the properties of a program?

8. How do you:

   a. Move a program item from one group to another?

   b. Copy a program item from one group to another?

   c. Delete a program item from a group?

9. Describe the process by which you would create a new program group window on your screen, copy some programs from other groups to the new group, and add to the new group new programs not previously part of your Windows environment.

Key Terms

Add/Remove Programs	Mouse trails	Shareware
Cobblestones	Password	Taskbar Properties
Desktop	Password Protected	Wallpaper
Event	Pattern	*.wav* file
Keyboard Properties	Regional Settings	
Mouse Properties	Screen saver	

Fine-Tuning Windows

Fine-tuning a computer system means customizing it so that it uses its resources most efficiently. These system resources include disk space and memory. In Windows, these available resources can affect the following:

- Which applications you can run

- How many applications you can run simultaneously

- How fast Windows and various Windows applications run

- How much data you can store between one session and the next

Optimizing your computer for Microsoft Windows 95 is intended to "balance" how your computer will accommodate speed, capacity, and free disk space. By *speed*, we mean the ability to run programs quickly, whether in the foreground or in the background. By *capacity*, we mean the ability to run many programs at the same time. By *free disk space*, we mean the amount of space on the drive not used by files. You can improve Windows' performance by configuring your computer system's memory properly.

Two ways in which you can optimize Windows are to free up conventional memory and to perform routine maintenance on your hard disk.

Learning Objectives

At the completion of this unit you should know

1. a typical systems management infrastructure,

2. how to install or connect Plug and Play devices,

3.   what localization of software applications means,

4.   how to configure accessibility options.

Systems Management

Windows 95 is the first version of Windows expressly designed for manageability. The design ensures that management of the Windows 95 PC is accessible both locally and remotely, via a network manager. Network security is used to determine administrator-privileged accounts using pass-through security. Windows 95 also provides for a logical separation of the user of the PC from the underlying configuration of the PC. This means that the PC and the user configurations and privileges can be managed independently. It also means that if a network manager chooses, a user can be enabled to "rove" on the network, that is, log on from virtually any PC on the network and operate in his or her desktop with the correct settings and network privileges. Additionally, it means that a single PC can be shared by multiple users, each with a different desktop configuration and differing network privileges.

Given the proliferation these days of PCs connected to a corporate network, it is key that the Windows 95 PC also be able to participate in any network-wide management schemes. Windows 95 is designed to meet these various network management standards. With this infrastructure built into Windows 95, network management applications are enabled so that they will provide tools for the network manager to keep the PCs and networks running more efficiently and more cost-effectively. The discussion of the management infrastructure in Windows 95 is organized as follows:

- Registry

- User management

- System management

- Network management

The Registry

The central repository in which Windows 95 stores the whole of its configuration data is known as the *Registry*. The Windows 95 system configuration, the PC hardware configuration, Windows 32-bit applications, and user preferences are all stored in the Registry. For example, any Windows 95 hardware configuration changes that are made via a Plug and Play device are immediately reflected in a configuration change in the Registry. Because of these characteristics, the Registry serves as the foundation for user, system, and network management of Windows 95.

The Registry essentially replaces the various MS-DOS and Windows 3.11 configuration files, including *Autoexec.bat*, *Config.sys*, ***Win.ini***, ***System.ini***, and the other applications *.ini* files. However, for compatibility purposes, instances of *Config.sys*, *Win.ini*, and *System.ini* files may exist on a Windows 95 PC for backward compatibility with either 16-bit device drivers or 16-bit applications that must run on Windows 95.

For example, it is expected that 16-bit applications will continue to create and write their own various *.ini* files.

The Registry concept is built on the Registry concept first implemented in Windows NT. The Registry is logically one datastore (a collection of information), but physically it consists of three different files to allow maximum network configuration flexibility. Windows 95 uses the Registry to store information in three major categories:

- User-specific information—user profiles contained in the file *User.dat*.

- Hardware or computer-specific settings—contained in the file *System.dat*.

- System policies—designed to provide an override to any settings contained in the above two components of the Registry. System Policies may contain additional data specific to the network or corporate environment as established by the network manager. This is contained in the file *Policy.pol*. Unlike *System.dat* and *User.dat*, *Policy.dat* is not a "mandatory" component of Windows 95 installation.

User Management

Windows 95 implements functionality for management of user-specific configurations and user-specific privileges. User management under Windows 95 is most evident with the introduction of a user log-on dialog box that minimally prompts the user for their log-on name and password each time they reboot Windows 95. This log-on dialog box captures the username and password that can trigger Windows 95 to dramatically reconfigure the desktop configuration and, as needed, limit access to either network or sharing capabilities from this Windows 95 PC. Windows 95 can also pass the user log-on name and password to registered applications and network services that use the log-on in Windows 95 as the "Master Key" to give the user access to these applications and services.

User management capabilities in Windows 95 are built on the following components:

- User Profiles

- System Policies

- Server-based security

USER PROFILES

In Windows 3.11 settings unique to a user were located in many disparate locations: *Autoexec.bat*, *Config.sys*, *Win.ini*, *System.ini*, and numerous application-specific *.ini* files. For example, this data was often intertwined with Windows' internal configuration data, thus making good user management with Windows 3.11 very difficult to achieve. For example, the simple task of allowing multiple users to use a single PC was not achievable with Windows 3.11 "out of the box." Managing multiple-user configurations on a network was even more difficult. Many companies out of necessity wrote their own user-management tools or used third-party tools to help manage multiple users on the network. Very often this user namespace did not leverage the existing namespace on the corporate network resident on the network servers. In some cases, the user management software was implemented as a replacement

Windows shell, with varying degrees of compatibility with the existing Windows applications and the underlying network client software. All of these tools and products attempted to retroactively address Windows 3.11's lack of user-management capabilities.

User management in Windows 95 is integral to the system, as implemented in a feature known as User Profiles. User Profiles are part of the Registry. They contain system, application, and network data that are unique to the individual user of a Windows 95 PC. These characteristics can be set by the user, by the network manager, or by the PC help desk staff. In contrast to Windows 3.11, the User Profiles in Windows 95 are contained within a single file named *User.dat*. By keeping all the user-specific data in one file, Windows 95 can provide a means for managing the PC separately from the configuration of the Windows 95 operating system and the PC hardware.

SYSTEM POLICIES

In conjunction with User Profiles and System Settings components of the Registry, System Policies are the final piece of the Registry. Like the other two Registry components, the System Policies consist of pairs of keys and values. Unlike the other two Registry components, however, System Policies are designed to override any settings that may exist in User Profiles or System Profiles. System Policies are not necessary to enable a Windows 95 system to boot (start). System Policies are loaded last, and are typically downloaded from a network server. Windows 95 provides a mechanism to allow the network manager to define a network location to find the System Policies and download to this PC. System Policies are designed to give the network manager the ability to customize control over Windows 95 for users of differing capabilities or network privilege level. These capabilities include controls of the user interface, network capabilities, desktop configuration, sharing capabilities, and so on.

Plug and Play

The technology named *Plug and Play* was jointly developed by Microsoft Corporation and a number of PC product vendors, to dramatically improve integration of PC hardware and software. Windows is a key enabling technology for Plug and Play. Plug and Play is built into all levels of Windows 95 and covers both common desktop and laptop devices, such as monitors, printers, video cards, sound cards, CD-ROM drives, SCSI adapters, modems, and PCMCIA devices.

With Windows 95, a user can easily install or connect Plug and Play devices to the system, letting the system automatically allocate hardware resources, with no user intervention. For example, by simply plugging in a CD-ROM and sound card, a desktop PC can easily be turned into a multimedia playback system. The user simply plugs in the components, turns on the PC, and "plays" a video clip.

Windows 95 also enables new Plug and Play system designs that can be dynamically reconfigured. For example, a Windows 95 Plug and Play laptop can be removed from its docking station while it is still running and taken to a meeting; the system automatically reconfigures to work with a lower-resolution display and adjusts for the absence of the network card and large disk drive.

Windows 95 together with Plug and Play devices will provide for complete *backward* compatibility to work with systems that were not designed according to the Plug and Play specification. When you purchase a Plug and Play device for a non–Plug and Play PC running Windows 95, for example, you still benefit from the automatic installation features of Plug and Play add-on devices.

If you have ever had to suffer through the experience of opening up a PC system unit to plug in a new device adapter card, you will understand why Plug and Play is important. The combination of Windows 95 and a PC that supports the Plug and Play specification will reduce your system setup and reconfiguration suffering to a minimum. You will still have to know how to use a screwdriver, but that is about the only extra skill you will need.

Typically, the process of adding a new device to a PC has involved figuring out how to set all the switches and jumpers on the new card, plugging the card in, installing software, rebooting the system, and hoping it works. The amount of time you could spend trying to resolve problems during installation of a new device could be extensive.

Examples of Plug and Play include the following:

- Applications running on portable systems that use PCMCIA cards for disk storage need to take account of the possibility that the user will try to eject a card when there are files open on that disk.

- User alteration of connectivity options—for example, exchanging a network card for a modem card—is likely to be of interest to both the network subsystem and any communications application. The application ought to try to adapt itself to the new speed of the connection, for example.

- Applications ought to adapt smoothly to changes in display resolution initiated by the user.

- The "disappearance" of network volumes when the user walks out of his or her wireless network should not result in misleading error messages.

Installing New Printers

Installing and configuring printers in Windows 95 is greatly simplified over Windows 3.1. As with other components of the Windows 95 system, setting up a new printer in Windows 95 benefits from Plug and Play capabilities. Windows 95 detects Plug and Play–compatible printers that return device ID values as described in IEEE Specification 1284 through bidirectional parallel communications. Bidirectional parallel communications with the printer will also aid in Plug and Play's querying of other physical attributes of the device.

Windows 95 detects a Plug and Play printer in several ways—when Windows 95 is first installed on a user's PC, during the boot cycle each time Windows 95 is started, or when a user explicitly requests a detection to be made.

When Windows 95 is first installed on a user's PC and when Windows 95 starts up, the Plug and Play detection code attempts to identify a printer connected to a bidirectional communications port. If the printer connected is not presently configured in the Windows 95 system, the user is asked whether the printer should be installed. If the user says yes and the appropriate printer driver is already present on the system, Windows automatically installs and configures the driver for the new printer. If the printer driver is not already present, Windows 95 prompts the user for the appropriate Setup and Installation disk for Windows 95. If the printer is not recognized by the Windows 95 system, the user is prompted to insert a disk containing the printer driver provided by the printer manufacturer.

While there will be much broader support and demand for Plug and Play printers, several printers on the market today provide varying degrees of true Plug and Play awareness. For example, the Hewlett-Packard LaserJet 4 models (4L, 4Plus, 4P, 4MP, 4mplus, and 4ML, 4si), LexMark 4039 and 4039+, and ValueWriter 600, which are presently shipping, are true Plug and Play peripherals.

International Language Support

With the growth of the worldwide PC market, the use of Microsoft Windows and Windows-based applications has made PCs easier to use for millions of people around the globe. Windows and Windows-based applications are sold and used worldwide. This poses some unique problems both for Microsoft as an operating system vendor, and for ISVs (independant software vendors) as applications developers.

When a new software application or operating system intended for a world market is developed, efforts must be undertaken to *localize* the software for a given country and for the written language in which it will be used. In many cases, this is as simple as changing the names of menus, menu items, and strings displayed by the software to match the foreign language used in the locale. However, as the features and functionality of a software product grow, so does the complexity required to tailor the application to characteristics of the native country. Since the start of the design work for the Windows NT operating system, Microsoft has been enhancing the level of support for international languages and cultural conventions in the 32-bit editions of the Windows family of operating systems.

Support for using Windows operating systems on a global basis is improved in Windows 95. Windows 95 offers benefits to both end-users and to software developers, which can be summarized as follows.

Benefits for Users

- Windows 95 makes it easy to use multiple language fonts and character sets, and easily switch between the different keyboard layouts required to support them; for example, Russian and English.

- Windows 95 substitutes fonts when switching between different languages if the original font is not present on the system.

Benefits for Developers

- It is easy for application developers to add international language support to their applications.

- Windows 95 provides services for application vendors to automatically switch between the proper fonts and keyboard layouts as users navigate through a multilingual document.

- Information can be passed through the Clipboard to other applications and will preserve language-specific attributes. Windows 95 provides additional services for application vendors to easily exchange information between internationally aware applications, while preserving all language formatting characteristics.

- *Multilingual*-aware applications can change the given language of the system under control.

Localized product versions for Windows 95 include German, French, Spanish, Swedish, Dutch, Italian, Norwegian, Danish, Finnish, Portuguese, Japanese, Chinese, Korean, Russian, Czech, Polish, Hungarian, Turkish, Greek, Arabic, Basque, Hebrew, Thai, Indonesian, and Catalan (as well as several other variations of some of these languages).

Mobile Computing

Windows 95 is designed to make PCs used "away from the desk" easier to operate and more powerful for everyone. Any notebook or portable computer user will benefit from improved support in three areas: remote network access (or "dial-up networking"), hardware support, and support for the mobile work environment.

Windows 95 includes a dial-up network client that allows a mobile or remote computer to dial into popular networking server products, such as Shiva Netmodem, NetWare Connect, and Windows NT Remote Access Services, using the same network protocols and advanced security features provided for desktop PCs.

The Plug and Play implementation in Windows 95 will support inserting, configuring, and removing devices such as PCMCIA cards while the operating system is running. Windows 95 will also support automatic reconfiguration of portable computers when they are inserted or removed from docking stations or port replicators.

Mobile computer users face special problems because of their work environment. Electronic mail and faxing work differently on a mobile computer than they do on a desktop system. Mobile computer users must contend with limited resources, such as disk space or battery power. Many mobile computers exchange files with a second desktop, PC, or file server.

The Microsoft Exchange includes features such as Remote Mail and Microsoft at Work Fax that make staying in touch while on the road easy and reliable.

An enhanced version of Advanced Power Management (APM) will further extend battery life. File viewers for the top 20 or 30 application file formats, plus support for integrated disk compression, reduce demands on hard disk space. Deferred printing support enables storage of print jobs while on the road, for eventual printing back in the office.

Finally, Windows 95 provides file-synchronization services and a direct-cable-file-transfer utility to simplify coexistence with other computers.

Using Briefcase

My Briefcase

Windows 95 introduces the Briefcase, an easy-to-use interface for keeping multiple versions of files "in sync." For example, if you copy several files from your desktop PC to your laptop, the Briefcase automates the process of comparing your (perhaps edited) files to the original versions, and performing any needed copy operations to keep all the files up-to-date. The Briefcase also enables applications to provide "reconciliation handlers" that merge documents together when both the original and the copy have been changed.

To simplify the process of exchanging files between two machines, Windows 95 implements "Direct Cable Connection." Direct Cable Connection provides a simple, fast, network-like connection (including security) between two machines, using a parallel or serial cable.

General Accessibilty Features

An accessibility section in the Windows 95 help contents and index provides a quick reference and pointer to topics that can help adjust the behavior of the system for people with disabilities.

Accessibility
Options

Most of the accessibility features are adjusted through the Accessibility Options icon in the Control panel in Windows 95. This allows you to turn the accessibility features on or off and to customize timings, feedback, and other behavior for your own particular needs.

Emergency Hotkeys

Most of the accessibility features are adjusted through the Control Panel. However, if a user is unable to use the computer until an accessibility feature is turned on, how can he or she use the Control Panel to activitate it? This chicken-and-the-egg problem is solved by providing emergency hotkeys that a user can press to temporarily turn on the specific feature needed. Then, once a feature is turned on, the user can navigate to the Control Panel and adjust the feature to his or her own preferences, or turn it on permanently. The same hotkey can be used to temporarily turn off one of the features, if it gets in the way, or to enable another person to use the computer.

Each hotkey is designed to be obscure key combinations or key sequences that should not conflict with applications. If such a conflict does arise, the hotkeys can be disabled and the user can still use the feature as needed.

Accessibility Status Indicator

FIGURE 15.1
Optional visual indicator

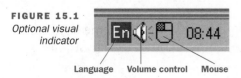
Language   Volume control   Mouse

An optional visual indicator is provided that tells the user which accessibility features are turned on (Figure 15.1), helping users unfamiliar with the features identify the cause of unfamiliar behavior. The indicator also provides feedback on the keys and mouse buttons currently being "held down" by the StickyKeys and MouseKeys features. The status indicator can be displayed on the system taskbar, or as a free-floating window, and can be displayed in a choice of sizes.

StickyKeys

Many software programs require the user to press two or three keys at one time. For people who type with a single finger or a mouthstick, that just isn't possible. StickyKeys allow users to press one key at a time and instruct Windows to respond as if they had been pressed simultaneously.

When StickyKeys is on, pressing any modifier key (Ctrl, Alt, or Shift) will latch that key down until you release the mouse button or a nonmodifier key. Pressing a modifier key twice will lock it down until it is tapped a third time.

StickyKeys functionality is adjusted using the Control Panel, or it can be turned on or off using an emergency hotkey, by pressing the Shift key five consecutive times.

SlowKeys

The sensitivity of the keyboard can be a major problem for some individuals, especially if they often press keys accidentally. SlowKeys instructs Windows to disregard keystrokes that are not held down for a minimum period of time. This allows a user to brush against keys without any ill effect, and when the user gets a finger on the proper key, the user can hold the key down until the character prints to the screen.

SlowKeys functionality is adjusted using the Control Panel, or it can be turned on or off using an emergency hotkey, by holding the right Shift key for 8 seconds (this hotkey also turns on RepeatKeys).

RepeatKeys

Most keyboards allow users to repeat a key just by holding it down. This feature is convenient for some, but can be a major annoyance for people who can't lift their fingers off the keyboard quickly. RepeatKeys lets users adjust the repeat rate or disable it altogether.

RepeatKeys is adjusted using the Control Panel, or it can be turned on or off using an emergency hotkey, by holding down the right Shift key for 8 seconds (this hotkey also turns on SlowKeys).

BounceKeys

For users who "bounce" keys, resulting in double strikes of the same key or other similar errors, BounceKeys instructs Windows to ignore unintended keystrokes.

BounceKeys is adjusted using the Control Panel, or it can be turned on or off using an emergency hotkey, by holding down the right [Shift] key for 12 seconds. You will hear an up-siren after 8 seconds and another double-tone after 12 seconds. Releasing the [Shift] key after the double-tone will activate BounceKeys.

MouseKeys

This feature lets individuals control the mouse pointer using the keyboard. Windows 95 is designed to allow the user to perform all actions without needing a mouse, but some applications may require one, and a mouse may be more convenient for some tasks. MouseKeys is also useful for graphic artists and others who need to position the pointer with great accuracy. You do not need to have a mouse to use this feature.

When the MouseKey is on, use the following keys to navigate the pointer on your screen:

- Press any number key except [5] (these are also called direction keys) on the numeric keypad to move the pointer.

- Use the [5] key for a single mouse-button click and the [+] key for a double-click.

- To drag and release an object, with the pointer on the object, press [Ins] to begin dragging, and then move the object to its new location and [Del] to release it.

- Select the left, right, or both mouse buttons for clicking by pressing the [/],[-],or [*] key, respectively.

- Hold down the [Ctrl] key while using the direction keys (numeric keys, except for [5]) to "jump" the pointer in large increments across the screen.

- Hold down the [Shift] key while using the direction keys to move the mouse a single pixel at a time for greater accuracy.

MouseKeys can be adjusted using Accessibility Options on the Control Panel, or it can be turned on or off using an emergency hotkey, by pressing the left [Alt], left [Shift], and [Num Lock] keys simultaneously.

ToggleKeys

This feature provides audio cues—high and low beeps—to tell the user whether a toggle key is active or inactive. It applies to the [Caps Lock], [Num Lock], and [Scroll Lock] keys.

ToggleKeys can be adjusted using the Control Panel, or it can be turned on or off using an emergency hotkey, by holding down the [Num Lock] key 8 seconds.

ShowSounds

Some applications present information audibly, as wave-files containing digitized speech or through audible cues that each convey a different meaning. These cues might be unusable by a person who is deaf or hard-of-hearing, someone who works in a very noisy environment, or someone who turns off the computer's speakers in a very quiet work environment. In Windows 95, you can set a global flag to let applications know that you want visible feedback—in effect, asking the applications to be "close captioned."

SoundSentry

This feature tells Windows to send a visual cue, such as a blinking title bar or screen flash, whenever there is a system beep. This allows users to see the message that they may not have heard.

SerialKeys

This feature, in conjunction with a communications aid interface device, allows the user to control the computer using an alternative input device. Such a device needs only to send coded command strings through the computer's serial port to specify keystrokes and mouse events that are treated like normal keyboard and mouse input.

Multiple Pointing Devices

The new Plug and Play architecture in Windows 95 inherently supports multiple pointing devices all cooperating together. This allows the seamless addition to the system of alternative pointing devices, such as head-pointers or eye-gaze systems, without the need to replace or disable the mouse.

GUIDED ACTIVITY 15.1

Typing with a Pencil

Suppose you could only type with a single finger, or with a stick held between your teeth. How would you press [Alt][Tab]?

1. Use the shortcut box in the Settings for StickyKeys to activate this option. Press a [Shift] key consecutively five times to try out StickyKeys.

2. Once it is activated, press the [Alt] key and see what happens.

3. Press [Tab] and you will have just typed two keys at once with a single finger.

4. Press [Alt] twice, then [Tab] a few times to see the [Alt][Tab] window and cycle through all the tasks you have running.

5. When you are satisfied, press ⟦Alt⟧ one more time to release it.

Backup

The Backup utility is a new 32-bit application for Windows 95 that makes it easy for users to "back up" information on their computer to another storage medium such as a floppy disk or to tape. The user interface in the Backup application takes full advantage of the new Windows 95 user interface, and uses standard controls such as the tree and list view controls to make it easy for novices and users familiar

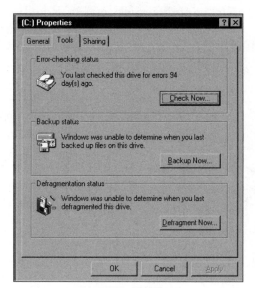

FIGURE 15.2
Backup options

with the controls in Windows Explorer as part of the Windows 95 shell. Usability studies have shown that the user interface is easy for novice users to understand and use, and thus will make it quick and simple for backups to be performed. Backup includes the ability to drag and drop file sets and backup sets onto a link to the Backup application, which can be placed on the desktop to make starting a backup operation much easier—this allows users to just "click and drag" to start a backup procedure. Access to the Backup application can also be invoked by running the Backup application, or by choosing the backup options from the Tools Tab on the Disk Property sheet (Figure 15.2).

Disk Utilities

Windows 95 includes a collection of disk utilities designed to keep your system performing optimally and error-free. In addition to the DriveSpace Disk Compression Tool, Windows 95 also includes a disk optimizer tool and a disk checking and repair tool.

Starting Disk Defragmenter (Optimizer)

The Disk Defragmenter (optimizer) tool in Windows 95 makes it easy for users to optimize their hard disk by rearranging information so that it is better organized. This helps to minimize the area on your disk where Windows 95 will look to load information that you request. Unlike the disk defragmenter utility provided with MS-DOS, the Disk Defragmenter utility in Windows 95 is a graphical application that runs within Windows 95. Users can defragment their disks in the background while other applications are running on their system, making it convenient for them to optimize

FIGURE 15.3
*Disk
defragmenting*

their system. Additionally, users can see details of the defragment process and watch the progress being made by the utility, or can display a minimal status box (Figure 15.3).

Using ScanDisk

The ScanDisk (disk checking and repair tool) provided with Windows 95 is designed to help users check the integrity of their disks and to remedy problems that are detected. Unlike the ScanDisk

FIGURE 15.4
*Checking for
errors with
ScanDisk*

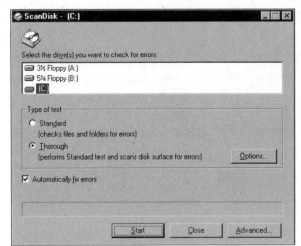

utility provided with MS-DOS, the ScanDisk utility in Windows 95 is a graphical application that runs within Windows 95. Users have the option of either running a standard scan, where ScanDisk will only check the files on the user's system for errors, or a thorough scan, where files are checked for errors and a disk surface test is performed to check for additional errors (Figure 15.4).

Understanding OLE

OLE (object linking and embedding) is a mechanism that allows applications to "interoperate" more effectively, thereby allowing users to work more productively. Users of OLE applications create and manage compound documents. These are documents that seamlessly incorporate data or objects of different formats. Sound clips, spreadsheets, text, and bitmaps are some examples of objects commonly found in compound documents. Each object is created and maintained by its server application, but through the use of OLE, the services of the different server applications are integrated. Users feel as if a single application with all the functionality of each of the server applications is being used. Users of OLE-enabled applications do not need to be concerned with managing and switching between the various server applications; they focus solely on the compound document and the task being performed using OLE-based features.

Features of OLE

With OLE, Microsoft Windows 95 increases the degree of application integration available to any applications that take advantage of the services. This gives users tangible benefits, allowing them to share data and functionality across applications and to combine them as they please. Because OLE is based on an open industry-standard, users can extend their applications with additional third-party products, further expanding their choice and flexibility.

OLE provides the following features to allow users to easily integrate information into multiple applications:

CROSS-APPLICATION DRAG-AND-DROP Users can drag and drop graphs, tables, and pictures directly onto slides, worksheets, and documents to mix text, data, and graphics into compound documents. Using drag-and-drop is faster and more intuitive than using Clipboard to cut and paste.

 NOTE *Users must drag to the desktop and then drop into other documents or programs.*

VISUAL EDITING With visual editing, the user can double-click on an object to directly edit while remaining in the original document. For example, double-click an embedded Microsoft Excel worksheet in a Word document and the Microsoft Excel menus and toolbars automatically appear within the context of Word. Unlike the first release of OLE technology, the user is not launched into a separate Microsoft Excel window to work on the spreadsheet data.

System Configuration Editor

From the Start button, choose the Run command. In the command line type: Sysedit. This will launch the System Configuration Editor (Figure 15.5), which will allow you to edit the following files: *Protocol.ini*, *System.ini*, *Win.ini*, *Config.sys*, *Msmail.ini*, and *Autoexec.bat*. It is strongly recommended that you do *not* make any changes in these files unless so directed by your instructor or laboratory manager. This

FIGURE 15.5
System Configuration Editor

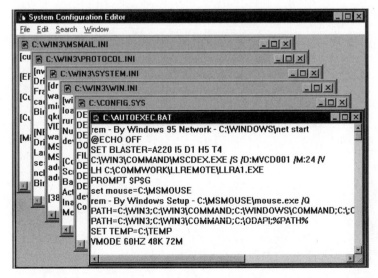

discussion is for information purposes and settings in these files should only be changed by an experienced or advanced user.

Review Questions

* *1.   List the Windows 95 system management infrastructure.

* 2.   What is Plug and Play technology?

* *3.   How can software applications or operating systems be made available for a world market?

* 4.   What is mobile computing?

* *5.   Give three examples of accessibility options.

* 6.   How can you check and repair a disk?

Key Terms

Multilingual	Registry	*User.dat*
Plug and Play	*System.dat*	*Win.ini*
Policy.pol	*System.ini*	

Transferring Data Using Clipboard

Clipboard is a utility program that acts as a temporary storage area for information being transferred between applications during a Windows session. You can cut or copy information from an application onto the Clipboard, and then transfer that information from the Clipboard into other applications or elsewhere in the same application.

Information you cut or copy onto the Clipboard remains there until you clear the Clipboard, cut or copy new information to the Clipboard, or exit from Windows. Clipboard can be used to transfer information from all windows except Clock and from most non-Windows applications. Clipboard retains its contents until you change them. Thus, you can paste the information into the designated area whenever you want to, as well as paste the same information repeatedly.

Clipboard provides a fast and convenient way to gather all the information required to complete a project in one place at one time. It can be used to move data between applications not specifically designed for Windows. Thus, it is a flexible and powerful tool for increasing your productivity.

Learning Objectives

At the completion of this unit you should know

1. how to start and exit Clipboard,

2. how to copy, cut, and paste information,

3. how to use Clipboard Viewer,

4. how to open and close the File, Edit, and Display menus.

Clipboard

The **Clipboard** is an area of memory in Windows that holds information that can be transferred from one application to another. If you have used a word processor, you will appreciate the ability to move or copy text and graphics from one location to another. This process is known as "cut and paste."

The procedures involved in using Clipboard are the same for all Windows applications. To cut or copy information from a Windows application:

1. Select the information you want to copy.

2. Choose the application's Cut or Copy command. (The **Cut** command is used if you want to move the information, while the **Copy** command is used to make a duplicate copy of the information.)

3. Switch to where you want the information copied. This might be elsewhere in the same document (or spreadsheet or graphic), to a different document in the same application, or to a different application.

4. Position the cursor or insertion point at the location where the information is to be placed.

5. Choose the receiving application's **Paste** command.

Copy, Cut, and Paste Commands

Almost all Windows applications have an Edit menu with Copy, Cut, and Paste commands. One of the few applications that does not have these commands is Clock, since it is not able to receive any kind of user input.

These commands work the same way in all applications. Copy puts the selected information on the Clipboard without removing it from the original document. Cut, on the other hand, puts the information on the Clipboard and at the same time deletes it from the source. Paste puts a copy of the Clipboard's contents into a designated area without removing anything from the Clipboard.

If you have not selected any information in the source document, the application's Copy and Cut commands will appear in gray. The Paste command will also appear in gray. Once you select information, the Cut and Copy commands will appear in the Edit menu as black. Once you have "cut" or "copied" to the Clipboard, the Paste command will be black.

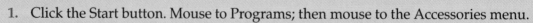

GUIDED ACTIVITY 16.1

Cutting and Pasting

1. Click the Start button. Mouse to Programs; then mouse to the Accessories menu.

2. Open WordPad from Accessories by double-clicking on its icon.

3. Click on Open in the File menu in WordPad.

4. Double-click on the file *C:\Windows\WDReadme.txt*.

5. Mark the first few lines of this file by dragging the mouse over the text. You should see the text selected as highlighted.

6. Click on Copy in the Edit menu.

7. Close WordPad.

8. Open Notepad from Accessories.

9. Click on New in the File menu.

10. Click on Paste in the Edit menu. The text copied from WordPad should now appear.

11. Click on Save in the File menu. Type a file name and click on OK to save the file.

12. Close Notepad.

COPYING AN ENTIRE SCREEN

To copy the image of the entire screen to the Clipboard, press the Print Screen key (sometimes labeled Prt Sc or Print Scrn). The Clipboard contents can then be pasted into Paint or another graphics program for editing, then cutting and pasting into a word processing document. That is the technique we used to reproduce the various program icons that you see in this text. To copy only the active window to the Clipboard (for example, the Virtual Memory window), press and hold the key before you press [PrtSc].

Using the Clipboard Viewer

Clipboard Viewer lets you see what is contained in Clipboard before you paste. To open Clipboard Viewer, double-click on its program item icon on the Accessories menu. The Clipboard window will appear as in Figure 16.1. The Clipboard window contains the usual parts: title bar, menu bar, Control menu box, sizing buttons, scroll bars, and the workspace.

FIGURE 16.1
Clipboard Viewer

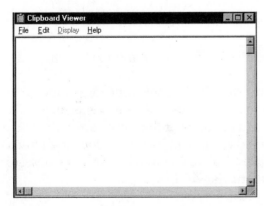

Starting Clipboard Viewer

1. Start WordPad from the Accessories program group.

2. Click on Open in the File menu and open a file by double-clicking on it.

3. Mark the text to be copied.

4. Click on Copy in the Edit menu.

5. Minimize WordPad to an icon by clicking on the minimize button in the upper-right corner of the window.

6. Click on the Clipboard icon on the Accessories menu.

7. The text you marked in step 3 should now appear in the Clipboard Viewer. Figure 16.2 shows a sample of text that was copied from WordPad to the Clipboard.

FIGURE 16.2
Text from WordPad copied to Clipboard

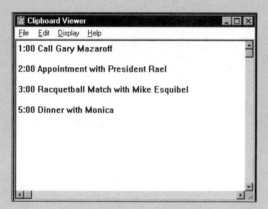

Clipboard Menus

Three of the menus in Clipboard—File, Edit, and Display—offer some flexibility in how you treat data or blocks of copy once they are on the clipboard.

File Menu

Commands in the File menu allow you to save and to reuse the current contents of the Clipboard.

Use the Save As command to store the current Clipboard contents to a disk file (see Figure 16.3). Clipboard automatically adds the file extension *.clp*. The Open command is used to replace the current contents of the Clipboard with an existing *.clp* file. The File menu's Exit command closes Clipboard, as does the Close command from the Control menu. Clipboard files are useful when creating and storing graphic images that can be placed several times within a document.

FIGURE 16.3
File Save As command

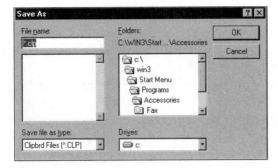

Edit Menu

The Edit menu in the Clipboard Viewer has only one command, Delete, which deletes the contents of the Clipboard. Information on the Clipboard uses a great deal of memory, thereby reducing the amount of available memory for other applications. If you get a warning message indicating that you do not have enough memory to

FIGURE 16.4
Clipboard's Delete command

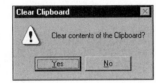

carry out a command, or if you notice your applications are running slower than normal, you should use Clipboard's Delete command to delete the current contents of Clipboard. When you click on Delete, you will get the warning message shown in Figure 16.4. If there is nothing on the Clipboard, the Delete choice will be gray as in Figure 16.5.

As you use the Delete command, a drop-down dialog box will appear, requesting that you confirm your selection. If you feel that you need to save the contents of Clipboard for future use, use the File menu's Save As command to create a disk file. You can now safely delete the contents of the Clipboard.

FIGURE 16.5
Delete command is gray

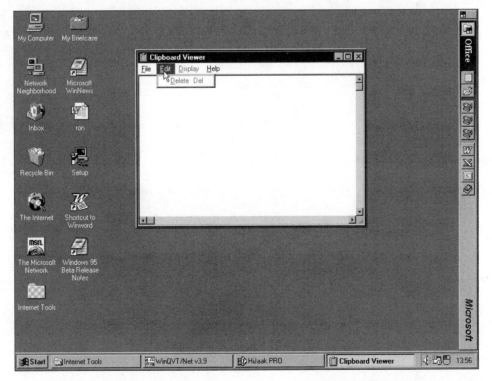

Display Menu

The Display menu lets you change the format by which Clipboard displays its contents. When you transfer data from one location to another through Clipboard, Windows attempts to maintain formatting. For example, if you copy text from a WordPad document to the Clipboard, and then paste it into another WordPad document, the paragraph retains all of its formatting characteristics. But if you copy text into another application that does *not* contain the same type of formatting characteristics, the actual transfer will be in plain text without the special formatted characteristics.

In the same manner, if you copy a drawing created in a *vector format* (a format that records a set of commands by which the drawing can be re-created), the source program supplies the selection in at least two versions, in vector format and as a bitmap (a format that records only the actual positions and colors of each dot in the drawing). The vector format is the more information-rich of the two, but if the receiving program uses only bitmaps, the Clipboard transfers a bitmap.

When a selection has been sent to the Clipboard in multiple formats, you can see what formats are available by viewing Clipboard's Display menu, shown in Figure 16.6.

For example, if you want to duplicate (copy) a document from Word for Windows with multiple fonts to Clipboard, Clipboard's Display will appear as Auto. The other selections on the Clipboard Display menu include Text and OEM Text.

A second type of Display viewer allows transferring of graphic images. Figure 16.7 shows the available options: Auto (default choice), Text, or OEM Text.

FIGURE 16.6
*Clipboard's
Display menu*

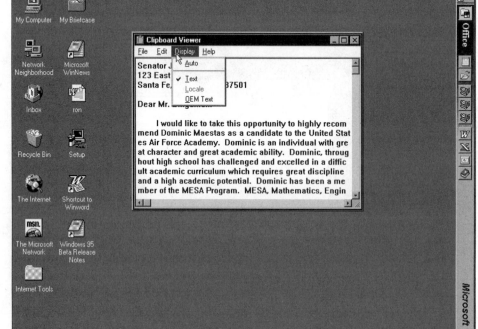

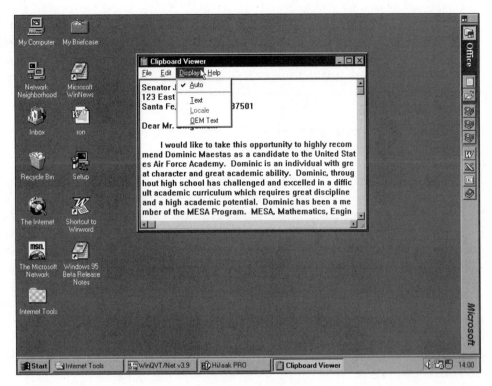

FIGURE 16.7
Display options

If you transfer copy from a Microsoft Word document, the Display menu will appear as in Figure 16.8. This allows you to transfer data in Text, Picture, and OEM Text formats.

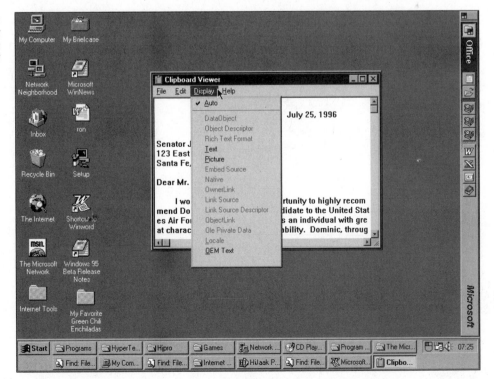

FIGURE 16.8
Transferring copy from a Word document

Owner Display refers to the way the information is sent to the Clipboard from Word for Windows with all formatting information intact. Text is the plain text version that Windows will transfer to a single font application, such as WordPad. *OEM Text* is a format that Windows will use if you transfer Clipboard's contents to a non-Windows application.

Using Clipboard with Non-Windows Applications

You can use the Clipboard to transfer information in and out of applications that were not designed specifically for Windows 95, although a few restrictions do apply. You can copy information from a non-Windows application to the Clipboard, but you cannot cut information from a non-Windows application to Clipboard. Also, if you are running Windows in either Real mode or Standard mode, your non-Windows applications will use the entire screen (you will not be able to run them in a window). Therefore, you will only be able to copy the entire screen to the Clipboard at a given time. Finally, you cannot copy information to the Clipboard from a non-Windows application that runs in graphics mode.

Review Questions

*1.   Explain the purpose of Clipboard.

*2.   What is the difference between Cut and Copy?

3.   How do you activate Clipboard Viewer?

*4.   Explain the importance of multiple formats while transferring information.

5.   How would you transfer data from an Excel worksheet?

Key Terms

Clipboard	Cut	Paste
Copy	OEM Text	Vector format

Windows Setup[1]

Windows Setup is a program that copies information from the original Windows disks, and then creates initialization files that instruct Windows how to act. It is different from Control Panel (see Units 5 and 14), which affects what you see on the screen. You can use Windows Setup to change system settings, set up applications to use with Windows, and add or remove optional Windows components.

Windows 95 Specifications

To use Microsoft Windows 95, you need:

- Personal computer with a 386DX or higher processor
- 4MB of memory (8MB recommended)
- Typical available hard disk space required: 35–40MB; 50–55MB for users not running Windows (actual requirements will vary based on features you choose to install)
- 3.5" high-density disk drive or CD-ROM
- VGA or higher-resolution graphics card

Options:

- Microsoft Mouse or compatible pointing device
- Modem or fax modem

---

1 Adapted from *Introducing Microsoft Windows 95*. Portions of the following are copyright © 1985–1995 by Microsoft Corporation.

- Audio card/speakers for sound

  To access Microsoft Exchange and The Microsoft Network:

- 8MB of memory

- 20MB of additional hard disk space

- Modem required for The Microsoft Network

Setting Up Windows 95

It's easy to set up Windows. There are two ways to do it, depending on whether you have an earlier version of Windows (version 3.*x* or Windows 3.11 for Workgroups) on your computer.

To Upgrade from an Earlier Version of Windows

1. Insert Setup Disk 1 in a floppy drive, or insert your Windows CD-ROM in a CD-ROM drive.

2. In File Manager or Program Manager, click File, and then click Run.

3. Type the drive letter, followed by a colon (:) and a backslash (\), and the word `setup`. For example:

   `a:\setup`

   Note that if you install from a CD-ROM, precede the word `setup` with `win95\`:

   `a:\win95\setup`

4. Follow the instructions on your screen. Click Next to continue through the Setup process.

   If you do not have a previous version of Windows, use the following procedure.

To Set Up Windows from MS-DOS

1. Insert Setup Disk 1 in a floppy disk drive, or insert your Windows CD-ROM in a CD-ROM drive.

2. At the command prompt, type the drive letter, followed by a colon (:) and a backslash (\), and the word `setup`. For example, your screen might look like this:

   `[C:\]a:\setup`

   Note that if you install from a CD-ROM, precede the word `setup` with `win95\`:

   `a:\win95\setup`

3. Press [Enter], and then follow the instructions on your screen. Click Next to continue through the setup process.

Setup prompts you to choose the type of installation you want. If you're not sure, choose the one that Windows selects for you. The following table describes these options.

This setup option	Does this
Typical	Sets up the most commonly used Windows components.
Portable	Sets up features that are most useful for a portable computer, while conserving disk space. This includes power management features and Briefcase, a program that helps you synchronize files between laptop and desktop computers.
Compact	Sets up only the basic files you need to run Windows. This is useful if you have very limited disk space.
Custom	Enables you to choose exactly which components to install. If you are an advanced user or system administrator and want to customize your Windows installation, choose this option.

If you encounter problems setting up Windows, see the *Setup.txt* file that comes with Windows.

Other Windows 95 Installation Issues

When you upgrade Windows 95 over a previous version of Windows, you will need 35–40MB of free disk space, as opposed to 50–55MB for a full installation to a different directory. Windows 95 can be installed in a new directory, or you can let Windows 95 replace the files in your Windows 3.1 directory. However, you will be better off installing Windows 95 in the same directory that contains Windows 3.1. This is the default setting when you install Windows 95. The advantage is that Windows 95 will use the Windows 3.1 settings to find all your hardware and software. If you want to be able to use both Windows 3.1 or Windows 95 on your PC, then you should install Windows in a new directory. You can only use Windows 3.1 and Windows 95 on one PC if the existing version of MS-DOS is 5.0 or higher. Assuming you have this, press [F8] when you see the Starting Windows 95 message at startup. You get a menu of options and select the Previous version of MS-DOS. Change to the Windows 3.1 directory, type WIN, press [Enter], and you are back on familiar ground.

Finally, Windows 95 will preserve your old software settings and everything should work fine, on one condition: that you installed Windows 95 over Windows 3.1 in the *same directory*. If you did not, all Windows applications and also any drivers for hardware peripherals (such as sound cards, modems, tape drives, and so on) will need to be reinstalled to work within Windows 95.

If you use Stacker to compress your hard disk, you shouldn't have any problems. Windows 95 is compatible with Stacker versions 2.*x* and greater. But it is a good idea to upgrade to Stacker 4.1, the latest version. It takes advantage of Windows 95's long file and folder names, offers better compression ratios, and makes moving to Windows

95 safe, fast, and easy. Upgrades for current users are available directly from Stac Electronics for $29.95 plus shipping and handling. For information, call Stac at (800) 522-7822.

To Find Out More About Windows 95

For more information about Microsoft Windows 95, take a look at Microsoft's *WinNews* section, which you will find on most major online services and networks:

- *Internet*

  FTP://FTP.MICROSOFT.COM/PEROPSYS/WIN_NEWS

- *World Wide Web* (Mosaic)

  HTTP://WWW.MICROSOFT.COM

- *The Microsoft Network*

  Open Computers and Software\Software\Microsoft\Windows 95\Win News

- *CompuServe*

  GO WINNEWS

- *Prodigy*

  JUMP WINNEWS

- *America Online*

  Use keyword WINNEWS

- *Genie*

  Download files from the *WinNews* area under the Windows RTC

- *RCS Online*

  Conference 2, File Area 167

- NEW SERVICE! To receive biweekly updates about Windows 95, suscribe to Microsoft's *WinNews* Electronic Newsletter. It will come directly to you via E-mail. To suscribe, send *Internet* E-mail to:

  ENEWS25@MICROSOFT.NWNET.COM. As the only text in your message, write:

  SUSCRIBE WINNEWS.

Answers to Common Questions If You've Used Windows Before

- *How do I start programs?*

  Your programs are in groups just as in Windows 3.1. To start a program, click on the Start button, point to Programs, point to the folder that contains the program you want, and then click the program.

- *What happened to my program groups?*

  You can find your program groups by clicking the Start button, and then pointing to Programs. Your program groups appear as folders on the Programs menu. Point to the folder that contains the program you want, and then click a program to open it.

- *What happened to File Manager?*

  Windows Explorer works a lot like File Manager but has the added benefit of displaying all of your drive connections in one window. To open Windows Explorer, click on the Start button, point to Programs, and then click on Windows Explorer.

- *What happened to Control Panel?*

  To open Control Panel, click on the Start button, point to Settings, and then click Control Panel.

- *Where did the MS-DOS prompt go?*

  The MS-DOS prompt is now located in the *Programs* folder. To open an MS-DOS window, click the Start button, point to Programs, and then click on MS-DOS Prompt.

- *What happened to the Run command?*

  To use the Run command, click on the Start button, and then click Run.

- *How do I copy files?*

  You can copy files the same way you copy and paste text. First, select a file in either My Computer or Windows Explorer. Click the Edit menu, and then click Copy. (A dialog box no longer appears.) Open the folder in which you want to put the file you are copying, click the Edit menu, and then click Paste.

- *How do I switch between windows?*

  Click the button on the taskbar that represents the window you want to switch to.

Tips, Hints, and Other Gems of Wisdom

To personalize windows

1. You can move the taskbar to any edge of your screen by dragging it with your mouse.

2. To set your computer's clock, you can double-click the clock on the taskbar.

3. To change the Windows color scheme, use your right mouse button to click the desktop; then click Properties.

4. To change your screen saver, use your right mouse button to click the desktop; then click Properties.

5. You can have programs start when you start Windows by dragging their icons to your StartUp folder.

6. You can switch mouse buttons if you are left-handed. Just double-click the Mouse icon in Control Panel.

7. The mouse pointer is easier to see on laptop computers if you turn on pointer trails. Just double-click the Mouse icon in Control Panel, and then click the Motion tab.

To optimize an MS-DOS program

1. In My Computer, click the icon for the program.

2. On the File menu, click Properties.

The settings you specify will be used each time you start the program by double-clicking its icon. If you start the program from an MS-DOS window, these settings won't be used.

To check your disk's surface, files, or folders for errors

1. Click Help and search for ScanDisk. Click on the Shortcut button to start ScanDisk.

2. Click the drive you want to check.

3. Click Thorough.

If you want to change the settings ScanDisk uses when checking the disk's surface, click Options.

If you want to change the settings ScanDisk uses when checking files and folders, click Advanced.

4. Click Start.

☞ **TIPS** *If you want to specify how ScanDisk repairs any errors it finds, make sure the Automatically Fix Errors box is not checked.*

For Help on an item in the main ScanDisk screen, use your right mouse button to click the item, and then click the What's This? command.

For Help on an item in the Surface Scan Options or ScanDisk Advanced Options dialog boxes, click on the question mark at the top of the dialog box, and then click the item.

To check files and folders for errors

1. Click Help and select ScanDisk. Click on the Shortcut button to start ScanDisk.

2. Click the drive that contains the files and folders you want to check.

3. Click Standard.

   If you want to change the settings ScanDisk uses when checking files and folders, click Advanced.

4. Click Start.

☞ **TIPS** *If you want to specify how ScanDisk repairs any errors it finds, make sure the Automatically Fix Errors box is not checked.*

For Help on an item in the main ScanDisk screen, use your right mouse button to click the item, and then click the What's This? command.

For Help on an item in the ScanDisk Advanced Options dialog box, click on the question mark at the top of the dialog box, and then click the item.

To set up your computer to connect to the network

1. Open Network properties from the Control Panel.

2. Click Add.

3. Click Client.

4. Click Add, and then follow the instructions on the screen.

✎ **NOTES** *The Client for NetWare Networks that is included with Windows 95 enables you to connect to Novell NetWare servers. To install this client, after you click Add in step 4, click Microsoft in the Manufacturers column, and then click Client for NetWare Networks.*

Two versions of the Novell NetWare workstation shell are also available. To install one of these instead of the Client for NetWare Networks, after you click Add in step 4, click Novell in the Manufacturers column.

If you have a network client that is not listed (but is written specifically for Windows 95), click Have Disk, and then follow the instructions on the screen.

Microsoft Plus! for Windows 95 [2]

The Microsoft Plus! for Windows 95 feature is a versatile companion to the Microsoft Windows 95 operating system that can make your 486 or Pentium computer run better, look better, and be much easier to maintain.

---

2 Adapted from *Introducing Microsoft Plus 95*. Portions of the following are copyright © 1985–1995 by Microsoft Corporation.

Microsoft Plus! includes enhancements to disk compression, visual enhancements, Internet tools, and more.

Desktop Themes and Other Visual Enhancements

Desktop Themes incorporate pictures, sound, and animation to give your computer screen a custom look. Microsoft Plus! also includes other visual enhancements.

System Agent

The System Agent runs in the background and performs system-maintenance tasks at regularly scheduled times, or when you are not using your computer.

Enhancements to DriveSpace

Microsoft Plus! includes DriveSpace 3, an enhanced version of Windows 95 DriveSpace that provides better disk compression and support for compressed drives up to 2 gigabytes (GB) in size.

Compression Agent

The Compression Agent utility can run on DriveSpace 3 compressed drives to compact your files while you are not using your computer.

Internet Explorer

You can use Internet Explorer to browse the World Wide Web, use Gopher, and explore other areas of the Internet.

Dial-Up Networking Server

You can use Dial-Up Server to set your computer so that you can dial into it from another location by using Windows Dial-Up Networking.

3D Pinball

The 3D Pinball for Windows 95 feature, a high-tech version of the classic arcade game, provides state-of-the-art graphics and sound.

APPENDIX

Keyboard Commands[1]

This Appendix lists the key sequences to accomplish the primary activities in all the programs furnished with Windows 95. The programs are grouped in the typical program group structure. When you see two keys together, you should press and hold the first key while you press the second (for example, Ctrl S). Two keys separated by a comma indicate that the first key is to be pressed and released before you press the second key (for example, Shift F1, F2). The term "arrow keys" used in the following lists means any of the following: ↑, ↓, ←, or →.

General Windows Keys

The following keys can be used from any window, regardless of the application you are using:

Key(s)	Function
F1	See Help on the selected dialog box item.
Alt F4	Quit a program.
Shift F10	View the shortcut menu for the selected item.
Ctrl Esc	Display the Start menu.
Alt Tab	Switch to the window you last used. Or switch to the next window by pressing Alt while repeatedly pressing Tab.
Ctrl X	Cut.

---

1 Adapted from *Introducing Microsoft Windows 95*. Portions of the following are copyright © 1985–1995 by Microsoft Corporation.

Key(s)	Function
`Ctrl` `C`	Copy.
`Ctrl` `P`	Paste.
`Del`	Delete.
`Ctrl` `Z`	Undo.
`Shift` while inserting the CD-ROM	Bypass auto-play when inserting a compact disc.
`Ctrl` + right-click	Put alternative verbs on the context menu (Open With).
`Shift` + double-click	Explore the object if it has an Explore command.

For the Desktop, My Computer, and Windows Explorer

When an item is selected, you can use the following shortcut keys:

Key(s)	Function
`F2`	Rename an item.
`F3`	Find a folder or file.
`Shift` `Del`	Delete immediately without placing the item in the Recycle Bin.
`Alt` `Enter` or `Alt` + double-click	View item properties.
`Ctrl` while dragging the file	Copy a file.
`Ctrl` `Shift`	Create a shortcut.

For My Computer and Windows Explorer

Key(s)	Function
`Ctrl` `A`	Select all.
`F5`	Refresh a window.
`Backspace`	View the folder one level up.
`Shift` while clicking the Close button	Close the selected folder and all its parent folders.
`F6`	Switch between left and right panes.

For Windows Explorer Only

Key(s)	Function
Ctrl G	Go to.
F6	Switch between left and right panes.
NumLock * (* on numeric keypad)	Expand all subfolders under the selected folder.
NumLock + (+ on numeric keypad)	Expand the selected folder.
NumLock - (– on numeric keypad	Collapse the selected folder.
→	Expand the current selection if it's collapsed, otherwise select the first subfolder.
←	Collapse the current selection if it's expanded, otherwise select the parent folder.

For Properties Dialog Boxes

Key(s)	Function
Tab	Move forward through options.
Shift Tab	Move backward through options.
Ctrl Tab	Move forward through tabs.
Ctrl Shift Tab	Move backward through tabs.

For Open and Save As Dialog Boxes

Key(s)	Function
F4	Open the Save In or Look In list.
F5	Refresh.
Backspace	Open the folder one level up, if a folder is selected.

For Accessibility Options Shortcut Keys

To use Accessibility Options shortcut keys, the shortcut keys must be enabled.

Key(s)	Function
Shift 5 times	Toggle StickyKeys on and off.
⬚ for 8 seconds	Toggle FilterKeys on and off.
NumLock for 5 seconds	Toggle ToggleKeys on and off.
← Alt ← Shift NumLock	Toggle MouseKeys on and off.
← Alt ← Shift PrtSc	Toggle High Contrast on and off.

For MS Natural Keyboard

Key(s)	Function
⊞ R	Run dialog.
⊞ M	Minimize all.
Shift ⊞ M	Undo Minimize All.
⊞ F1	Windows Help.
⊞ E	Explorer.
⊞ F	Find Files or Folders.
Ctrl ⊞ F	Find Computer.
⊞ T	Cycle through taskbar buttons.
⊞ Break	PSS Hotkey ... (System Properties).

Answers to Selected Review Questions

1-2. The recent success of Microsoft Windows 95 is attributable to: (1) the enormous range of Windows applications now available; (2) the fact that Windows 95 runs on millions of DOS-based machines; (3) the ability of Windows 95 to push any PC to its limit in ways that few other programs can. Windows 95 lets you multi-task Windows applications and access up to 16MB of RAM.

1-3. Windows 95 features include: (1) compatibility with existing MS-DOS and Windows-based applications; (2) new user interface; (3) Plug and Play capability; and (4) long file names.

The new capabilities of Windows 95 include Explorer, a program that allows a full range of mouse operations to copy and move files and folders by dragging their icons with your mouse. Control Panel lets you connect to network printers, set up additional ports, set multitasking options, and customize the appearance of your desktop.

1-4. The steps required for starting Windows 95 are as follows:

a. Turn on your PC and monitor. Your computer will begin to load the various programs, drivers, and so on. After a couple of minutes, Windows will automatically load.

b. The monitor will display the Windows 95 copyright screen.

c. You will see a dialog box requesting your username and password. If this is the first time you have used Windows 95, press the Enter key.

d. After a short pause, the Windows desktop appears. On the desktop, you will see the My Computer icon.

2-2. The chief advantage for using the keyboard for input versus using the mouse is that, occasionally, the keyboard allows you to use a single-key shortcut, replacing many mouse movements. The purpose of the ⌊Alt⌋ key or the ⌊F10⌋ (function) key in keyboard commands is to let you obtain menu names in the menu bar.

2-4. A menu command with an ellipsis (...) after the name means that a dialog box will appear when the command is chosen, asking for information the application requires to carry out the command. A grayed-out (dimmed) command is one that is not currently available as an option. When a menu command has a check mark next to the name, the command is active; this convention is used for commands that toggle (switch) between one state and another.

A key combination after the name is a shortcut for this command; one can use this key combination to choose the menu command without first opening the menu.

2-5. Windows utilizes a dialog box both to request information from the user and to provide information to the user. A dialog box appears whenever you choose a command that is followed by an ellipsis (...).

3-2. The taskbar is used as a program launcher. Windows 95 uses the taskbar as a common storage point for several different types of objects. The taskbar is always visible. The major function of the taskbar is to provide a consistent home position or anchor point for the user. Like a bank of TV monitors, taskbar in Windows 95 gives the user a visual cue as to which windows or applications are presently open. To change tasks, select the desired "channel". No matter where the user is, he or she can see all of his or her active tasks simply by looking at the taskbar.

3-3. Shortcuts can be used to print several documents. To print a document, you would open the folder, click on the document icon, drag the icon to the printer icon, and drop it. The document would begin printing. The shell takes care of loading the appropriate application and starting the printing.

3-4. Program group windows can be arranged by the Cascade and Tile commands. The Cascade command layers the open program group window, whereas the Tile command divides the desktop workspace into smaller windows of similar sizes for each program group window that is open.

3-5. The five typical program groups are: (1) My Computer; (2) Accessories group, which includes WordPad, Paint, HyperTerminal, and Calculator; (3) Windows Applications group, which may contain such programs as Word for Windows (word processing) and Excel (spreadsheet)—although the programs in this group vary from one organization or system to another depending on what has been purchased, and are not included in the basic Windows package; (4) Non-Windows Applications group, which contains programs such as WordPerfect, Quattro Pro, dBASE IV, Lotus 1-2-3, and Norton Utilities—these also vary from one system to another; (5) Games group, which displays three games: Solitaire, Minesweeper, and Hearts (others might be added).

4-1. Explorer's principal role is to help you organize files and folders, by allowing you to view them and then build a structure for those files and folders in a fashion that makes sense to you. In other words, it is a shell program that permits you to convert abstract commands into understandable English.

4-3. Subfolders are indicated by the + (plus) sign on the folder.

4-5. To see the list of individual files in a particular folder, simply click on its folder.

4-6. Folder icons are listed first, in alphabetical order; Program file icons include those files with *.exe*, *.com*, *.pif*, and *.bat* extensions. Usually these are executable files used to start applications. Document item icons are created by specific applications. Open file-folder icons indicate current open folders. Data file icons are used for other files.

4-9. The maximum number of characters that a file name may contain is 255.

The types of characters that can begin a file name are either a letter or a number.

The reserved words that cannot be used as file names are: CON, AUX, COM1, COM2, COM3, COM4, COM5, LPT1, LPT2, LPT3, LPT4, PRN, and NUL. These words cannot be used as file names because they are commands intended to address hardware devices.

4-13. When deleting files, you must be absolutely sure that you want to delete a particular file, especially since files being deleted will be erased from the disk directory and become virtually unrecoverable.

5-1. Thirteen or more icons are in the Control Panel, depending on your PC configuration. Below is a description of their functions:

a. The Add Hardware icon allows you to install new hardware devices.

b. The Accessibility Options are for people with disabilities, restricted movements, low vision, or impaired hearing.

c. The Add/Remove Programs icon installs a windows component after Windows 95 has been installed.

d. The Mouse icon allows you to set up the mouse, including speed.

e. The Date icon allows you to change the computer's date and time.

f. The FindFast icon allows you to create an index for locating files quickly.

g. The Display icon permits you to change the way items on your desktop look.

h. The Joystick icon permits you to calibrate your joystick.

i. The Keyboard icon allows you to set repeat speed.

j. The Mail icon connects to The Microsoft Network.

k. The Post Office icon allows you to specify settings for a network client.

l. The Modem icon allows 32-bit PC card support.

m. The Multimedia icon allows you to use a CD player to play compact discs.

n. The Network icon lets you use a cable to connect the computer to a network.

o.   The Password icon permits you to assign or change computer passwords.

p.   The Printers icon lets you change printer settings.

q.   The Regional Settings icon lets you change number, currency, time, date settings, and so on.

r.   The Sounds icon lets you access audio features and customizes the computer to use sounds.

s.   The System icon provides general properties pertaining to the system being used.

5-2.   A font is a graphic design that affects the appearance of numerals, symbols, and characters. Fonts allow you to give your work a professional or casual appearance. It is recommended that you remove any fonts that are not being used, since fonts take up valuable memory that may be required for other applications.

5-3.   With Microsoft Exchange, you can send and receive electronic mail or fax messages.

5-4.   An empty color palette is called Custom colors.

6-1.   Printing in the background means that once you send a document to the printer, you can continue with another application. You do not have to wait until the print job is completed to continue with your work.

6-2.   Windows 95 has two types of print queues, local and network. The local queue means that a printer is connected directly to your computer with a cable. The network queue refers to the print queue on a network server. It is managed by a completely separate print manager, which is different from the one found in Windows 95.

6-5.   Four problems that may occur while printing are:

a.   My document didn't print at all.

b.   My document printed, but it doesn't look right, or it printed only partially.

c.   Printing is unusually slow.

d.   Printer is offline.

7-2.   To erase a large area of text efficiently, mark the text you want to erase. Position the cursor on the first character and drag it to the last line of text that you want erased. The block of text will be shaded in black. Press [Del] to erase this block of text.

7-3.   Yes, formats do transfer if formatted text is copied or moved to another location and/or to WordPad.

7-5.   Text that is left-aligned will possess a straight edge on the left margin, but the right margin will be uneven or jagged.

Text that is aligned at the middle of the page is centered.

Text that is right-aligned is the opposite of text that is left-aligned, since the right edge is even and the left margin is jagged.

Justified means that both margins (left and right) are straight.

8-1. Raster graphics are based on movements (the electronic beam that paints on any CRT). Files are saved as bitmap. Vector graphics deal with objects that can be scaled (sized) such as lines, arcs, and polygons.

8-3. The elements of the Paint Window are the workspace, cursor, toolbox, palette, and the line size box. The workspace is the area where you will create your drawings. The cursor indicates where a line or other object will be placed when you begin your drawings. (The cursor shape may be different, depending on the tool that is being used.) The toolbox contains the tools that you use to create drawings. These tools include Fill, Airbrush, Erase, Enter Text, Cut, and so on. The palette contains the colors and patterns available. The line size box contains the available drawing widths.

8-5. The Copy command will make an exact duplicate of the material designated to be copied, and place it at the desired destination. By contrast, Cut will remove the selected material from its present location and place it temporarily on the Clipboard.

8-7. Using the mouse to select a tool from the toolbox, click on the tool that you want.

9-1. a. A modem (*mo*dulator/*dem*odulator) is a hardware device that is used to tele-communicate data. It converts digital signals (data) to analog signals that can be sent over telephone lines at the sending end. At the receiving end, analog signals are converted back into digital signals used by terminals and computers.

   b. Baud rate is the measure of the speed at which data are sent or received over a telephone line. The higher the rate, the faster the data are sent.

   c. Data bits are data sent through the modem in a series of ones and zeros (digits). The number of data bits equals the number of ones and zeros in a piece of data, such as a character sent via a telephone line. Two types of data bits are 7 bits (which represents all the letters of the alphabet, numbers, punctuation marks, and some special symbols) and 8 bits (which is large enough for the entire IBM-PC character set).

   d. Stop bits are used as a signal to tell the receiving computer where one character ends and another begins.

   e. Parity is a method of detecting errors in the data being transmitted. By adding a one or a zero after the data, the software alters the total number of ones into even or odd numbers. The choices for parity checking are Odd, Even, or None.

   f. Data flow control is designed to notify the remote computer when Hyper-Terminal's buffer capacity has been reached. HyperTerminal needs to notify the remote system to pause momentarily before sending any more characters; otherwise, incoming data will be lost.

   g. "Pause" and "resume" signals are known as handshaking. The method of hand-shaking used is determined by the Flow Control setting. HyperTerminal's default choice (Xon/Xoff) is the method most commonly used.

9-4. The HyperTerminal Emulation setting reflects the type of terminal of the remote computer. The information on terminal type is available from the online service to which you are connecting. The choices for terminal type include Auto Detect, TTY, VT-100, MiniTel, View Data, and VT-52. If you are not sure which terminal type to use, select TTY.

9-5. Configuring the communications settings will determine how your data are packaged and sent over the telephone line. Modem settings identify for Hyper-Terminal what signals it needs to initiate a call, receive a call, dial the telephone, and hang up.

10-1. Once you have opened Calculator, you can switch from standard calculator to a scientific calculator by choosing View from the Calculator menu.

10-4. To avoid entering text beyond the right edge of the window, set Word Wrap from the Edit menu. This option automatically wraps text to the next line when you reach the right-hand border of the window.

10-5. A time log file is created by entering .LOG in capital letters at the beginning of the file. Notepad will automatically add the current time and date to the file.

11-1. The Windows family of products includes the following:

a. Word for Windows is a word processing application.

b. Excel is a spreadsheet application.

c. Project is an application for managing schedules and resources and for graphically communicating project planning.

d. PowerPoint is an application that allows you to create and manage high-quality overhead and 35mm slide presentations.

11-3. a. Microsoft Excel.

b. Microsoft PowerPoint.

c. Microsoft Word for Windows.

d. Microsoft Project for Windows.

12-1. The Internet was developed by Bolt, Beranek, and Newman (BBN) for the Advanced Research Projects Agency of the U.S. Department of Defense.

12-2. Internet services or protocols include:

a. E-mail.

b. TCP/IP.

c. Telnet.

d. FTP.

e. Gopher.

12-4.   Three examples of emoticons are:

    a.   Smile   :.)

    b.   Yelling   :-o

    c.   IMHO   In My Humble Opinion

12-6.   To join a chat session, you must have an account with The Microsoft Network. Chat rooms can be found in MSN Categories.

13-1.   A program information file (PIF) is a file that contains special information regarding Windows' requirements to run a non-windows application.

14-1.   The desktop is the area of the Windows screen that borders any particular window or icon. It is the background area where you create and work with Windows applications.

14-2.   The options available for customizing the Desktop are as follows:

    a.   Pattern lets you cover your desktop with a repeating dot pattern. You can create the pattern yourself or use a pattern furnished by Windows.

    b.   Wallpaper provides a scenic design for your desktop.

14-6.   You can determine that the sound is off when you select a command that is not valid and the warning beep does not come on.

15-1.   Windows 95 system management infrastructure includes the Registry, User Management, System Management, and Network Management.

15-3.   Efforts must be taken to *localize* the software to a given country and written language in which it will be used. In many cases, this is as simple as changing the names of menus, menu items, and strings displayed by the software to match the foreign language used in the locale.

15-5.   Accessibility options can be set for:

    a.   StickyKeys.

    b.   SlowKeys.

    c.   MouseKeys.

16-1.   Clipboard is a utility program that acts as a temporary storage area for the information you are transferring between applications during a Windows session. Information can be copied or cut from an application onto the Clipboard and then transferred into other applications. Clipboard can be used to transfer information among Calculator, WordPad, Paint, HyperTerminal, and most non-Windows applications. Clipboard also provides a fast and convenient way to gather in one place at one time all the information required to complete a project. It can be used to move data between applications not specifically designed for Windows.

16-2.   Copy puts the selected information in the Clipboard without removing it from the original document. Cut, on the other hand, puts the information on the Clipboard and at the same time deletes it from the source.

16-4.   Multiple formats are important because when you are transferring data to the Clipboard you are allowed to identify which formats are available, by pulling down Clipboard's Display menu. In other words, you are given a broader range of formats from which to choose.

Index

Notes

Notes

Notes

Notes

Notes

Notes

Notes

Notes

Notes

Notes

Notes